REAGAN
AND THE
CITIES

REAGAN

AND THE

CITIES

Edited by

George E. Peterson and Carol W. Lewis

The Changing Domestic Priorities Series
John L. Palmer and Isabel V. Sawhill, Editors

 THE URBAN INSTITUTE PRESS · WASHINGTON, D.C.

Copyright © 1986
THE URBAN INSTITUTE
2100 M Street, N.W.
Washington, D.C. 20037

Library of Congress Cataloging in Publication Data
Main entry under title:

Reagan and the cities.

(The Changing domestic priorities series)
1. Urban policy—United States—Addresses, essays,
lectures. 2. Intergovernmental fiscal relations—United
States—Addresses, essays, lectures. 3. Federal-city
relations—United States—Addresses, essays, lectures.
I. Peterson, George E. II. Lewis, Carol W. (Carol
Weiss), 1946–   . III. Series.
HT123.R39   1986   307.7'64'0973   85-29525
ISBN 0-87766-384-X
ISBN 0-87766-385-8 (pbk.)

Printed in the United States of America
9 8 7 6 5 4 3 2 1

THE URBAN INSTITUTE is a nonprofit policy research and educational organization established in Washington, D.C., in 1968. Its staff investigates the social and economic problems confronting the nation and government policies and programs designed to alleviate such problems. The Institute disseminates significant findings of its research through the publications program of its Press. The Institute has two goals for work in each of its research areas: to help shape thinking about societal problems and efforts to solve them, and to improve government decisions and performance by providing better information and analytic tools.

Through work that ranges from broad conceptual studies to administrative and technical assistance, Institute researchers contribute to the stock of knowledge available to public officials and to private individuals and groups concerned with formulating and implementing more efficient and effective government policy.

Conclusions or opinions expressed in Institute publications are those of the authors and do not necessarily reflect the views of other staff members, officers or trustees of the Institute, advisory groups, or any organizations that provide financial support to the Institute.

THE CHANGING DOMESTIC PRIORITIES SERIES

Listed below are the titles available, or soon to be available, in the Changing Domestic Priorities Series

Books

THE REAGAN EXPERIMENT
An Examination of Economic and Social Policies under the Reagan Administration (1982), John L. Palmer and Isabel V. Sawhill, editors

HOUSING ASSISTANCE FOR OLDER AMERICANS
The Reagan Prescription (1982), James P. Zais, Raymond J. Struyk, and Thomas Thibodeau

MEDICAID IN THE REAGAN ERA
Federal Policy and State Choices (1982), Randall R. Bovbjerg and John Holahan

WAGE INFLATION
Prospects for Deceleration (1983), Wayne Vroman

OLDER AMERICANS IN THE REAGAN ERA
Impacts of Federal Policy Changes (1983), James R. Storey

FEDERAL HOUSING POLICY AT PRESIDENT REAGAN'S MIDTERM
(1983), Raymond J. Struyk, Neil Mayer, and John A. Tuccillo

STATE AND LOCAL FISCAL RELATIONS IN THE EARLY 1980s
(1983), Steven D. Gold

THE DEFICIT DILEMMA
Budget Policy in the Reagan Era (1983), Gregory B. Mills and John L. Palmer

HOUSING FINANCE
A Changing System in the Reagan Era (1983), John A. Tuccillo with John L. Goodman, Jr.

PUBLIC OPINION DURING THE REAGAN ADMINISTRATION
National Issues, Private Concerns (1983), John L. Goodman, Jr.

RELIEF OR REFORM?
Reagan's Regulatory Dilemma (1984), George C. Eads and Michael Fix

THE REAGAN RECORD
An Assessment of America's Changing Domestic Priorities (1984), John L. Palmer and Isabel V. Sawhill, editors (Ballinger Publishing Co.)

ECONOMIC POLICY IN THE REAGAN YEARS
(1984), Charles F. Stone and Isabel V. Sawhill

URBAN HOUSING IN THE 1980s
Markets and Policies (1984), Margery Austin Turner and Raymond J. Struyk

MAKING TAX CHOICES
(1985), Joseph J. Minarik

AMERICA'S CHILDREN: WHO CARES?
Growing Needs and Declining Assistance in the Reagan Era (1985),
Madeleine H. Kimmich

TESTING THE SOCIAL SAFETY NET
The Impact of Changes in Support Programs during the Reagan Administration
(1985),
Martha R. Burt and Karen J. Pittman

REAGAN AND THE CITIES
(1986) edited by George E. Peterson and Carol W. Lewis

Conference Volumes

THE SOCIAL CONTRACT REVISITED
Aims and Outcomes of President Reagan's Social Welfare Policy (1984), edited
by D. Lee Bawden

NATURAL RESOURCES AND THE ENVIRONMENT
The Reagan Approach (1984), edited by Paul R. Portney

FEDERAL BUDGET POLICY IN THE 1980s (1984), edited by
Gregory B. Mills and John L. Palmer

THE REAGAN REGULATORY STRATEGY
An Assessment (1984), edited by George C. Eads and Michael Fix

THE LEGACY OF REAGANOMICS
Prospects for Long-term Growth (1984), edited by Charles R. Hulten and Isabel
V. Sawhill

THE REAGAN PRESIDENCY AND THE GOVERNING OF AMERICA
(1984), edited by Lester M. Salamon and Michael S. Lund

CONTENTS

TABLES

FIGURES

FOREWORD

This book is part of The Urban Institute's Changing Domestic Priorities project. The project is examining changes that are occurring in the nation's domestic policies under the Reagan administration and is analyzing the effects of those changes on people, places, and institutions.

Few places or institutions have been more affected by the changes in federal policy than cities or city governments. For most of the 1970s, cities were treated as special cases in federal domestic policy. They were thought to require special aid formulas in federal grants, special programs of emergency assistance (for example, federal guarantees for New York City debt), and special programs of long-range assistance. Development of a formal federal urban policy was one of the first promises of the Carter administration when it came to office, reflecting both the priorities and the political indebtedness of the new administration.

Since those heady days less than a decade ago, the cities have had to face a new political reality. They have borne a more than proportionate share of federal budget cuts. They have found the promise of supportive federal urban policy not only unrealized but specifically disavowed by the new administration. And although it is always difficult to distinguish the transient from the permanent in politics, it now appears that it will be a long time before ''cities'' reappear as an influential interest group or as the special target of new federal spending programs.

Through all these changes, the cities have survived. An overview of the research findings indicates that in some respects—financial condition, economy, self-sufficiency—cities are stronger now than they were at the height of federal intervention. In other respects—for example, the public capacity to assist certain classes of the poor—they are weaker. Above all, the cities of the second half of the 1980s are different, in what they do for themselves and for their populations and in what urban leaders expect from other levels of government.

The authors of this volume attempt to take stock of the many dimensions of change that have occurred in city economies, city politics, and city social programs. The reading is an empirical one, drawing upon a diverse set of data sources, tempered by intensive case studies of particular locations. It aims to give a better understanding of how far we have come during the past decade in urban policy and city realities, and how the changes in the federal role promoted by the Reagan administration fit into that evolution. There can be no guarantee that clarifying the implications for cities of recent policy changes will help the process of making public choices in the future, but before embarking on a new round of domestic policy change, we owe it to ourselves to take a dispassionate look at the consequences of change thus far.

John L. Palmer
Isabel V. Sawhill
Editors
Changing Domestic Priorities Series

ACKNOWLEDGMENTS

We wish to acknowledge the critical reading given to these chapters by John L. Palmer, co-director of the Changing Domestic Priorities project, Harold Wolman, and an anonymous external reviewer. Their suggestions have sharpened the focus of the volume. Priscilla Taylor and Karen Wirt skillfully edited the volume for publication. The manuscript was typed and prepared for typesetting by Dorothy Cheek and Frankie J. Worthy and proofread by Alden Woodbury. Funding for the project was provided by The Ford Foundation and the John D. and Catherine T. MacArthur Foundation.

George E. Peterson
Carol W. Lewis
Editors

INTRODUCTION

When Ronald Reagan took office, his administration laid down a challenge to those sectors of the economy that relied on large amounts of federal program assistance. Within the first sixty days, the president issued a plan for domestic budget cuts and announced his intention to reduce and index taxes in a way that would place constraints on federal spending for at least the rest of the decade.

No sector of the economy felt more threatened by these budget initiatives than the nation's cities. Older cities in particular seemed to have more programs that were singled out for domestic budget reductions. In giving priority to the war on inflation, the new administration seemed to be accepting the inevitability of recession without offering cities any of the battery of targeted antirecession assistance programs that had marked the policies of both parties in the 1970s. In fact, the administration expressly disavowed "urban policy," in the sense of trying to compensate cities through special federal assistance for high costs or for poor economic growth prospects, either in the long run or during the course of recession. As a result, many of the cities' leaders predicted a harrowing period for urban America.

We now know that most of the early predictions about how cities would fare under the Reagan administration were too pessimistic. It is less clear why the forecasts were in error. Was it simply that the president's budget cuts were diluted by Congress? Congress restored a significant amount, but by one tally (see the chapter by George Peterson), funding for specifically urban programs nonetheless fell some 23 percent in fiscal 1982 from what it would have been had fiscal 1980 policy continued in effect. Or did the conventional understanding fail in its diagnosis of how city governments, urban households, and other organizations would react to policy change?

1

One goal of this volume is to take stock of the impact of the Reagan administration's programs on the cities. The cities, of course, are not neutral ground. At a time when the president was receiving two overwhelming electoral mandates from the rest of the nation, he was losing the presidential balloting in the big cities of the Northeast and Midwest by an even larger margin. Although the Reagan message was received more favorably in cities in other parts of the country, it would not be fair to judge whether the new domestic policies worked in the nation as a whole by looking only at the cities, the toughest place for a field test.

The cities nonetheless are the best location for testing the fundamental propositions that underlie the Reagan administration's domestic policy reforms. Too much can be made of the budget cuts by themselves; the enduring effects of President Reagan's domestic policy lies as much in its predictions about how people and institutions will respond to policy change. In any attempt to field-test presumptions about behavior, it is all to the good that the political and institutional issues are intensified in the cities and that groups adversely affected by budget cutbacks are overrepresented in the cities relative to the rest of the nation. The most common complaint among social scientists is that by the time any policy change reaches the individual citizen or the local organization it has become lost in the stream of other events, making it extremely difficult to identify the impact of public policy alone.

In this book we collect as much of the empirical evidence as possible on what happened in cities when federal policies were changed. The authors all try to pierce through first-round budget effects—to use household surveys of how citizens thought the quality of services changed when local spending was reduced, to draw on surveys of hospitals and interviews with hospital officials to find out how provision of hospital charitable care changed when state or federal incentives were altered, or to uncover data on the employment choices made by individual firms in cities and suburbs over the economic cycle. Because our principal interest is to observe responses to the policy principles advocated by the Reagan presidency, we have expanded the meaning of "Reagan and the Cities" to look not only at local responses to federal policy initiatives, but at the local responses to analogous initiatives by state governments, such as state revenue limitations, or state and federal changes in Medicaid policy.

Assessing the Reagan Policy

Cutting across the chapters of this volume are five themes—five tests of propositions central to the Reagan policy—that may be usefully described here at the outset.

Budget Perspective

One theme is a perspective on the budget cuts. Fundamental to the Reagan administration's domestic policy reform is the contention that merely toting up the dollar reductions in federal program spending misrepresents the impact of policy change. Some federal programs are not valued by the organizations in whose budgets they appear. Other programs are riddled with inefficiences, making it possible to reduce spending without affecting service quality. Most important, it is argued, households and institutions do not judge the desirability of policy change narrowly, as if all that mattered was the net sum of the change in their personal taxes and benefits. There has been a tendency to dismiss this position as public relations puffery—on a par with the industrialist in a Dickens novel who accompanies wage reductions with a homily on the virtues of abstinence. But the proposition that people and organizations appraise policy change from a perspective other than budgetary self-interest deserves serious consideration.

The studies in this volume bear out this first Reagan proposition to a considerable degree. The single biggest cut in federal aid to cities came from the elimination of public service employment under the Comprehensive Employment and Training Act (CETA). Yet at the time these cuts were initially proposed, most city officials *favored* them, as well as federal budget reductions for legal services and regional cooperation. The local officials responding to surveys displayed a complete neutrality toward federal cuts in public housing support and were almost completely neutral toward cuts in youth unemployment programs. It is not necessary to search for arcane explanations of this willingness to accept funding reductions. The first three program categories—public service employment, legal services, and regional cooperation—represent areas in which cities typically have perceived themselves as agents for carrying out federal policy or areas in which federal funds have gone to strengthen organizations that are often at odds with the city government itself. The last two categories—low-income housing and youth unemployment—represent social issues in which city involvement initially was stimulated by federal policy and federal funding. Apparently, the officials in some cities did not mind being relieved of these responsibilities through federal defunding.

In the chapter by Sarah F. Liebschutz and Alan J. Taddiken, a survey was made of all families in Rochester, New York removed from the welfare rolls by the tightening of income eligibility restrictions. The study documents the income loss for these families, their loss of other government benefits, and the problems suffered by family members. Yet 34 percent of the welfare mothers regarded themselves as better off, despite their removal from the welfare rolls (versus 41 percent who believed they were worse off), and by a margin of almost three to one, respondents who had been terminated from Aid to Families with Dependent Children (AFDC) believed that life would be better for them in the future rather than worse. In part this attitude indicates the economic adjustments the families had made and were making, as well as an improving economy. In part it reflects an apparent sharing of the cultural value that families should not be dependent on government assistance and relief at having ended such dependence. In either case, to look only at the dollar value of the lost federal program benefits oversimplifies the impact of policy change.

If there is evidence that affected parties often do not evaluate federal policy simply in terms of the first-round budget effects on them, there is good evidence too that the critics of government spending have exaggerated the capacity of local governments to absorb budget reductions without having an adverse impact on local service quality. In their stronger claims, partisans of budget cuts in the public sector sometimes affirm that governments are such inefficient providers of services that local governments could absorb substantial budget reductions without having to make changes in service provision that local citizens would notice.

In the chapter by John M. Greiner and George E. Peterson, service delivery in Massachusetts municipalities is examined in the wake of Proposition 2½. The authors find that, although in some cases reorganization of service delivery allowed maintenance of or even improved service quality in the face of budget cuts, most budget reductions were accompanied by objective deterioration in service quality or reduced citizen satisfaction with service characteristics. Such findings do not rebut the claim that productivity improvements *could* offset spending reductions, but they do tend to establish that, at the actual margin, public spending and service quality go together in ways that consumers recognize.

Financial Self-Sufficiency

No disagreement between the Reagan administration and its critics surfaced more swiftly than differences over the ability of the institutions hit by federal budget cutbacks to make the necessary financial adjustments on their own—and this brings us to the second cross-cutting theme of this book. True, the reductions in federal aid to cities and to nonprofit organizations did not, in the first Reagan term, approach the proportions that the president proposed or the city spokesmen feared. Nevertheless, the Reagan budget cuts rendered permanent the reductions in federal aid that had begun in 1978 when the antirecession programs of the Carter administration were dismantled; and, by the standards of federal budgets of the past half-century, the cuts were large.

The subsequent financial experience of both the cities and the nonprofit organizations is so at odds with the pessimistic predictions made at the time that it obliges reconsideration of what we know about the response to recession and external financial pressure. The chapter by Peterson considers these issues from the standpoint of the cities. A systematic look at the economic cycles since 1969 reveals that cities have been less vulnerable to recession than commonly believed. Central cities have actually experienced less steep cyclical fluctuations in income earned than the rest of the economy and much less cyclical volatility than suburban areas. The movement of economic activity out of the central city to the suburbs slows during recessions, only to revive in full force during subsequent cyclical recoveries. The fundamental premise of federal urban policy in the 1970s—that antirecession aid should be directed toward the cities, especially old and declining cities, because they are the most cyclically vulnerable components of the national economy— seems to be wrong.

Moreover, the capacity of city governments to handle financial vicissitudes strengthened remarkably after the mid-1970s. At the end of fiscal 1982, when the nation was in the trough of recession and federal budget cutbacks were at their peak, city governments were in better financial shape by almost all indicators than they had been during any year of the 1970s. Much of the improved performance was owing to better and more sober financial management. But part of the difference reflected, as the Reagan diagnosis predicted, a previously untapped capacity of cities to provide their own fiscal shock absorbers. In 1981–82, cities and states acted much more swiftly to raise taxes and set aside emergency funds from their own revenues than they had done in the 1973–74 recession. In retrospect, it is difficult to avoid the conclusion that in the earlier recession cities postponed their own fiscal adjustments with the expectation that antirecession federal assistance would make such adjustments unnecessary, whereas in 1981–82 they accelerated those adjustments because they did not expect that federal assistance would be forthcoming. The proposition was vindicated—cities, despite their previous dependence on federal assistance, could adjust financially to cutbacks in federal aid while simultaneously coping with recession.

The ability of nonprofit institutions to survive financially was equally impressive. Despite predictions that funding for these institutions would fall by as much as 20 percent or more, careful comparisons of the budgets of nonprofit organizations (see, for example, the chapter by W. Wayne Shannon et al.) reveal very little erosion in the total budgets of these organizations. Many nonprofit organizations demonstrated an unsuspected ability to enhance their own revenues by establishing (or raising) fees and charges for their services. Of course, this financial maneuverability was not open to all organizations and it frequently altered clientele groups when it was implemented. Once again the direct budget effects of federal cuts were only the beginning of the story.

Substitution of Private Charity for Public Programs

A third theme of the Reagan administration's public philosophy holds that when federal funding is reduced, private charity will step in to replace important public programs in support of the poor. The imagery surrounding private charity encourages one to think in terms of individual donations or neighborhood volunteer programs.

If the choice in fact were simply between government programs and strictly voluntary individual action, considerable skepticism would be appropriate. Both national and local surveys (the chapter by Shannon et al.) indicate that three out of four citizens think people are less willing to help their neighbors today than they were twenty-five years ago. The scale of individual voluntarism is very modest. In a 1982 survey conducted in Stamford, Connecticut, for example, the median charitable contribution of the households surveyed was $200, with only 30 percent of the population reporting any volunteer time, and a median of three hours per week contributed by persons who did volunteer. No plausible increase in these voluntary efforts could replace significant budget reductions through the public sector.

But the most important choices between private charity and public programs occur on a much larger scale, in a framework of institutions rather than individual citizens. In the chapter by Judith Feder and Jack Hadley, one of these choices is examined, hospital care for the poor. In 1980 the nation's total hospital care for the poor amounted to $14.4 billion—$9.1 billion paid by the federal, state, (and occasionally local) Medicaid program, and $5.3 billion paid through hospital charitable care. The latter was both voluntary charity (care for which hospitals did not expect to receive payment) and involuntary (through bad debts for care for which the hospitals expected but did not receive payment).

When the public sector cut back on Medicaid eligibility in the face of federal and, more important, state budget restrictions, the hospitals did not increase their charitable care commensurately. Even when there were steep increases in the poverty population because of the recession, there was little growth in hospital charitable care. In fact, charitable care did not *substitute* for Medicaid at all. In locations where Medicaid coverage declined, the proportion of private hospital revenues devoted to care for the poor also declined. In areas where Medicaid coverage expanded, private hospital charitable care also increased. The conception of separate public and private charitable sectors, with an elastic line of demarcation between them, is misleading. The mere shrinkage of public sector care for the poor does not create a vacuum that private philanthropy rushes to fill. Rather, the public and private sectors are linked by a grant-in-aid system and a structure of financial incentives. These make public and private sector actions as often complements as substitutes for each other.

Only the public hospitals in large cities were an exception to the pattern of charitable hospital care. The share of public hospitals' revenues devoted to charitable care rose sharply during the recession, regardless of a state's Medicaid policy. Hospitals in large cities apparently do see themselves as providers of last resort that must step in to provide care if other public programs fail. But even this type of substitution for state or federal funding cutbacks was limited. Although the *share* of public hospital revenues devoted to charitable care rose considerably, the net effect was mitigated by a scaling back in total public hospital activity (and occasional closings of city public hospitals) dictated by city governments' stringent budgets.

Urban Development

The Reagan philosophy also contains an urban development strategy. Part of the emphasis on self-reliance holds that cities should compete with one another for economic growth as vigorously as do private firms, and without subsidies. In the words of the Reagan administration's *1982 National Urban Policy Report*, instead of vying for federal grants, state and local governments should recognize that "it is in their interests to concentrate on increasing their attractiveness to potential investors, residents and visitors." Beyond this, the administration has advanced an analogue to the supply-side theory of firms' response to tax reductions. Its enterprise zone proposals (see the chapter by Marc Bendick, Jr., and David W. Rasmussen) are premised on the assumption that by lowering tax burdens and removing regulatory restrictions cities not only can attract a greater share of business growth but also can help unleash an entrepreneurial spirit of small business formation that is being frustrated by current public policy.

The Reagan theory of enterprise zones cannot receive a direct empirical test because a federal law authorizing establishment of enterprise zones still has not been enacted. The policy debate over these zones, however, has stimulated a good deal of state legislation. But the form in which states' enterprise zone policy has developed deviates greatly from the original federal theory. Under the rubric of enterprise zones, states and cities have returned to an older view that—far from promoting development primarily by removing the public sector presence—successful enterprise zones require special public support through land assembly or complementary public investment, as well as through geographically directed tax reductions. The most promising enterprise zone programs adopted by cities conform to a public plan for retaining the city's growth industries and allowing for their systematic further expansion through active public sector help, rather than through reliance on a hands-off policy designed to stimulate creation of new small businesses by getting government out of their way.

A few cities have turned the thesis of urban self-reliance on its head. Instead of committing themselves wholeheartedly to the market and trying to compete for footloose private firms, they have attempted to frame a public sector version of local economic self-sufficiency. No large city has gone further in this direction than Chicago (see the chapter by Dennis R. Judd and Randy L. Ready). The city has established components in its public sector budget—to focus city procurements on minority firms, and Chicago businesses—in an effort to make local government the engine of growth. It has announced a policy of using city funds to stimulate the creation of small enterprises, minority enterprises, and neighborhood cooperatives, as well as to improve the technological capability of such firms—all in an effort to make the Chicago economy more self-sufficient and more insulated from national economic trends. Whether this economic development strategy can succeed remains to be seen; at this point it must be classified as a speculative long shot.

One aspect of Chicago's development dilemma is similar to that confronted by other cities that Judd and Ready examine. If the role of government in redistributing income through public sector budgets is to be reduced, and if cities have no choice but to turn to local economic development to generate wealth, how will they ensure that some of that wealth reaches minority groups? The Reagan hypothesis that small enterprises in general can flourish as a means of wealth spreading is only now beginning to receive a serious test as the economy moves into longer-term expansion. However, it is clear that the minority constituencies that dominate policies in many big cities distrust this solution. Judd and Ready examine the efforts of minority mayors and others to target the growth of bigger business to the benefit of the special urban community and to test the tools of local economic development to favor certain kinds of firms or certain types of owners.

Federalism

A fifth proposition of the Reagan presidency, which runs through many of the papers in this volume, is the inherent strength of American federalism, and in particular the key role of state government in mediating between the federal government and the cities. When the citizens of Massachusetts voted to impose extreme limitations on the local ability to raise property taxes, the state government intervened (as the California state government had done before it in response to Proposition 13) to lessen the blow to local governments and smooth out the adjustment process. When the federal government converted some categorical grants to block grants, while simultaneously cutting funding levels, it was the states that determined the ultimate structure of grant changes for cities and usually came up with some additional funds to mitigate the full impact of federal budget policy. By the time national Medicaid policy changes reached local hospitals, they reflected at least as much state response to federal funding changes as the federal initiatives themselves.

The record of state and local adjustment to the policy initiatives of Reagan's first term reaffirms the critical role of state government in American federalism, just as the president himself has reaffirmed the states' role in his public statements. But the record challenges the president's interpretation of federalism. The New Federalism proposals of the first term advocated a clean, logical division among local, state, and federal governments—in service responsibilities as in funding. In contrast, the federalism that demonstrated its virtues during the first Reagan term was Old Federalism, with all its complexities, overlapping responsibilities, and confusions. Public managers were able to absorb the sudden cuts in grants-in-aid in part because they discovered in the cracks of the federal system unspent carryover funds from the past that both outside analysts and federal program managers had almost forgotten. When federal policy change buffeted local governments, they turned to the state, and when states received funding cuts too large to handle on their own, they shared them with localities. In the negotiation process that ensued, the worst effects on either level of government almost always were averted.

As John Stuart Hall writes in his chapter on the adjustments made by Phoenix, American federalism at its best is a sort of catastrophic insurance plan. "When depression, recession, budget cuts, political error, and pure human stupidity seem about to unravel the American political fabric, federalism compensates. When the dam breaks, federalism fixes it. Under stress, American federalism forces American governments to cooperate." These virtues depend on the many informal arrangements that have sprung up among different levels of government and the lack of rigorous lines of demarcation among them. In the end, the fact that so many New Federalism proposals died stillborn may reflect as much basic satisfaction with the old collaborative arrangements as unhappiness with the prospective loss of federal aid.

Organization of the Book

All studies of cities show a tension between the desire to generalize and the desire to be true to the institutional and programmatic detail of a particular place. The authors in this book all try to resolve this tension by carrying out case studies against a background of comparative analysis. In the earlier chapters the emphasis is on comparative analysis—of all big cities, of city hospitals, of Massachusetts municipalities, and so on. The case studies in these chapters are used to illustrate the actual policy decisions that lie behind the analytical results. In the later chapters, the emphasis is on particular places—Stamford (Connecticut), Rochester (New York), Phoenix, Louisville, Chicago, Denver, or Saint Paul. In these studies, the comparative background helps place the individual city or institution in a broader range of city experience. The authors and editors have tried to keep in mind that the most valuable analyses are those that permit generalization, but the most valuable insights often are those that come from plunging into local complexities free from preliminary generalization.

URBAN POLICY AND THE CYCLICAL
BEHAVIOR OF CITIES

George E. Peterson

One of the most encouraging developments of the Reagan presidency, yet one that requires a rethinking of city behavior as we understand it, was the favorable economic and fiscal position that cities found themselves in at the beginning of the president's second term.

To most spokesmen for urban America, the economic and fiscal policies of the administration, when they were first articulated, seemed to foretell crisis for the cities. The board of directors of the National League of Cities contended than the administration had adopted a " 'radical' economic program, (with) a 'radical' view of American cities." The president-elect of the league, Charles Royer, mayor of Seattle, described the administration's *1982 National Urban Policy Report* as "not an urban policy, Mr. Chairman. It is a blueprint for surrendering America's cities. With this document, the federal government admits it is incapable of winning the battle for the cities, and announces its intention to go AWOL. It is ironic that so much effort by so many creative minds has been expended to rationalize this desertion."[1]

The "radical" nature of the Reagan administration's urban program, as perceived by Royer in 1982, lay in two elements: its resolve to let recession run its course, without providing cities with antirecession programs of job creation or emergency fiscal assistance, and its proposals to dissolve most of the programs of direct federal assistance to cities. One indication of how greatly expectations have changed in just three years is that the word "radical" now seems oddly disproportionate in describing this agenda, but at the time

---

1. Prepared statement of the Honorable Charles Royer, Mayor of Seattle, Washington, in *The Administration's 1982 National Urban Policy Report*, Hearings before the Joint Economic Committee, 97th Cong. 2d sess., 1983, pt. 1, p. 36.

the measures did represent a sharp break with federal policy that stretched back at least to the mid-1960s.

As fiscal entities, and as locations for jobs and investment, most cities entered the period of President Reagan's second term of office in far better condition than mayors and others predicted in 1982. Much of the credit, of course, belongs to the general economy. From the outset, the Reagan administration announced that its principal urban policy was to promote national economic recovery and long-term growth.

There is more than economic recovery to the story, however. Cities weathered the recession, coped with the withdrawal of federal programs, and emerged better off than most analysts had foreseen. The very failure of the predictions raises the question of what accounts for the difference between expectation and reality. Was the administration correct when it asserted that cities had at their command a capacity for controlling local fiscal conditions that past federal policy had underestimated and even frustrated? Did the federal policy of the 1970s err in the assessment that cities suffer most from recession, so that countercyclical policy should be focused there?

The Effects of Recession on Cities

Federal urban policy during the 1970s was based on the assumption that cities are especially vulnerable to economic cycles. The largest urban aid programs were the antirecession programs designed to create temporary jobs and provide cities with a fiscal cushion to help survive recession.[2] Not only did these programs concentrate their benefits on urban areas, but they went further than any other programs in directing aid to central cities with high rates of unemployment, slow growth, and poor fiscal conditions.

The intellectual underpinnings of countercyclical urban policy were fairly casual. The simultaneous appearance of recession and severe city fiscal problems, first in 1974 with New York City's financial crisis and then later spreading to other cities, persuaded many observers that older cities could not cope on their own with a cyclical loss of economic activity in addition to weak secular performance.

There emerged, too, the outline of an analytical argument as to why old cities should be more vulnerable to economic cycles than the rest of the country. Slow-growth areas or declining metropolitan areas were thought to possess greater proportions of old, marginal capital facilities and high-cost unionized labor. When demand slackens during recession, this high-cost cap-

---

2. These programs were Public Service Employment, Emergency Local Public Works, and Anti-Recession Fiscal Assistance.

ital and labor are the first to be removed from production. During recovery they are the last to be reemployed. Such behavior would make the cyclical swings of slow-growth or declining Standard Metropolitan Statistical Areas (SMSAs) especially volatile.[3] Conversely, the scarcity of skilled labor in fast-growth areas should provide a source of cyclical stability, since firms would hoard labor during periods of recession lest they have an inadequate labor supply during recovery.[4] Finally, the fact that metropolitan areas and central cities in general produce for national markets was thought to link them to national cyclical fluctuations more strongly than locations that have a larger share of production for local or regional markets.[5]

Reasoning like this produced strong expectations about how local areas should perform during the cycle. Three premises were put forth:

- Metropolitan areas in general should be more vulnerable to recession than the rest of the country;

- Slow-growth metropolitan regions should suffer more from recession than fast-growth areas;

- Business activity in the central city should be more cyclically sensitive than business in the suburbs.

The cyclical instability of city economies was expected to spill over to city finances, making them especially precarious during recessions.

The relatively good performance of many cities during the recession of 1981–82 prompts a reexamination of cities' exposure to national economic cycles, but it is still too early to have complete data on economic performance by geographic location for the cycle that began in 1981 and was continuing in the growth stage (though with signs of slowdown) as this was written in June 1985. For some of the detail of testing we must return to data on the two cycles of the 1970s. The remainder of this chapter explores the three stated premises.

---

3. For the argument on age of capital, see Prarin Varaiya and Michael Wiseman, "The Age of Cities and the Movement of Manufacturing Employment, 1947–72," working paper 77-1 (Berkeley, California: Institute of Business and Economic Research 1977).

For the argument on labor costs and unionization, see Martin Feldstein, "The Effect of Unemployment Insurance Temporary Layoffs and Unemployment," *American Economic Review*, vol 68 (1978), pp. 834–46; and James Medoff, "Layoffs and Alternatives under Trade Unions in U.S. Manufacturing, *American Economic Review*, vol. 69 (June 1979), pp. 380–95.

4. A. P. Thirwall, "Regional Unemployment as a Cyclical Phenomenon," *Scottish Journal of Political Economy*, vol. 13 (1966), pp. 205–19.

5. For a consideration of this hypothesis, see Howard Friedenberg and Robert Bretzfelder, "Sensitivity of Regional and State Nonfarm Wages and Salaries to National Business Cycles, 1948–79," *Survey of Current Business* (May 1986), pp. 15–27.

Cyclical Sensitivity of Regions and Metropolitan Areas

The traditional theory of subnational economic cycles holds that wide differences exist in cyclical sensitivity across regions and between metropolitan and nonmetropolitan areas, reflecting primarily the geographic concentration of durables manufacturing. The Great Lakes states, where such manufacturing is most intensive, have been found to display above-average cyclical sensitivity as far back as 1914.[6] Since World War II, cyclical swings in the Great Lakes region have had a magnitude about one and a half times the national average.[7] Accompanying this finding is the interesting corollary that in the Great Lakes region other industries besides durables manufacturing experience larger-than-expected cyclical swings, presumably because they are more likely to be suppliers to regional durables manufacturers, which themselves are subject to wide cyclical swings.

Recent periods have witnessed some significant shifts in the traditional pattern of regional cyclical volatility. In 1973–79 the cyclical sensitivity increased in Tennessee, Mississippi, and Arkansas because of increased levels of cyclically sensitive manufacturing in these southern states. In 1980–81 the Great Plains region went from a normally below-average response to one that exceeded the national average, apparently because of the sensitivity of durables manufacturing linked to agriculture.

Because metropolitan areas traditionally have been the manufacturing centers of the United States, these also have been thought to be more sensitive to national economic cycles than the rest of the country. There is evidence indicating that this, in fact, was the case for the early post-World War II cycles. But since 1969—during the era when the federal government under both parties was developing its countercyclical urban policy—metropolitan areas emphatically have not been more cyclically vulnerable than the rest of the nation. Just the reverse has been true. The greatest cyclical vulnerability had been suffered by nonmetropolitan regions.[8] Thus, the first premise ex-

---

6. George H. Borts, "Regional Cycles of Manufacturing Employment in the United States, 1914–1953," *American Statistical Association Journal* (March 1960), pp. 151–211; and Lynne Browne, "Regional Industry Mix and the Business Cycle, "*New England Economic Review* (November-December 1978), pp. 35–53.

7. Robert B. Bretzfelder, "Sensitivity of State and Regional Income of National Business Cycles," *Survey of Current Business* (April 1973), pp. 22–23; and Robert B. Bretzfelder and Howard Friedenberg, "Sensitivity of Regional and State Nonfarm Wages and Salaries to the National Business Cycle, 1980:I-1981:III," *Survey of Current Business* (January 1980), pp. 22–29.

8. See Donald M. Manson, *The Sensitivity of Income in Cities and Suburbs to National Business Cycle Fluctuations*, working paper (Washington, D.C.: Urban Institute, 1983); and George E. Peterson, et al., *Economic Analysis of Effects of Business Cycles on the Economy of Cities*, working paper (Washington, D.C.: Urban Institute, 1984).

plored in this discussion—that metropolitan areas should be more vulnerable to recession and cyclical change than the rest of the country—has been shown to be incorrect.

There are many ways to measure economic activity during a cycle, but the most comprehensive ones are income earned by place of work and personal income received by place of residence. In table 1 cyclical sensitivity is shown in terms of the cyclical swing of personal income—that is, the difference between the growth of real personal income at annual rates during the cyclical expansion and the growth at annual rates during the recession. In all periods shown in the table, cyclical swings for nonmetropolitan areas far exceeded those for metropolitan areas. If anything, the relative volatility of nonmetropolitan regions appears to have intensified during the thirteen years examined.

Several factors appear to account for most of the growth in the relative cyclical volatility of nonmetropolitan areas. One factor is the decentralization of durables manufacturing and construction. These are the most volatile elements of the economy, and as they have decentralized, so has the pattern of cyclical sensitivity. Agriculture has also undergone change; it has become a more industrialized and export-oriented activity, with a consequent increase in vulnerability to economic cycles. The growth in service employment, however, has been a stabilizing element in metropolitan economies. Income from service employment is the most stable component of private income and the most highly concentrated in metropolitan areas. The assumption that

TABLE 1

CYCLICAL BEHAVIOR OF PERSONAL INCOME IN
METROPOLITAN AND NONMETROPOLITAN AREAS, SELECTED PERIODS,
THIRD QUARTER OF 1969 THROUGH 1982

	Cyclical Swing[a]	
Period	*Metropolitan*	*Nonmetropolitan*
1969:3–1973:3	2.63	5.46
1973:3–1980:1	5.23	11.30
1980–1982[b]	1.96	5.21

SOURCES: Based on a 1969–80 Urban Institute analysis of unpublished local area quarterly income data compiled by the Bureau of Economic Analysis, 1980–82; annual local area data are from *Survey of Current Business* (April 1984) pp. 32–35.

a. Difference between real quarterly growth at annual rates during cyclical expansion and real quarterly growth during recession.

b. Economic activity in 1980–82 is measured in terms of annual growth, treating 1981 as an expansion year and 1982 as a recession year. The actual quarterly dates of expansion and recession are expansion, 1980:1–1981:4; recession, 1981:4–1982:4.

TABLE 2

CYCLICAL SWINGS OF SMSAs BY POPULATION GROWTH RATE,
SELECTED PERIODS, THIRD QUARTER OF 1969 TO FIRST QUARTER OF 1980[a]

Population Growth Rate, 1970–80	Number of SMSAs	1969:3 to 1973:4		1973:4 to 1980:1	
		Total Private Income	Personal Income	Total Private Income	Personal Income
Decline	24	4.92	2.19	8.83	5.36
0–5 percent	55	4.79	2.08	8.32	5.08
5–15 percent	72	7.01	3.65	8.89	5.12
15–25 percent	47	5.88	3.31	9.22	4.76
25–50 percent	43	4.77	2.32	9.49	4.62
More than 50 percent	16	5.34	2.77	16.55	8.22
All SMSAs	257	5.46	2.63	9.14	5.23

SOURCES: Same as table 1.

    a. Total private income is by place of work; personal income is by place of residence.

counter cyclical assistance needs to be directed to metropolitan areas, because
that is where cyclical volatility is greatest, does not stand up to the recent
facts. Instead, the pattern of antirecession aid in the 1970s further widened
the advantage in cyclical stability that metropolitan areas already possessed.

Cyclical Sensitivity of Slow-Growth and Fast-Growth SMSAs

A second premise of countercyclical urban policy has been that slow-
growth or declining metropolitan regions are more vulnerable to cyclical
fluctuations than fast-growth metropolitan areas and therefore require special
assistance to combat recessions. At the regional level, Borts, Engerman, and
Tideman each found for earlier cycles that regions experiencing slow-growth
generally had large cyclical fluctuations, whereas those that enjoyed rapid
growth usually had smaller swings.[9] Extension of the pattern to the metropolitan scale, and for later cycles, seemed a reasonable extrapolation.

Experience since 1969 does not sustain this presumption. One way to
measure secular growth is through population change. In all three cycles—
1969–73, 1973–80, and 1981–82—metropolitan areas that lost population
during the 1970s or had extremely slow population growth experienced below-
average cyclical swings. Table 2 shows a detailed comparison of cyclical

---

9. Borts, "Regional Cycles of Manufacturing;" Stanley Engerman, "Regional Aspects of
Stabilization Policy," in Richard A. Musgrave, ed., *Essays in Fiscal Federalism* (Washington,
D.C.: The Brookings Institution, 1965); and T. Nicolaus Tideman, "Defining Area Distress in
Unemployment," *Public Policy*, vol. 24 (Fall 1973), pp. 441–92.

swings by population growth rate. In the 1973–80 cycle, a construction-dominated cycle, the fastest-growing SMSAs had by far the largest cyclical swings, though in the 1969–73 cycle medium-growth SMSAs were most cyclically unstable. The pattern of relative volatility is true both of private income earned (by place of work) and of personal income received (by place of residence) after inclusion of government transfers and income earned from public sector employment. The adjustments made to arrive at personal income remove a good deal of the cyclical swing from household income, but do not alter greatly the relative sensitivity of different types of SMSAs.

These results imply that the problems of urban secular decline are largely separable from the problems of cyclical fluctuations, at least at the metropolitan scale.

Cyclical Sensitivity of Central Cities

The last premise in the traditional understanding of urban areas has been that the central areas of SMSAs, as a group, are more vulnerable to economic cycles than are suburbs. Academic economists have speculated that central city markets are especially vulnerable to national economic cycles.[10] It is from this perspective that the nation's mayors criticized the Reagan administration's urban program. In the words of Coleman Young, mayor of Detroit, and then president of the U.S. Conference of Mayors:

> It seems to me that one of the major arguments for federal assistance to cities is the role of the federal government in managing, or as is currently the case, in mismanaging the economy. High unemployment, high interest rates, trade policy, and federal budget and tax cuts have adversely and disproportionately affected the cities—some cities and regions more than others. Moreover, current economic and fiscal policies have particularly hurt the residents of cities. The negative effects of federal policies on cities and their residents argue for special efforts to ameliorate the effects of these policies.[11]

Empirical evidence does not support the conclusion that the central area of SMSAs, as workplaces, are more vulnerable to economic cycles than are the suburbs or the rest of the nation. Income data are collected at the county level so that central counties have to serve as proxies for actual cities in comparisons. As workplaces central counties, as opposed to suburban coun-

---

10. John F. Kain, "This Distribution and Movement of Jobs and Industry," in John F. Kain, *Essays on Urban Spatial Structure* (Cambridge, Massachusetts: Ballinger, 1975); and Roger Noll, "Metropolitan Employment and Population Distribution and the Conditions of the Urban Poor," in John P. Crecine, ed., *Financing the Metropolis*, vol. 4 (Beverly Hills, California: Sage Publications, 1970).

11. Prepared statement of the Honorable Coleman A. Young, mayor of Detroit, in *The Administration's 1982 National Urban Policy Report*, pp. 110–11.

TABLE 3

CYCLICAL SWINGS OF CENTRAL AND SUBURBAN COUNTIES,
SELECTED INCOME AGGREGATES, SELECTED PERIODS,
THIRD QUARTER OF 1969 TO FIRST QUARTER OF 1980[a]

Period and Location	Total Private Income	Labor Income		Personal Income	Personal Income per Capita
		Place of Work	Place of Residence		
1969:3 to 1973:4					
Central counties	4.91	4.02	4.09	2.53	3.41
Suburban counties	5.64	4.70	3.72	2.50	3.37
1973:4 to 1980:1					
Central counties	8.26	7.15	7.40	4.84	4.74
Suburban counties	10.37	9.19	8.14	5.73	5.18

SOURCE: Based on Urban Institute analysis of local area personal income data compiled by the Bureau of Economic Analysis.

a. Total private income is taken from place of work; personal income is taken from place of residence.

ties, have had markedly more stable income generation over recent economic cycles. This is shown in table 3 by the greater cyclical swings of suburbs in the aggregate.

One reason for the greater cyclical sensitivity of suburbs is the decentralization of manufacturing that has occurred. The suburban counties of SMSAs now have a higher share of income generated from manufacturing than do central counties. They also have a higher share of income from construction, the other most cyclically volatile element of income. In the next section the openings and closings of firms are shown to be especially sensitive to the economic cycle. Because the average rates of openings and closings of firms are higher in the suburbs, these locations are especially vulnerable during cyclical downswings but rebound more vigorously during upswings. Once again, slow secular growth and secular decline do not go hand-in-hand with cyclical volatility.

The greater cyclical vulnerability of suburbs virtually disappears when income by place of residence is analyzed rather than income by place of work. Suburban residents tend to commute to the central county to fill many of the cyclically stable jobs in transportation, finance, insurance, real estate, and services, while there is reverse commuting of central county residents to more cyclical suburban jobs in manufacturing and construction.

When cyclical intensity is measured by the unemployment rates of residents, rather than by their income, central counties show a somewhat greater cyclical swing than suburban counties. This difference is explained by the fact that outright unemployment is concentrated in lower-income and minority groups that are overrepresented in central areas, whereas cyclical variations in income are spread throughout the population.

The lesser volatility of central areas over the cycle is not a quirk of aggregation. During the 1973–80 cycle, central county income was more stable than suburban county income in all nine census regions. A comparison between central counties and suburban counties of the same SMSAs offers further evidence. Of the 137 metropolitan areas that have more than one county, the central county had a smaller cyclical swing in income by place of work than its own suburban counties in 78 metropolitan areas during the 1969–73 cycle. The central county had a smaller cyclical swing in 97 of the 137 metropolitan areas in the 1973–80 cycle.

The fact that income measures are available only for central counties makes a precise analysis for central *cities* impossible, except in the handful of cases in which central city and central county boundaries coincide. However, the evidence strongly suggests that the more stable cyclical behavior of central counties is also true of central cities. In the sixteen SMSAs in which the central county coincides with the central city, the central counties have shown an especially pronounced pattern of greater stability relative to the rest of the SMSA. This is also true of the seventeen SMSAs in which the central city accounts for 80 to 99 percent of the central county population (see table 4).

Secular decentralization of economic activity from the central city to the suburbs has continued throughout all stages of the economic cycle, but it has proceeded more swiftly during expansions than during contractions. Central counties see their share of SMSA income decline most rapidly during cyclical upswings, when new investment and new firm start-ups are most vigorous. In contrast, during the 1973–75 recession, decentralization of income generation within metropolitan areas came to a virtual halt.[12] A comparison of rates of metropolitan decentralization during the 1969–80 period shows that the slowdown in outward movement of economic activity during recessions holds true for most individual sectors, as well as for income in the aggregate (see table 5). By every empirical measure available, it simply is not true that

---

12. Donald M. Manson, Marie Howland, and George E. Peterson, "The Effect of Business Cycles on Metropolitan Suburbanization," *Economic Geography* (January 1984), pp. 71–80.

TABLE 4

CYCLICAL SWINGS OF CENTRAL AND SUBURBAN COUNTIES WITH POPULATIONS THAT
APPROXIMATELY MATCH THOSE OF CENTRAL CITY BOUNDARIES, SELECTED INCOME
AGGREGATES, SELECTED PERIODS, THIRD QUARTER OF 1969
TO FIRST QUARTER OF 1980[a]

		1969:3 to 1973:4			1973:4 to 1980:1		
Ratio of Central City to County Population	Number of Counties	All Private Income	Labor Income	Personal Income	All Private Income	Labor Income	Personal Income
Central counties							
100 percent	16	1.32	1.15	0.44	6.47	5.32	3.36
80–99 percent	17	5.68	4.95	3.13	9.01	7.95	4.56
Suburban counties							
100 percent	16	3.22	2.84	0.84	8.90	7.83	4.84
80–99 percent	17	7.99	5.31	3.81	11.74	9.64	7.19

SOURCE: Sources and notes same as table 3.

central cities, as places of work, suffer more from modern economic cycles than the rest of the country.

Behavior of Firms During the Business Cycle

The cyclical sensitivity of cities ultimately depends on the cyclical behavior of firms. To better understand the behavior that underlies cyclical fluctuations, The Urban Institute examined a sample of 53,929 individual business establishments in three industries.[13] The data base was constructed from four Dun and Bradstreet market indicator files, 1973, 1975, 1979, and1982, merged with the U.S. Bureau of the Census City Reference File to determine the geographic location of each establishment. These firms essentially make up the universe of establishments in three industries during the period studied: the merged file contains information on 27,014 machine tool, 14,067 electronic components, and 11,909 motor vehicle and parts establishments. The industries were selected to represent an average-growth industry (machine tools), a fast-growth industry (electronic components), and an industry that was stagnating during this period (motor vehicles and parts). We limited the sample to manufacturing industries in order to concentrate on

13. George E. Peterson, Marie Howland, and Donald M. Manson, "Economic Analysis of the Effects of Business Cycles on the Economy of Cities," working paper (Washington, D.C., Urban Institute, 1985).

TABLE 5

ANNUAL PERCENTAGE CHANGE IN CENTRAL COUNTY SHARE OF
SMSA INCOME EARNED IN THE PRIVATE SECTOR,
SELECTED INDUSTRIES AND PERIODS,
THIRD QUARTER OF 1969 TO FIRST QUARTER OF 1980

	1969:3–1973:4		*1973:4–1980:1*	
Industry	*Recession*	*Expansion*	*Recession*	*Expansion*
All private	−0.26	−0.39	−0.03	−0.42
Construction	−0.47	−0.46	0.24	−0.46
Manufacturing	−0.32	−0.30	−0.24	−0.41
Transportation, communications, and utilities	−0.52	−0.36	−0.25	−0.43
Retail	−0.64	−0.48	−0.26	−0.39
Finance, insurance and real estate	−0.18	−0.44	0.44	−0.72
Other services	−0.24	−0.32	0.07	−0.36

SOURCE: Same as table 3.

industries that had displayed cyclical volatility at the national level. The Dun and Bradstreet source provides information only on the number of employees by establishment, so total employment was used as the measure of economic activity.

When these data are analyzed in table 6, a surprisingly clear pattern of cyclical performance emerges. The cyclical volatility of industry employment comes from the openings of new establishments and the closings of old ones. Both these elements of employment change are highly sensitive to the national economic cycle. In contrast, net employment change within existing establishments shows a *countercyclical* tendency—pronounced in the case of machine tools, less pronounced in electronic components, and overwhelmed by declining industry employment in motor vehicles and parts. As production is eliminated at marginal branch plants or other marginal locations, some of the demand is diverted to continuing establishments, allowing them to sustain or even increase employment during recessions.

The rates of openings and closings of establishments are closely linked to each other for the simple reason that newly created establishments are the most likely to fail. When the establishments are new firms, they tend to be small, precariously financed, and reliant on growth in demand that spills over from the existing firms in an industry. Often these firms are created to pick up contracts that the well-established firms cannot fully handle during periods of economic expansion. Many new establishments are new branch plants set up by multilocation firms; these establishments are the first to disappear during

TABLE 6

ANNUAL AVERAGE NATIONAL EMPLOYMENT GROWTH RATES: EXPANSIONS,
OPENINGS, AND CLOSINGS OF FIRMS IN THREE INDUSTRIES, SELECTED PERIODS,
1973–82

Industry and Employment Measure[a]	Recession, 1973–75	Expansion, 1975–79	Recession, 1979–82
Machine tools			
Net expansions	2.08	0.63	1.76
Opening	3.76	5.99	5.35
Closing	−8.32	−4.67	−7.57
Total	−2.48	1.95	−0.46
Electronic components			
Net expansions	2.68	1.92	2.13
Opening	3.30	7.15	6.22
Closing	−10.36	−6.32	−6.74
Total	−4.38	2.75	1.61
Motor vehicles			
Net expansions	1.44	−0.78	−2.57
Opening	0.24	0.47	0.56
Closing	−4.13	−5.19	−7.17
Total	−2.45	−5.50	−9.18

SOURCE: Urban Institute analysis of Dun and Bradstreet files.

a. Net expansions are in continuing establishments. Change of establishment location is included in openings and closings.

recessions. For example, in 1975, 24 percent of machine tool establishments had been in business less than five years, yet this group accounted for 38 percent of all closings during the recession. Small establishments closed at a much higher rate and were more cyclically sensitive than large establishments. Branch plants in all three industries closed at a higher rate and their closures were more cyclically sensitive than individual establishments or headquarters plants.

The importance of openings and closings of establishments in the net employment change of an industry means that the industry tends to be more cyclically volatile in those locations where it is growing fastest. For most industries this is the suburbs, which have displayed the strongest swings in industry employment (see table 7). Electronic components employment, however, continues to grow fastest in the central cities—perhaps because it is an industry in which establishments are of much smaller average scale and therefore more reliant on face-to-face contact with suppliers and purchasers. For

TABLE 7

CYCLICAL SWINGS IN EMPLOYMENT BETWEEN RECESSION AND EXPANSION,
CENTRAL CITIES AND SUBURBS, 1973–79 AND 1975–82[a]

Cycle and Average Growth Rate	Central City	Suburbs
Machine tools		
1973–79	4.89	5.13
1975–82	3.55	5.36
Average growth rate, 1975–82	−2.4	4.00
Electronic components		
1973–79	9.70	5.50
1975–82	6.19	−0.38
Average growth rate, 1975–82	2.2	0.50
Motor vehicles		
1973–79	−8.00	11.60
1975–82	1.84	8.47
Average growth rate, 1975–82	−6.50	−3.70

SOURCE: Same as table 6.

a. Annual average employment growth rate during expansion minus annual average growth rate during recession.

electronic components, cyclical employment fluctuates most strongly where secular growth is highest; thus employment is more cyclically variable in the central city.

The data presented here call into question the widely held perception that central city employment, by industry, is more cyclically volatile than employment in the same industries in other locations. Perhaps more important, this observation raises questions as to whether such variability, if it were present, would be undesirable. High rates of cyclical fluctuation appear to go hand-in-hand with higher rates of employment creation through firm openings, a sign that an area is performing the "incubator" function traditionally held to be a strength of central cities. More concern, perhaps, should be expressed over the fact that this incubator function in many industries has moved out of the central city, taking with it cyclical instability of employment.

The Appropriateness of Anticyclical Urban Policy

Care must be taken to avoid exaggerating the importance of a theory of city cyclical behavior in formulating federal urban policy in the 1970s. Although the major elements of this policy were introduced expressly as parts of an antirecession package, the argument for countercyclical aid did not rest solely in the belief that cities were more cyclically sensitive than the rest of the nation.

Underlying the countercyclical programs, too, was a special concern over the long-run position of older, poorer cities. Urban policy during the Carter and Ford administrations was intended to help revitalize places that had been losing jobs and population over the longer term. This purpose might have been submerged beneath language stating that the urban programs were temporary programs designed to help cities combat the effects of recession, but the secular commitment to assist distressed cities was always evident.

Still, all qualifications aside, the major elements of urban policy in the 1970s were advanced as countercyclical measures and were tied to a widely accepted theory that it was cities that suffered most from national economic cycles, and that cities with the poorest secular performance also displayed the greatest cyclical volatility. That theory now appears to have been wrong.

The Fiscal Position of Cities and the State-Local Sector

During the aftermath of the 1973–74 recession the federal government had in operation an unprecedented array of countercyclical programs designed to help protect the state-local sector, and particularly cities, from the effects of recession. During the 1981–82 recession the Reagan administration let the state-local sector resist recession on its own. In fact, the largest domestic budget cuts of President Reagan's first term were delivered in fiscal 1982 to coincide with the recession. The 1983 Emergency Jobs Appropriations bill that eventually was passed by Congress, over the president's objections, was but a weak reminder of the countercyclical efforts of the 1970s. How did state and local governments react fiscally to the two cycles, and what lessons are to be learned from this behavior?

The Cyclical Pattern of State-Local Surplus

To measure aggregate state and local financial condition we analyzed the balance between general revenues and general expenditures. This figure is reported in the national income accounts as the general surplus—that is, the balance between revenues and expenditures after exclusion of changes in the financial position of state and local government pension and other trust funds.

The growth path of the general surplus as reported in the national income accounts is not easy to interpret. One problem is that the surplus is not a running index of fiscal health in a sector. Most local governments, and all states except one, require balanced budgets. Therefore, over any extended period of time, annual surpluses tend to gravitate toward zero. There is nothing in a surplus number to indicate how difficult it was to achieve the reported balance—whether it was produced by "automatic" revenue gains resulting from economic growth or created by increases in tax rates or cutbacks in expenditures. There are also technical difficulties in the measure. Capital *spending* is counted as part of sectoral expenditures in the national income accounts, but sectoral borrowing (mostly through bond issues) to finance capital outlays is not counted as revenue. Repayments of debt are not included as expenditures. Thus the reported surplus is not a current account surplus, a cash flow surplus, or a combined funds surplus. Nevertheless, the general surplus does measure the excess of revenues over current plus capital expenditures in the state-local sector, and thus gives an indication of the sector's overall financial condition. It is best interpreted as the amount of money the sector generates in a given year, after paying current and capital costs, and therefore has available to retire debt or set aside for other purposes.

The national income accounts surplus responds systematically and predictably to the business cycle. On average, the state and local government sector has shown a surplus during expansionary periods and a deficit during national contractions. This pattern held true in all four expansions since 1969 and in three of four contractions. The only exception was the very brief (one quarter) 1980 contraction, when the surplus fell sharply but remained positive. Moreover, the annual and quarterly movements of the surplus have tracked the economic cycle quite faithfully.

The greatest deviations from regular cyclical surplus behavior occurred in the quarters after the national recession trough of 1974 and in the quarters beginning with the national recession trough of 1982 (see table 8). Paradoxically, after the 1974 recession, despite the unprecedented amounts of countercyclical federal aid that became available, the state-local sector ran the largest deficits of the post-World War II period. The sector remained in deficit for six quarters after the recessionary trough was reached. In contrast, during the recession of the first Reagan term, and despite contemporaneous cuts in federal aid, the state-local sector ran deficits for a total of only three quarters. During the early recovery stages of the cyclical expansion, it produced national income accounts surpluses that ran several billion dollars above the level predicted by a regression equation fit for the entire 1974–84 period.[14] The difference in state-local surplus position over the two cycles are shown clearly in table 8.

---

14. Ray Bahl, "Business Cycles and the Fiscal Health of State and Local Government" (Washington, D.C.: Urban Institute, 1985).

TABLE 8

STATE-LOCAL AGGREGATE BALANCES IN LAST TWO MAJOR RECESSIONS,
QUARTERLY SURPLUS AT ANNUAL RATES
(*Billions of Dollars*)

Quarter, in Relation to Recession Trough	1974–75 Recession	1981–82 Recession
Quarters preceding trough		
First	−3.0	1.0
Second	−6.8	−1.0
Trough of Recession	−7.6[a]	−3.7[b]
Quarters following trough		
First	−7.2	−1.9
Second	−5.8	7.0
Third	−4.2	9.5
Fourth	−4.5	12.0
Fifth	−1.6	13.4
Sixth	−1.4	12.6
Seventh	8.4	4.3

SOURCE: National income accounts, as revised in July 1984.

    a.   First quarter of 1975.
    b.   Fourth quarter of 1982.

It seems evident in retrospect that in the 1974–75 recession congressional passage of the antirecession fiscal legislation, most elements of which were not finally approved until 1976 (over President Ford's veto), encouraged states and localities to wait for fiscal help from Washington rather than act swiftly on their own to close their budget gaps. The anticipation of federal funds, as well as the delay in approving the federal antirecession package, caused the state-local sector to prolong and deepen its deficits. During the 1981–82 recession the reverse incentives were at work. States and localities were convinced that no countercyclical assistance would be provided by the administration (although eventually the Emergency Jobs Appropriations bill was passed), and they expected still deeper cuts in existing federal aid programs. Discerning no choice but to solve their own budget problems, they acted with unprecedented speed to raise taxes and cut spending.

The Financial Position of Cities

The aggregate state and local surplus is not a good measure of the financial position of individual cities or even of cities as a class. Analysis of financial data for cities has been troublesome until recently because of the difficulty of obtaining records for individual cities. One analyst, Philip Dearborn, has been successfully tracking several measures of finances in large cities since the early 1970s, so that a decade-long time series is now available for several of the most important indicators of financial conditions in cities.[15]

These measures reveal a striking secular improvement in the finances of large cities that continued, and perhaps even accelerated, through the first two years of the Reagan administration, despite recession and cutbacks in federal aid. At the end of fiscal 1982—in the trough of the national recession and after the year of steepest federal aid reductions—finances of large cities were in better shape than during any year of the 1970s.

Table 9 compares several indexes of financial distress for the thirty largest cities in the United States for three periods: at the beginning of the 1970s, in 1976 after the recession of 1974–75, and at the end of fiscal 1982. The measures reflect the financial position of cities' general funds, those funds that are available for the provision of general services.

The first section of the table considers general fund operating deficits. A single year's deficit is not unusual. Indeed, in cities that have an accumulated surplus, a single year's excess of expenditure over revenue may be a planned event. However, a deficit of significant size dictates the need for budget adjustment and is a harbinger of possible financial trouble. In the table, a "significant" deficit is defined as one in which general fund expenditures exceed revenues by more than 5 percent. Both the number of cities finding themselves in this position, and the severity of their deficits, have declined greatly since the 1970s. A related measure of financial risk is the occurrence of two consecutive years of general fund deficits, with the deficit larger in the second year than in the first. This measure, too, reveals improvement in city financial conditions, though the number of cities falling into this position has never been very large.

"Accumulated deficits," the third measure shown in the table, carry forward the sins of past budgets and represent the inherited constraint on current finances. In most states, cities are required by law to maintain positive accumulated balances in their general funds. Again, an overall improvement in city finances is evident. In fact, special circumstances mark some of the cities that face accumulated deficits in the most recent period. The city of Chicago, for example, operates under an unusual state law, according to which expenses are incurred in one year and property taxes are collected to pay for these expenses in the *next* year. This arrangement perpetuates a cumulative deficit in the general fund, which is covered through short-term borrowing in anticipation of future property tax levies.

---

15. Philip Dearborn, *Bankruptcies, Defaults, and Other Government Financial Emergencies* (Washington, D.C.: U.S. Advisory Commission on Intergovernmental Relations, 1985).

TABLE 9

MEASURES OF FINANCIAL DISTRESS IN THIRTY LARGE CITIES, 1971, 1976, AND 1982
(Percentage)

Status of General Funds	1971		1976[a]		1982	
Expenditures exceed revenues by more than 5 percent	Cleveland	-16.1	New York	-9.3	Cincinnati	-5.2
	Philadelphia	10.2	Boston	-9.0		
	New York	-9.2	Cincinnati	-7.7		
	Buffalo	-7.3	Milwaukee	-6.1		
			New Orleans	-5.7		
Expenditures exceed revenues for two consecutive years[b]	Cleveland	-16.1	Boston	-9.0	Cincinnati	-5.2
	New York	-9.2	Milwaukee	-6.1	Denver	-2.8
	Buffalo	-7.3	New Orleans	-5.7	New Orleans	-2.6
Accumulated deficits, shown as a percentage of revenues	Chicago	-47.5	New York	-31.1	Cleveland	-11.8
	Cleveland	-16.6	Chicago	-24.8	Chicago	-10.6
	New York	-9.2	Buffalo	-15.0	Boston	-4.7
	Philadelphia	-6.1	Boston	-10.7	St. Louis	-1.5
	Detroit	-3.7	Philadelphia	-10.2	Columbus	-1.0
	St. Louis	-2.9	Detroit	-5.6	New York	-0.2
	New Orleans	-1.2	San Antonio	-3.9		
Five cities with lowest liquidity, as a percentage of expenditures			New York	-8.1	Chicago	11.7
			Chicago	-4.0	Los Angeles	11.8
			Boston	0.8	New York	12.8
			Philadelphia	6.6	Boston	18.1
					Detroit	27.0

SOURCE: Philip Dearborn, *Bankruptcies, Defaults, and Other Government Financial Emergencies* (Washington, D.C.: U.S. Advisory Commission on Intergovernmental Relations, 1985).

a. Cleveland's true financial condition was subsequently judged inauditable. However, it would have appeared on all four distress measures for 1976.

b. With the second year showing a larger percentage of expenditures.

The last measure of financial condition shown is liquidity—the ratio of a city's cash and cash equivalents on hand to general fund spending. This is a measure of a city's financial cushion. It was the loss of liquidity that finally triggered financial crises in New York City and Cleveland during the 1970s. Overall liquidity ratios have improved since the mid-1970s, and the number of cities operating with dangerously low liquidity positions has declined greatly.

On the basis of these data, cities were in better financial position in 1982, the most difficult year of adjustment to the Reagan economic and fiscal program, than in the late 1970s when federal urban assistance was at its height. There is only one sense in which federal policy could be said to be responsible for this improvement. The belief that federal aid was going to be cut by an uncertain but probably large amount led cities to manage their finances carefully to guard against this risk. Like the rest of the state and local sector, cities raised taxes and cut expenses faster during the 1981–82 recession than in any of the other recessions after World War II. This fiscally conservative behavior undoubtedly reflected city officials' appraisal that the external funding environment contained more uncertainties than in the past.

The financial experience of cities since the mid-1970s seems to bear out one tenet of the Reagan administration's domestic policy: that cities are able to look out for themselves fiscally, with emergency help from the states if necessary. Since the mid-1970s the basic financial management of cities has changed. The defaults of New York City and Cleveland provided the initial impetus for taking financial management more seriously. But private financial markets have been largely responsible for perpetuating the new attitude. The markets now demand far more complete disclosure of city financial condition than formerly, including timely financial reports prepared according to generally accepted accounting principles and external audits. In states like New York and Ohio where more than one city has come to the brink of financial disaster, the state legislatures have enacted special measures establishing the terms for state assistance in regaining financial equilibrium and also reporting and auditing requirements to avoid financial crises in the future.

The Effects of Cutbacks in Federal Aid

Although recession proved to have the more serious impact on city budgets during President Reagan's first term of office, at the outset of that term reductions in federal aid were viewed as equally threatening. Now that the administration has produced in its second term a new list of proposed federal aid cuts, once again seemingly focused on city programs, it is fitting to look back on the experience of the first four years. Why did the worst fears of city leaders fail to materialize?

TABLE 10

CURRENT POLICY BASELINE AND ACTUAL FUNDING,
SELECT URBAN PROGRAMS, FISCAL 1982
(*Millions of dollars*)

Urban Program	Fiscal 1982 Policy Baselines[a]		Actual Fiscal 1982		Percentage Reduction	
	Budget Authority	Outlays	Budget Authority	Outlays	Budget Authority	Outlays
Community development block grant	3,886.0	4,656.0	3,456.0	4,127.7	−11.1	−11.3
Urban Development Action Grant	662.0	729.0	439.7	500.3	−33.6	−31.4
Comprehensive Employment and Training Act, Public Service Employment	366.2	3,868.0	0.0	139.0	−100.0	−96.4
Mass transit	4,997.7	4,011.0	3,497.7	3,868.9	−30.0	−3.5
Wastewater treatment	3,544.0	4,133.0	2,400.0	4,300.0	−32.3	4.0
Economic Development Administration	610.0	537.0	198.5	405.0	−67.5	−24.6
Compensatory education	3,884.2	3,403.0	3,033.9	3,105.0	−21.9	−8.8
Social services block grant	3,279.0	3,266.0	2,580.0	2,567.0	−21.3	−21.4
Community services block grant	586.0	591.8	348.0	376.0	−40.1	−36.5

SOURCE: Unpublished data, Office of Management and Budget.

a. Based on policies in effect at the end of fiscal 1980.

Part of the answer, of course, lies in the fact that the first-term federal budget cuts never reached the proportions that the president proposed. Some of the proposed program terminations—for example, wastewater treatment grants—never took place. Other programs listed for extinction or sharp cutbacks—such as urban highway aid, mass transit capital support, and low-income energy assistance—actually grew in budget scope, when Congress passed the Surface Transportation Assistance Act of 1982 and the Emergency Jobs Appropriations act of 1983.

Nevertheless, in purely budgetary terms, President Reagan achieved a large share of his initial goal for funding reductions in domestic aid programs. For the set of urban programs listed in table 10, the president requested a cut of 44 percent in budget authority from the pre-Reagan "baseline" level and achieved a cut of 36.5 percent. The reductions in outlays from baseline levels were smaller (23 percent), but came even closer to the president's proposals. Although the Emergency Jobs Appropriations Act temporarily restored some of the grant funding for social programs and the boost of five cents in the gasoline tax restored and augumented capital grants for highways and mass transit, a large departure from past trends in urban aid funding was apparent.

One reason the budget cuts of the first term did not have more impact on city governments was that the federally assisted programs proved readily detachable from the rest of a city's activities. Reductions in federal aid were swiftly passed on to individual programs, many of which city officials often regarded as marginal to their principal service responsibilities, without necessitating general budget readjustments. The importance of this "detachability" shows up repeatedly in the case studies of local responses to federal aid reductions conducted by The Urban Institute and in case studies of the state and local impacts of the Reagan domestic program directed by Richard Nathan.[16]

Typical was the assessment of San Diego's city manager, who observed: "We don't find ourselves affected much by Reagan's budget policies. Part of the ongoing approach of the mayor and council for the past several years has been to avoid great dependence on the federal government."[17]

Echoing the same view of federal assistance was the Boston city treasurer: "We got out of running the city on basic federal funds five years ago. The fiscal problems of the city, since 1979, have not been attributable to decreases in federal aid. The federal cuts have simply meant that we provide far fewer special services than we used to provide. It's the service populations for these programs, not the city budget or the city taxpayers, that has had to make the adjustments."[18]

Since the termination of Carter's antirecession federal aid, federal categorical assistance in most cities has not been used to support basic services like police or fire protection, sanitation, financial management, or even schools to a great extent. Federal grants typically were handled through separate funds and were used to finance auxiliary activities whose spending could be adjusted upward or downward to reflect federal assistance levels. By 1981, for example, almost all cities had moved their Public Service Employment (PSE)

16. Richard P. Nathan and Fred C. Doolittle, "Overview: Effects of the Reagan Domestic Program on States and Localities," working paper (Princeton, New Jersey: Princeton Urban and Regional Research Center, June 1984).

17. Harold Wolman, "The Effect of President Reagan's Domestic Policy on San Diego's Fiscal Circumstances," working paper (Washington, D.C.: Urban Institute, September 1983).

18. Kim Warshaw, "The Effect of President Reagan's Domestic Policy on Boston's Fiscal Circumstances," working paper (Washington, D.C.: Urban Institute, September 1983).

workers out of general government services, in anticipation that federal funding for the program would be terminated at some point.

Often the managerial organization of a city dramatized the separate treatment of federal programs. Boston, for example, established separate agencies to administer the major federal grant programs. As federal assistance diminished, a parallel administrative consolidation took place, which shrank the special agencies to a single one charged with overseeing most federal programs. The city of Los Angeles established a Community Development Department to administer most federal grants and ensure their isolation from regular city operations. In fiscal 1983 this entire department received no general fund support from the city. Its isolation from general city operations was symbolized by its location nearly a mile from city hall, in the only leased office space that the city government used.

Of course, not every city was able to isolate federal aid programs in a way that made it easier to absorb funding reductions. The cities under the greatest fiscal pressure had to continue to try to convert federal grants into support for basic services, wherever possible. Their success in this endeavor made them specially vulnerable to aid reductions. One extreme example of such dependence on federal aid is Detroit. The city finance director reported that even in 1981, "CETA [Comprehensive Employment and Training Act] workers were spread throughout the departments and were used for essential services."[19] When the PSE program was terminated in September 1981, the city lost funding for more than 1,800 CETA Comprehensive Employment and Training Act employees working in general city positions, more than 10 percent of the city's work force. (The single largest CETA employer was the police department.) In 1978 or 1979 this direct dependence on federal dollars would have been typical of many cities, but by 1981 it was a rare exception.

The political maneuvering over the first-term budget cuts reinforced the separability of federal aid reductions. When the final pattern of budget reductions is compared with the pattern that the president initially advocated, it can be seen that the actual cuts came to be concentrated on programs that were most readily detachable from general city functions and commanded the best local political support. Funding for community services agencies, legal aid societies, low-income housing assistance, and temporary public employees was cut severely. These activities served special constituencies without much political clout. Cities by and large simply reduced local spending to reflect the lower levels of federal assistance. By contrast, in the first term cities

---

19. Kim Warshaw, "The Effect of President Reagan's Domestic Policy on Boston's Fiscal Circumstances," working paper (Washington, D.C.: Urban Institute, October 1983).

successfully resisted most of the cuts planned for wastewater treatment plants, general revenue sharing, or mass transit aid.

In a survey of local government officials in Pennsylvania and Texas, Taebel and Cole found that the majority of local officials *favored* federal cuts in many programs that were independent of city government.[20] The program areas from this survey are ranked below by city officials' attitudes toward federal funding reductions. A score of 5.0 indicates a "very favorable" attitude toward federal spending reduction; a score if 1.0, a "very unfavorable" attitude. A score of 3.0 is neutral. Although the president proposed funding reductions in all these programs, the final pattern of cuts in the first term of the Reagan administration corresponds closely with the local political attitudes toward them that were reported in the survey.

Program Area	*Attitude Rating*
Legal services	3.64
CETA public service employment	3.22
Regional activities	3.09
Low-income housing	3.00
Youth employment	2.97
Mass transportation	2.79
Sewage treatment plant construction	2.22
Average	3.01

The experience of cities with the Reagan administration's first-term budget cuts may have limited relevance in predicting the effects that another round of major cuts in the second term would have. The most readily separable programs already have absorbed their cuts. Further funding reductions must come from programs more important to the general budget and to core city services. General revenue sharing, for example, which finally was eliminated in the federal budget for fiscal 1986, constituted 5 to 6 percent of the income of the typical big city's general fund. Its elimination is likely to necessitate local tax increases or general service reductions, although the cities' surplus position will permit gradual adjustments. Mass transit operations also are services of central importance to most city governments. Federal aid reductions in these areas will be much more difficult to pass on directly to a specialized service population, without affecting the general city budget. The

20. Delbert Taebel and Richard L. Cole, "State Legislators and City Officials: A Comparison of Perceptions of Urban Problems and New Federalism Budget Cuts," paper prepared for the Urban Institute, February 1984.

TABLE 11

STATE AND LOCAL REPLACEMENT, HEALTH AND HUMAN SERVICES BLOCK GRANTS,
STATE FISCAL YEARS 1981–83
(*Number of Sample States*)

Block Grant	Funding Replacement (Current Dollars)			Full Replacement of Lost Federal Dollars (with Adjustment for Inflation)	
	Full	Partial	Zero or Negative	Yes	No
Social services	11	4	3	3	15
Community services	0	0	18	0	18
Maternal and child health	8	2	3	4	9
Preventive health and health services	9	1	3	5	8
Alcohol, drug abuse, and mental health	12	2	0	5	9

SOURCE: George Peterson et al., *The Reagan Block Grants: What Have We Learned?* (Washington, D.C.: Urban Institute Press, forthcoming).

Note: Data represent actual expenditures by states plus local governments for programs funded by predecessor categorical grants. Full sample consists of eighteen states. Data were collected by The Urban Institute, General Accounting Office, and Association of State and Territorial Health Officials. Where results are reported for fewer than eighteen states, data collection has not been completed.

removal of state and local tax deductibility from the federal income tax, as proposed in the administration's tax simplification plan, would have perhaps the most serious effect on city revenue-raising capacity.

One other reason that cities survived the first-term budget cuts with so little financial disruption is the greater-than-expected help they received from state governments in replacing federal aid reductions. State behavior toward the Reagan block grants provides one index of state replacement. For most block grants a majority of states replaced at least part of the federal funding losses. A number of states increased own-source spending sufficiently to offset the entire dollar loss from federal funds or even to preserve the real value of program spending in the face of both inflation and federal grant reductions. The block grant responses of eighteen states through fiscal 1983 are summarized in table 11. The pattern of replacement strongly reinforces localities' own efforts to preserve general government activities at the expense of detachable federal programs. The community services block grant—used to fund community service agencies outside the local government structure—was the only block grant to receive no replacement funding from state governments.

Conclusions

In sum, cities appeared to fare better in the first Reagan term than might have been expected, certainly better than most advocates of city interests had predicted. Cities do not seem to have suffered more from recession than the rest of the country. In fact, a review of experience back to 1969 shows that city economies have been less sensitive to economic cycles than has the national economy as a whole. Despite the economic and policy shocks they had to absorb, city finances were in better shape at the end of 1982 than at any time in the 1970s, and they were showing a strong trend toward improvement. Even city budgets managed to survive the first Reagan term of office with far less damage than most observers had predicted.

These conclusions seem to me to be important and should be taken into account in framing federal domestic policy for the rest of the 1980s. There may be a temptation, however, to read too much into such conclusions. Although the federal system worked to protect city budgets, the type of cuts made in the first term were the easiest ones for city governments to handle. The experience probably is not a realistic precedent any future budget reductions. The fact that city budgets escaped relatively unscathed from the first term of federal policy reform reflects, to a significant degree, the ability of city governments to pass on the effects of program reductions directly to program beneficiaries. This perspective should remind us that scrutiny of city budgets can only begin the inquiry into the effects of federal program change. The most important consequences are likely to lie outside budget numbers, in the effects on people and institutions, as explored in the other chapters of this volume.

CUTBACKS, RECESSION, AND HOSPITALS' CARE FOR THE URBAN POOR

Judith Feder and Jack Hadley

Currently and historically the financing of hospital care for the urban poor has been both a public and a private function. Governments pay private hospitals to serve some of the poor; private hospitals serve some poor people free of charge; and, in most big cities, governments own hospitals whose primary purpose is to serve people regardless of their ability to pay.[1]

Although critics have always questioned how well this system serves the poor, in the early 1980s concern seemed particularly justified. In that period economic recession substantially increased the number of poor people. At the same time, recession and political pressure reduced the ability and willingness of governments to finance health care for the poor. Most important, changes

---

Preparation of this chapter was supported by grant 18-P-07728/3-01 from the Health Care Financing Administration and grants from The Robert Wood Johnson, Ford, and MacArthur Foundations.

The authors gratefully acknowledge the assistance and advice of Sidney Lewine, whose knowledge and experience in hospital administration greatly enhanced our ability to understand hospital behavior, and of Jack Cooke, who helped us interpret the interaction between hospital rate setting and care available to the poor. We also thank the hospital and public officials who shared their experiences with us. We owe a particular debt to the following hospital association officials for arranging interviews with hospital representatives in their respective cities: Mark Collins, Howard Cook, Stephen Gamble, Irving Gitlin, David Kinzer, and Carol McCarthy. We also appreciate helpful comments from Drew Altman, Randall Bovbjerg, Charles Brecher, John Holahan, William Scanlon, and Rosemary Stevens, and the valuable research assistance provided by Ellen Pisarski.

1. In 1982 there were public hospitals in seventy-two of the hundred largest cities and in forty-three of the fifty largest cities. Among the twenty largest cities, only Philadelphia and Detroit do not have public hospitals, though Detroit's former public hospital, Detroit General, was replaced by a quasi-public, private, nonprofit hospital that has major responsibility for indigent care.

in federal law and pressure on state budgets brought major cutbacks in the federal-state Medicaid program that provides health insurance to the eligible poor.[2] Although the population in poverty increased 13.4 percent between 1980 and 1982, the population with Medicaid coverage remained essentially unchanged.[3]

The Medicaid population remained steady despite poverty growth—in part because of a 1981 federal law that reduced the federal share of Medicaid costs, required states to limit the working poor's eligibility for welfare and Medicaid, and allowed states to make other eligibility reductions; and in part because many states decided not to increase income eligibility standards to keep pace with inflation. State cuts were not necessarily limited to Medicaid. Several states also limited their state-funded health benefit programs that were offered to the poor who were ineligible for Medicaid (such as single adults and childless couples aged twenty-one to sixty-four, and intact families).

At the same time that eligibility restraints were imposed, several states also reduced their Medicaid payments to hospitals and increased their efforts to control hospital use. Between 1980 and 1982, eleven more states (making a total of nineteen) adopted constraints on hospital payment—about half of these spurred by 1981 federal legislation expanding the freedom of states to design their own methods of hospital payment. In addition, many states restricted the number of hospital days covered by Medicaid or narrowed the definition of Medicaid-covered hospital care.

In this chapter we look at what happened to hospital service to the urban poor when there were more people seeking care and fewer public resources to pay for it. Simply stated, the question we seek to answer is, did hospitals use their own resources to support care for the poor when public financing failed to keep pace with the demand for care?

Although this analysis deals exclusively with hospital care, it fits into a larger inquiry about the ability and willingness of private and nonprofit institutions to "replace" federal and state programs when these are cut back. Many analyses have demonstrated than when government hospital financing was first introduced, in addition to augmenting hospital care for the poor, it displaced the charitable care offered by hospitals. Have the local private or

---

2. Randall R. Bovbjerg and John Holahan, *Medicaid in the Reagan Era: Federal Policy and State Choices* (Washington, D.C.: Urban Institute Press, 1982); and John Holahan, "The 1981 Omnibus Reconciliation Act and Medicaid Spending," Working Paper (Washington, D.C.: Urban Institute, May 1984).

3. Judith Feder, Jack Hadley, and Ross Mullner, "Falling through the Cracks: Poverty, Insurance Coverage and Hospitals' Care to the Poor, 1980 and 1982," *Milbank Memorial Fund Quarterly/Health and Society*, vol. 62, no. 4 (Fall 1984), pp. 544–566.

nonprofit sectors stepped in to replace federal and state hospital financing now that this financing has been constrained?

We start the analysis with the presumption that both demand and financing influence how much hospital care the poor receive. If we assume that the incidence of ill health among the poor remains roughly constant over time or fluctuates randomly around an average level, the demand or "need" for hospital care for the poor depends on the proportions of city populations that are poor and unable to pay for care. If hospitals respond to demand, there should be proportionately more care offered to the poor when there are proportionately more poor people.[4] Financing, however, is necessary to support this response. Hospitals' provision of care is likely to depend heavily on the availability of funds from public sources (including Medicaid, and state and local government appropriations) or private hospitals' net revenues (both from net revenues earned on services to privately insured patients and from grants, gifts, and endowment income).[5]

To examine the responses of hospitals to demand and financing, we drew information from two sources. One was a survey of nonprofit, nonfederal hospitals of one hundred or more beds, located in the one hundred largest cities. This survey, conducted jointly by The Urban Institute and The American Hospital Association, obtained hospital data for fiscal years 1980 and 1982 on the volume of charity care and bad debts, revenues by source, and overall financial status. The second source was interviews with selected hospital administrators and financial officers as well as with public officials. These were conducted in twelve of the largest cities.

The survey data provide statistical information on how the volume of hospitals' care to the poor changed between 1980 and 1982 in response to changes in the demand for care by poor people (measured by the percentages of the population below 125 percent of the poverty line) and changes in Medicaid coverage. The interviews reveal hospitals' behavioral responses to changes in demand and financing during the period. Although interviews provide less reliable data, the perceptions of hospital and public officials are

---

4. Not all of the potential demand for hospital care will be translated into actual demand because persons without the ability to pay adjust downward their own attempts to use hospital care. As long as these downward adjustments are distributed evenly over the poverty population, however, actual demand for hospital care for the poor will rise in proportion to the poverty population.

5. Although Medicare finances hospital care for poor elderly persons, we exclude it from this discussion for two reasons: it is available to all elderly persons, not just the poor; and its comprehensive coverage puts the poor elderly on essentially equal terms with other elderly persons in purchasing hospital care.

a basis for interpreting survey results and for identifying hospitals' strategies for addressing the problems of serving the poor.

Our statistical analyses show that hospitals did not respond to increases in poverty with more care for the poor. Public hospitals did increase the share of their resources for the poor, but decreases in their overall resources limited the effects of their efforts. By contrast, private hospitals barely changed the share of their resources for the poor between 1980 and 1982. In fact, in areas where Medicaid assistance did not keep pace with poverty, private hospital care for the poor actually declined. In short, cutbacks in public programs mean less care for the poor.

These findings suggest that hospitals manage or ration their care for the poor when demand increases. Our interviews support this conclusion. Private hospitals in the cities we visited consistently reported efforts to keep care to the poor—notably free care—in check.

The rationing efforts of private hospitals probably increased the demand for stays in public hospitals and contributed to the increase in the share of public hospitals' revenues used to provide care for the poor. Our analysis indicates that public as well as private institutions ration care, and that less service for the poor, not burden shifting, is the major consequence of private hospital rationing. Although data are not currently available to assess the health consequences of hospitals' actions, increased poverty in the absence of increased public financing means that the poor have less access to hospital care.

The next two sections of this chapter present the evidence supporting these conclusions, with an examination of the various factors that influence hospitals' care for the poor. The first section draws on the survey of nonprofit, nonfederal hospitals to describe the hospitals' response to changes in demand for and financing of care for the poor between 1980 and 1982. The second section describes hospitals' behavioral responses to changes in demand and financing, summarizing the information obtained from interviews with hospital and public officials. In addition to documenting that rationing occurs, we relate the way in which private hospitals ration care, the consequences of private rationing for the poor population as well as for public institutions, and the likelihood of political action to avoid rationing and to maintain service to the poor.

Hospitals' Care for the Poor, 1980–82

Hospitals' care for the poor, as we define it, has two components: care financed by Medicaid and care that hospitals deliver without charge—the sum of charity care (for which hospitals expected no payment because patients were unable to pay) and bad debt (for which hospitals expected but did not receive payment).[6] In 1980 the nation's total hospital care for the poor amounted to $14.4 billion—$9.1 billion in Medicaid and $5.3 billion in charity and bad debt—valued at hospitals' full established charges. The one hundred largest cities accounted for more than half of the nation's total hospital care for the poor, $7.7 billion in that year, a share exceeding their shares of the poor's hospital beds (35 percent) and poor people (29.8 percent).

By 1982 the nation's total hospital care for the poor had risen to $20.5 billion, $10.3 billion in the one hundred largest cities. That difference, however, was primarily the result of inflation. Despite an increase in the number of people in poverty of 13.4 percent between 1980 and 1982, the real quantity of the nation's hospital care to the poor increased only 1.5 percent. In the one hundred largest cities, where the population in poverty increased 18.1 percent, the volume of care for the poor was actually lower in 1982 than it was in 1980.

Care for the Poor and Urban Economic Conditions

Not all cities, however, experienced the same economic changes. How did changes in the volume of care for the poor vary with cities' changes in poverty? To answer this question, we ranked the hospitals in the one hundred largest cities by the changes in the poverty population in their respective cities between 1980 and 1982 and divided the hospitals into two groups.[7] The first group, which represented fifty-six cities that experienced little or no change in poverty between 1980 and 1982, averaged an increase of 3.9 percent. The second group represented thirty-six cities that experienced a sizable change in poverty in the two-year period, 46.5 percent increase on average. In 1980, however, the two groups of cities experienced very similar levels of poverty (23 and 25 percent).

Table 12 describes the characteristics of the two groups of cities and their volume of care for the poor in 1980 and 1982. The data show that in both types of cities the amount of care that poor people received declined relative to the change in the poverty population. In cities where poverty rates

---

6. Although people who are able to pay can incur bad debts, our survey found that three-quarters of all bad debt was attributable to the uninsured, most of whom we assume lack the resources to pay full hospital bills. Furthermore, hospitals do not apply consistent definitions of bad debt and charity. What one hospital refers to as bad debt another calls charity; and at different times similar care in the same hospital could fall into either category. For these reasons we have combined bad debts and charity into a single measure.

7. There were no responding hospitals, public or private, in eight of the one hundred largest cities. The numbers of cities in the two groups are unequal because the groups were defined to produce approximately equal numbers of hospitals in both sets.

increased only slightly, the volume of care for the poor dropped about 8 percent, from 3.8 million adjusted patient days in 1980 to 3.5 million adjusted patient days in 1982. In cities with dramatically increased poverty levels, care for the poor did increase but by a much smaller proportion—only 5.6 percent, compared to the 46.7 percent growth in the number of persons with low incomes.

Public versus Private Hospitals

Why was the response of hospitals in these cities so small? The table addresses this question by examining the behavior of public and private hospitals—specifically, the share of their care devoted to Medicaid and free care, their financial status as measured by "percent total margins" (defined as the

TABLE 12

HOSPITALS' CARE FOR THE POOR IN THE HUNDRED LARGEST CITIES,
BY CHANGE IN POVERTY, 1980 AND 1982[a]

Community Characteristics and Hospital Care	Cities with Little or No Change in Poverty (56 Cities)		Cities with High Increase in Poverty (36 Cities)	
	1980	1982	1980	1982
City characteristics				
Percentage below poverty[b]	28.3	23.3	25.7	36.2
Percentage with Medicaid	11.6	9.4	15.2	18.3
Percentage change in Poverty 1980–82[c]	. . .	3.9	. . .	46.7
Hospitals' volume of care for the poor (thousands of adjusted patient days)[d]				
Public hospitals	1,252	1,134	1,140	1,297
Percentage change, 1980–82	. . .	−9.4	. . .	13.8
Private hospitals	2,541	2,354	3,993	4,126
Percentage change, 1980–82	. . .	−7.4	. . .	3.3
All hospitals	3,793	3,488	5,133	5,243
Percentage change, 1980–82	. . .	8.0	. . .	5.6
Hospitals' volume of care for all persons (thousands of adjusted patient days)[d]				
Public hospitals	3,604	3,714	3,384	3,243
Private hospitals	17,591	18,036	23,654	23,741
All hospitals	21,195	21,750	27,038	26,984

TABLE 12 (*Continued*)

Community Characteristics and Hospital Care	Cities with Little or No Change in Poverty (56 Cities)		Cities with High Increase in Poverty (36 Cities)	
	1980	1982	1980	1982
Hospitals' effort in caring for the poor and financial experience				
Number of public hospitals	25	25	19	19
Free care (percentage of charges)	18.0	17.8	17.7	22.8
Medicaid (percentage of charges)	15.7	12.8	17.5	17.2
Government funds (percentage of revenues)	19.0	17.9	19.0	15.3
Total margin (percentage of revenues)	2.1	2.4	1.8	−0.2
Number of private hospitals	145	145	171	171
Free care (percentage of charges)	4.1	4.1	4.3	4.6
Medicaid (percentage of charges)	10.0	8.9	12.5	12.8
Government funds (percentage of revenues)	1.3	1.1	1.1	1.4
Total margin (percentage of revenues)	5.2	4.8	3.2	3.2

SOURCES: Hospital data are from the American Hospital Association and from The Urban Institute, "Survey of Medical Care for the Poor and Hospitals' Financial Status," 1980 and 1982. City characteristics are from the U.S. Department of Commerce, Bureau of Labor Statistics, "Current Population Survey," unpublished data (March 1981 and March 1983).

a. Data are weighted by hospitals' total volume of care.
b. Percentage with income below 125 percent of the poverty income level.
c. The mean of the percentage changes in individual hospitals' city poverty rates.
d. Adjusted patient days are a weighted sum of hospitals' inpatient and outpatient care.

difference between total revenues and expenses, as a percentage of total revenues) and their appropriations from all levels of government.[8] Only public hospitals in cities with large increases in poverty substantially increased their effort to serve the poor between 1980 and 1982. The share of resources they devoted to free care increased almost 30 percent, from 17.7 to 22.8 percent

---

8. Shares are measured by Medicaid and free-care charges as a proportion of total charges. Percent total margins are defined as the difference between total revenues and expenses, as a percentage of total revenues. Appropriations came from all levels of government. Local funds account for about 66 percent of the total.

of total charges.[9] The impact of this increased effort, however, was mitigated by declines in these public hospitals' total volume of care; between 1980 and 1982 this care decreased from 3.4 million to 3.2 million adjusted patient days.[10]

Further evidence of limits to these hospitals' resources is the failure of government appropriations to keep pace with free care. Between 1980 and 1982 government revenues actually fell as a share of total revenues. As a result, these public hospitals spent more than they earned in 1982, incurring negative total margins of 0.2 percent, fully 2.0 percentage points lower than their margins in 1980.

In contrast to public hospitals, private hospitals in cities with large increases in poverty made very little effort to step up their service to the poor between 1980 and 1982, despite positive net margins that stayed consistent throughout the period. In cities in which poverty did not increase, both private and public hospitals reduced their care for the poor. The biggest drops came in Medicaid assistance, which reflected the decrease in the proportion of these cities' populations receiving Medicaid benefits, from 11.6 percent in 1980 to 9.4 percent in 1982. Margins for both public and private hospitals were well above those of hospitals in the cities with high poverty rates.

Medicaid's Role

It is interesting that in cities that experienced an upsurge in poverty the share of hospitals' charges derived from Medicaid barely changed, despite the fact that the proportion of the population receiving Medicaid assistance in these cities grew, on average, from 15.2 percent to 18.3 percent. This average increase, however, disguises the fact that in some cities where poverty rose, Medicaid assistance did not expand, while in other cities this assistance increased along with poverty.

A clear picture of Medicaid's role in supporting care to the poor is presented in table 13, which is based on data from hospitals in two groups

---

9. These data exclude one of the nation's largest public hospitals—University of Southern California Medical Center in Los Angeles County. It changed its funding of free care between 1980 and 1982 as a result of policy changes instituted by the newly elected county commissioners and the state government. Much of the care for medically indigent persons reported as free care in 1980 was designated as care under the newly created county medical program to serve these indigents in 1982. Consequently, reported free care fell, but total care to the medically indigent actually increased. Despite this increase, the hospital's total revenues from governments fell. Thus its experience was consistent with the general pattern for city public hospitals—increased efforts to provide free care despite declining resources.

10. Adjusted patient days represent a weighted sum of hospitals' inpatient and outpatient care.

TABLE 13

Hospitals' Care for the Poor in Cities with Increased Poverty, by Change in Medicaid Coverage, 1980 and 1982[a]

Community Characteristics and Hospital Care	Cities with Decreased Medicaid (6 Cities)		Cities with Increased Medicaid (17 Cities)	
	1980	1982	1980	1982
City characteristics				
Percentage below poverty[b]	24.9	30.8	27.9	34.7
Percentage with Medicaid	15.1	14.0	16.4	18.4
Percentage change in Poverty				
1980–82[c]	. . .	28.1	. . .	25.8
Hospitals' volume of care for the poor (thousands of adjusted patient days)[d]				
Public hospitals	224	267	466	624
Percentage change, 1980–82	. . .	19.2	. . .	33.9
Private hospitals	810	782	2,062	2,233
Percentage change, 1980–82	. . .	3.5	. . .	8.2
All hospitals	1,034	1,049	2,528	2,857
Percentage change, 1980–82	. . .	1.5	. . .	13.0
Hospitals' effort in caring for the poor				
Number of public hospitals	2	2	10	10
Medicaid				
(percentage of charges)	18.1	20.7	13.6	15.2
Free care				
(percentage of charges)	24.6	30.1	14.7	22.8
Number of private hospitals	39	39	70	70
Medicaid				
(percentage of charges)	14.9	14.4	14.1	15.1
Free care				
(percentage of charges)	3.4	3.3	4.5	5.0

Source: Sources and notes are the same as table 12.

of cities with approximately equal and large increases in poverty rates but different changes in Medicaid assistance. The table shows that Medicaid is critical to sustaining care to the poor when poverty rises. In the six cities in which Medicaid assistance declined, care to the poor grew only 1.5 percent while poverty rose 28.1 percent. In the seventeen cities where Medicaid coverage expanded, care to the poor increased 13.0 percent, compared with a 25.8 percent growth in poverty. Although Medicaid expansion did not produce a greater effort to provide care commensurate with the upswing in poverty, without that Medicaid support, hospitals' care to the poor appeared to be almost totally unresponsive to changes in poverty.

This lack of response is the result of private, not public hospitals' behavior. Public hospitals appear to have stepped up their efforts to serve the poor when there was greater poverty, regardless of changes in Medicaid assistance. (Note, however, that only two public hospitals are represented in the six cities where poverty increased and Medicaid declined, so it is difficult to generalize from their experiences.)

Private hospitals, in contrast, reduced the share of care they devoted to Medicaid and free care when Medicaid assistance was reduced. In cities experiencing an expansion of Medicaid, private hospitals increased both their Medicaid services and free care in response to greater poverty. Not surprisingly, for these hospitals the change in Medicaid funding was twice as large as the change in their resources for free care, but they still provided a large amount of free care compared with the amount provided by private hospitals generally. This difference may be due to a relatively high representation, over 25 percent, of private teaching hospitals in this group in the Northeast. These hospitals have traditionally played a prominent role in caring for the poor in their cities.

The responsiveness of public hospitals in large cities to poverty in their communities becomes even more noteworthy when these hospitals are compared with public hospitals in other parts of the country. Table 14 shows changes in public hospital care for the poor *outside* the hundred largest cities between 1980 and 1982, for communities with and without major increases in poverty. The lack of response to poverty is striking. These public hospitals provided almost the same levels of care to the poor—both Medicaid and free care—in 1982 as in 1980 whether or not poverty increased. Public hospitals' total margins remained strongly positive and actually increased over the period in both groups of communities in our study. This behavior is consistent with these public hospitals' low proportions of government revenues—levels suggesting that communities as well as hospitals outside the hundred largest cities are unwilling to guarantee that the poor will have a provider of last resort.

In summary, our analysis shows that between 1980 and 1982, hospital care for the poor in large cities barely increased in response to the substantial rise in poverty. The small amount of increase in hospital care was largely attributable to more free care offered by public hospitals and to the willingness of private hospitals to provide more Medicaid-supported care in cities in which Medicaid coverage increased with poverty levels. But the efforts of public hospitals' were mitigated by reductions in their total resources. Private hospitals, whose resources were less constrained, did not greatly enlarge their effort to provide free care in areas where poverty rose but Medicaid fell.

TABLE 14

<small>Public Hospitals' Care for the Poor in Communities Outside the Hundred Largest Cities, by Change in Poverty, 1980 and 1982[a]</small>

Hospital Care and Community Characteristics	Areas Showing Little or No Change in Poverty		Areas Showing an Increase in Poverty	
	1980	1982	1980	1982
Hospital care for the poor				
Free care (percentage of charges)	9.0	9.3	6.6	6.6
Medicaid (percentage of charges)	8.3	8.5	8.7	8.8
Government revenue (percentage of revenues)	4.5	3.6	3.4	3.5
Total margin (percentage of revenues)	3.0	3.1	4.5	4.7
Community characteristics				
Percentage below poverty[b]	18.8	18.2	17.9	23.5
Percentage with Medicaid	8.0	6.5	7.4	8.2
Percentage change in poverty, 1980–82[c]	. . .	−0.9	. . .	34.1
Number of hospitals	76	76	110	110

SOURCE: Same as table 12.

   a.   Data are weighted by hospitals' total volume of care.
   b.   Percentage with incomes below 125 percent of the poverty income level.
   c.   The mean of the percentage changes in individual inpatient and outpatient care.

Overall, then, experience shows that if government financing—from Medicaid, government appropriations, or grants—is not forthcoming to support care for the poor, the poor will receive less hospital care.

Hospitals' Response to Changes in Financing and Demand for Care of the Poor

To understand how urban hospitals are actually coping with increased demand for free care between 1980 and 1982, we conducted interviews in twelve cities during fall 1982 and winter 1983. The cities and some of their characteristics are listed in table 15. As the table shows, we concentrated our attention on cities with high levels of poverty, because we believed that the capacity of hospitals to provide care to the poor would be most threatened in these cities. Persons interviewed included chief executives and financial officers of private hospitals, local government officials responsible for public hospitals, and state Medicaid administrators.

TABLE 15

CHARACTERISTICS OF TWELVE CITIES VISITED IN 1982–83 TO DETERMINE HOW URBAN HOSPITALS COPE WITH INCREASED DEMAND FOR FREE CARE

City	Total Population 1980	Percentage of Population In Poverty		Percentage of Population Unemployed		Percentage of Population With Medicaid		Income per Capita (dollars) 1980	Percentage of Beds in Private Hospitals 1980
		1980	1982	1980	1982	1980	1982		
Atlanta	425,022	33.0	25.2	7.0	7.5	21.8	12.9	6,550	67.2
Boston	562,994	23.2	33.4	6.2	9.2	13.3	13.9	6,555	91.7
Chicago	3,005,072	29.9	35.4	8.0	10.8	17.5	16.8	6,939	88.9
Cleveland	573,822	25.3	39.0	7.2	10.4	13.9	24.8	5,770	88.8
Denver	491,396	18.3	24.4	5.9	7.0	5.6	4.6	8,556	85.3
Detroit	1,203,339	36.6	43.2	14.1	15.8	22.0	27.3	6,215	100.0
Los Angeles	2,966,763	23.1	32.1	6.6	9.3	13.8	15.2	8,442	69.3
Miami	346,931	48.3	37.3	6.0	10.1	23.1	13.4	6,179	68.7
New Orleans	557,482	28.5	36.4	6.1	9.2	7.5	20.4	6,547	71.0
New York	7,071,030	31.7	38.0	7.7	9.1	20.9	22.7	7,273	73.5
San Francisco	678,974	18.5	21.7	6.5	8.4	15.7	8.4	9,267	89.1

SOURCE: Based on U.S. Department of Commerce, Bureau of Labor Statistics, *Current Population Survey* (March 1981 and March 1983).

Interviews revealed that most private hospitals were actively engaged in limiting their provision of care to the poor. Although public hospitals were less likely to limit service, in some cities they too had to constrain care in response to budget cuts. Even in areas where local governments maintained funding, participants in the health care system did not believe that public hospitals substituted fully for constraints imposed in private hospital care. In general, when hospitals—public or private—limited their services, poor people tended to receive less care.

The following discussion outlines why and how private hospitals "ration" their care for the poor; how constraints on the free care provided by private hospitals affect public hospitals; how public hospital constraints affect hospitals in the private sector; and when (and how) provision of care to the poor becomes a political issue, involving both public and private institutions.

Rationing Care for the Poor

Historical research on urban hospitals demonstrates that the care that voluntary hospitals provide to the poor has never been truly unconstrained. In the nineteenth century, when the poor were the only users of hospitals, voluntary hospitals limited their services to the poor who were considered deserving—"hard working and church-going citizens [who] did not belong in the company of paupers, prostitutes, alcoholics and the dependent generally."[11] The second group, along with the incurable and chronically ill, went to the almshouse, which became the public hospital.[12]

Over time, as the hospital developed from "a well of sorrow and charity" into a "workplace for the production of health," financial pressures also influenced the characteristics of the patient population.[13] Curative medicine meant higher costs, exceeding what hospitals could collect in philanthropy and government funds. To relieve their "chronically strained budgets," hospitals therefore charged fees to patients and began "enforcing a prudent ratio of pay to indigent patients."[14] Different hospitals calculated "prudent ratios" at different levels; older, well-endowed institutions in the Northeast were more inclined to assist the poor than newer hospitals in the Midwest and

11. Charles E. Rosenberg, "From Almshouse to Hospital: The Shaping of Philadelphia General Hospital," *Milbank Memorial Fund Quarterly/Health and Society*, vol. 60, no. 1 (Winter 1982), p. 114.

12. Paul Starr, *The Social Transformation of American Medicine* (New York: Basic Books, 1982), p. 151.

13. Ibid, p. 146.

14. Charles Rosenberg, "Inward Vision and Outward Glance: The Shaping of the American Hospital, 1880–1914," in David J. Rothman and Stanley Wheeler, eds., *Social History and Social Policy* (New York: Academic Press, 1981), p. 32–34.

West. But even in older cities with traditions of serving the poor, financial pressures brought less service. As the demand for care from paying patients grew, "the poor became the residual beneficiaries of care in voluntary hospitals."[15]

In this respect, hospital behavior in the 1980s bears a strong resemblance to behavior in the 1920s and can be understood in similar terms: care to the poor is only one of the goals of a hospital and may be subordinated to the overall survival and well-being of that hospital. Although hospitals obviously have different definitions of well-being (while some relatively affluent hospitals found it necessary to limit care, other hospitals already in deficit were unwilling to alter behavior) most staff members we interviewed said that their hospitals were either considering or had already implemented actions to limit free care.

Strategies for reducing this care fall into two broad categories, restricting access to particular services by the poor and making certain types of services less available. To restrict use of services by persons unable to pay, many hospitals reported adoption (or greater enforcement) of a rule requiring that nonemergency patients without insurance must pay part of their bills in advance. Hospitals varied in the scope and enforcement of their initial cash payment requirements. Some hospitals would give no nonemergency care without some payment; others reported exceptions to that rule. For example, medical considerations took precedence over financial ones in specified circumstances (unique cases valued for teaching purposes and cases in which patients received care that was a continuation of earlier treatment) or, as one financial officer described, "whenever the physicians screamed." Some hospitals applied the initial cash payment rule to all departments. One hospital applied the rule in all departments *except* one in which free care was considered practically unavoidable—that is, obstetric care by the sole hospital in a poor neighborhood. Many hospitals directed the policy specifically to departments with heavy losses, with the outpatient departments as prime candidates. Some hospitals also extended the rule to their emergency rooms, screening patients in order to eliminate nonemergency care for the uninsured.

One hospital reported a more elaborate approach to control of admissions, which included allocation of a fixed budget for care to the poor. To enforce a large reduction in its free care (necessitated by a deficit), this hospital adopted formal priorities for delivery of nonemergency care (first priority to neighborhood residents receiving primary care from hospital-affiliated phy-

---

    15. Rosemary Stevens, "A Poor Sort of Memory: Voluntary Hospitals and Government before The Depression," *Milbank Memorial Fund Quarterly/Health and Society*, vol. 60, no. 4 (Fall 1982) p. 569.

sicians; last priority to persons with self-inflicted injuries or illnesses), with selection of cases made by a committee on a biweekly basis.

A more subtle approach to limiting charity care adopted by hospitals in some cities (particularly those facing low Medicaid payments for outpatient care) was to transfer some of the responsibility for decisions on free care from hospitals to physicians—basically by making physician groups the owners of outpatient departments. Despite the ownership transfer, the hospital continued to influence provision of free care—primarily by subsidizing what physician groups pay the hospital in rent. But formal decisions on the amount of free care to offer and on the enforcement of these decisions became the responsibility of the doctors, not the hospital. Hospital officials who used this approach believed it gave them a way to limit their free care losses while reducing their liability for community or board complaints.

The restrictions placed on free care discussed thus far affected patients with no private or public insurance, not patients covered by Medicaid or general assistance programs. Almost invariably, hospitals did not limit access for the publicly insured, even in cases in which Medicaid paid less than Medicare. Although hospitals in some states refused to treat other states' Medicaid patients, for the most part, less Medicaid revenue tended to mean less care for the uninsured, not for the Medicaid population.

The only exception to this rule occurred in Illinois in 1982, when Medicaid reduced both the number of days it would cover and the rate per day. Chicago hospitals reported their primary methods for reducing Medicaid use to be careful scheduling of elective procedures (delaying admissions to the next month once a given month's quota was reached) and active monitoring of longer stays.

Together with or independent of such controls on utilization, several hospitals reported an alternative approach to reducing free care—a cutback or elimination of services heavily used by the poor. As one hospital administrator explained: "The most efficient way to cut costs is to eliminate services that don't generate revenues." Obviously, services directed to the uninsured satisfy this criterion. Examples that hospitals gave of such services included social services, hospice care, drug treatment, psychiatric care, and outpatient services.

Cutting services offered or service use by the poor may have negative consequences, even in hospital departments that do not generate revenues. Hospitals that value comprehensive training programs, as many major teaching hospitals do, may prefer to sustain money-losing services rather than reduce or eliminate particular training programs. In general, however, hospitals appear willing to subordinate educational objectives to financial soundness when the pressure is on.

The Consequences of Limiting Charity Care

The most commonly cited consequence of the limits placed on charity care by private hospitals is an increased burden on public hospitals. In part this greater responsibility of public hospital reflects patients' behavior—as people without resources or insurance seek care in public rather than private institutions—and in part it reflects the tendency of private hospitals to transfer uninsured patients (or uninsured people seeking admission) to public hospitals.

Private and public hospitals alike acknowledge that transfers do occur. In fact, transfers appear to be a part of hospitals' regular pattern of doing business. Some transfers occur for medical reasons and some for financial reasons, but for the most part, transfers are treated as a matter of course. In most cities, the public hospitals routinely accept transfers when beds are available and when physicians in the transferring and receiving hospital have agreed to the arrangements.

Data on the increased free care provided by public hospitals suggest that number of transfers may have grown substantially between 1980 and 1982. Our interviews suggested, however, that transfers were not the primary problem created by limits on private charity; the more significant consequence seems to have been a reduction in overall care for the poor.

People who are denied nonemergency service by one hospital do not necessarily seek care at another. Instead, they may forgo or defer care. Deferral is consistent with 1980 survey data showing much lower service use by the uninsured[16] and with 1982 survey data indicating that about half of the one million uninsured who needed medical care but did not receive it for financial reasons did not even try to obtain care.[17]

Chicago's recent experience provides an instructive example of the mix of transfers and reduced service likely to occur in response to cutbacks in public financing and private charity. Following major cutbacks in Medicaid, which were announced in summer 1981, transfers to Cook County Hospital rose from between 50 and 150 transfers per month to about 500 in August 1981. As a result, Cook County Hospital experienced record levels of Medicaid patient days (hospital inpatient days used by Medicaid recipients).

That Medicaid boom, however, was short-lived; it was associated with the period of negotiations between the hospital industry and the state over

---

16. In 1980, insured persons received 90 percent more hospital days per capita than did the uninsured. See Karen Davis and Diane Rowland, "Uninsured and Underserved: Inequities in Health Care in the U.S.," *Milbank Memorial Fund Quarterly/Health and Society*, vol. 61, no. 2 (Spring 1983) pp. 149–76.

17. Robert B. Blendon, Drew E. Altman, and Saul M. Kilstein, "Health Insurance for the Unemployed and Uninsured," *National Journal* vol. 15, no. 22 (May 28, 1983), pp. 1146–49.

Medicaid changes. Once an agreement was reached, transfers and overall Medicaid volume fell. Transfers never dropped as low as their previous levels (continuing to range between 250 and 400 per month), but both the hospital's total census and its Medicaid patient days decreased.

This drop occurred even though the negotiated changes in Medicaid meant fewer days of Medicaid service in private hospitals. To stay within limits on total Medicaid patient days, private hospitals reported that they delayed nonemergency admissions when the census was running high and attempted to shorten Medicaid patients' stays. But these actions affected the poor (in reduced service) far more than they affected the public hospital. The continued relatively high level of transfers suggests that the public hospital's responsibility for nonpaying (if not Medicaid) patients did increase with Medicaid cuts.

Acceptance of transfers is not mandatory, however, and public hospitals can reduce both the number of transfers and service delivery to public hospitals' regular clientele. Although in some cities—for instance, Cleveland, Chicago, and New York—public hospitals reported no major new funding problems in 1982, in other cities, limited funds brought efforts to cut back service use and availability.

The revenue pressures on public hospitals are both similar to and different from the pressures that private hospitals face. Medicaid cuts hit public and private hospitals alike, but Medicaid is typically a more important revenue source for the public hospital, so the cuts have a larger impact. Recession and lower incomes can also reduce some public hospitals' service use, as paying patients defer hospital care when their resources are strained. Where local governments offset these reductions (as in Chicago in 1982), public hospitals maintain their spending levels despite lower patient revenue. When local funds fail to keep up or are cut (as in Boston, Denver, and Los Angeles), public hospitals must constrain their spending and may limit their service.

In 1982, public hospitals were taking actions that affected service in Boston, Denver, and Los Angeles. In all three cities, hospitals introduced payment requirements intended to bring in revenue from patients who could pay and reduce service to patients who could not. These actions accompanied staff reductions and other efforts to reduce costs. In Los Angeles and Denver, such efforts included major cutbacks in the number and hours of outpatient clinics; these cutbacks restricted the availability of service to the poor.

Theoretically a cutback in one type of service (for example, outpatient care) could lead to substitution of another (like care in the emergency room or an inpatient stay). In both Denver and Los Angeles, however, public hospital officials reported that contractions were effective. Service reductions were real, and the poor received less care.

It is also theoretically possible (and sometimes argued) that just as private hospitals' cutbacks transfer responsibility to public hospitals, the reverse is true—public hospitals' contractions can shift burdens to private institutions. But again, experience generally fails to bear this out. Hospital administrators in both Denver and Los Angeles indicated that cutbacks in public services generally failed to produce any increase in private hospitals' service delivery. As in private hospitals, public hospitals' cutbacks tend to affect nonemergency care that can be deferred. In these circumstances, a Denver public official explained, not only can private hospitals refuse care (as already described); but poor patients, uncomfortable in hospitals not accustomed to serving them, may not even seek private care. As long as the public hospital treats the most serious cases first, transfers from public to private hospitals seem unlikely.

Exceptional circumstances, however, can produce such transfers. Denver General Hospital's experience with a maternity service emergency offers an example. On a holiday weekend in 1979, Denver General had forty patients in labor and only twenty-four beds. At that point, they closed the hospital to deliveries, had guards intercept arrivals, and diverted emergency ambulance cases to other hospitals. Private hospitals provided the necessary service, under the watchful eye of the Denver press.

But once having accepted this public hospital responsibility at their own expense, private hospitals took action to prevent its recurrence. Private hospitals successfully pressed for legislation to establish a special fund to support maternity care for the poor in private institutions. The lesson is clear: if private institutions are forced to deliver care to the poor, they expect to be paid for it. Otherwise, public cutbacks are likely to mean less service.

California's experience with a formal transfer from private to public institutions offers a final example of the way patient and institutional behavior tend to reduce service delivery when cutbacks occur. In 1982 California transferred responsibility for medically indigent adults (poor people who fail to satisfy Medicaid's non-income-related eligibility criteria) from the state (which had paid for care in private and public institutions) to the counties— specifically, to county hospitals. Although the state and some counties (including Los Angeles) reported an active effort to inform people of the change and to facilitate transfers of patients traditionally served by some private hospitals (especially through outpatient clinics) to the county hospital, the transfer was incomplete. The information effort appeared to sustain inpatient service levels for the medically indigent, but a significant volume of outpatient service did not "transfer" to the public hospital.

A greater service decline could be expected in counties (like San Francisco) that made lesser efforts to notify patients and facilitate transfer. Interviews indicated that the San Francisco government was intentionally "undermarketing" to the medically indigent to avoid overtaxing the public hospital's capacity. The result could be less inpatient as well as outpatient care.

These examples lead to the perhaps unsurprising conclusion that people more than institutions are affected when public financing for health care is cut.

Care for the Poor as a Political Issue

Recognition that care to the poor is *not* unavoidable has significant political implications. Were it true that public hospitals and private institutions serving the poor "protected" other private hospitals (who might have to provide more care to the poor if these institutions did not exist), all hospitals would have a stake in assuring adequate financing for this care. Care to the poor would then be a major political issue for the hospital industry.

But neither the data nor participant perceptions support this point of view. To the extent that private hospitals can limit their care to the poor, the hospital industry as a whole is unlikely to make adequate government aid a high political priority.

When, then, does financing for the poor become a political issue? In two circumstances: (1) when private institutions either want to maintain their service to the poor and find that their resources are inadequate (as in the case of hospitals wanting to maintain a tradition of service to the poor or teaching hospitals, which assign interns and residents to poor patients for teaching purposes) or have no other patients (some community hospitals in poor neighborhoods); and (2) when local governments are either unwilling or unable to maintain their financing and want another level of government (typically the state) to share the burden. In both cases, the hospitals serving the poor must raise the issue of financing for themselves. Because most hospitals neither have to nor want to serve the poor, there is no common front.

Affected hospitals have taken action to sustain or improve their financing. In general, those actions take two forms: an effort to obtain more public funds through some type of special treatment for a given hospital or group of hospitals; or an effort to redesign hospital payment mechanisms in a way that not only brings in additional resources but redistributes resources from "rich" hospitals to "poor" hospitals.

Brooklyn Jewish Hospital. Brooklyn Jewish Hospital offers a visible example of an individual hospital pleading its own case for more aid. In 1979, Brooklyn Jewish—a major nonprofit teaching hospital in the Bedford-Stuyvesant neighborhood of New York City—filed for bankruptcy. Its fiscal status in large part reflected its inability or failure to manage its care for the poor.

As its neighborhood and clientele shifted from middle-class, paying patients to poor and uninsured ones, the hospital did not limit its volume of care for the poor, did not maximize public payments for this population, and did not cut back its teaching programs or tertiary services to live within its means.[18]

Political resistance to closure of a major provider and employer in a poor and medically underserved area produced local and state aid for Brooklyn Jewish Hospital in 1978. When more aid was needed, the city and the state took the hospital's case to the federal government and obtained a demonstration grant in 1979. Generally regarded as the product of electoral politics, the grant was nevertheless touted as a demonstration and accompanied by requirements for management and delivery reform.

This action stimulated broader political interest in the financial status of hospitals serving the poor, and, following the Brooklyn Jewish Hospital demonstration, the federal government launched the Distressed Hospitals Initiative, making four additional awards. Although somewhat different in design, each of these demonstrations construed federal aid as the means to allow greater efficiency in management and delivery, thereby freeing additional resources to finance care for the poor. In fact, some efficiencies have been achieved, but they have not been sufficient to resolve the basic problem—the need for more resources to sustain care for people unable to pay. Despite their demonstration label, these grants are more accurately characterized as aid to specific institutions than as an experimental effort.

At the state level, aid to individual institutions is less frequently packaged as a demonstration. As noted, Brooklyn Jewish Hospital received state aid before federal aid through a special state program to assist institutions in poor neighborhoods (the Ghetto Medicine Program) and through Medicaid. Special grant programs like this are unusual; rate adjustments are not. New York's rate-setting program has an emergency relief provision that adjusts rates for hospitals whose financial soundness is threatened by pressure to provide care to the poor. And in some other states, Medicaid programs have adopted explicit rate adjustments or made allowances to hospitals with a substantial volume of Medicaid and charity care.

This special treatment results, in part, from 1981 federal Medicaid legislation that expanded states' authority to set hospital rates, and, at the same time, required states to take into account high-volume providers to the poor in initiating new payment methods. Although federal officials do not interpret

---

18. Arthur D. Little, Inc., "Evaluation of the Bedford-Stuyvesant/Crown Heights Demonstration Project: Final Report," Report to Department of Health and Human Services, Office of the Assistant Secretary for Planning and Evaluation (Cambridge, Mass.: A.D. Little, March 1983).

this provision as *requiring* adjustments to rates for these hospitals (assessing likely impacts and asserting their acceptability to the state would suffice), in 1982 about two-thirds of the states with state-designed Medicaid hospital payment systems made special allowances for hospitals serving low-income patients.

Sometimes hospitals regard other hospitals' special allowances as a desirable precedent. As one observer explained, "We could be next." But in other cases, deciding who receives these allowances and how much they get can be quite controversial. Extra payments to some are likely to mean lower rates for others, whether the trade-off is implicit or explicit (as in Pennsylvania, where the annual rate of increase in Medicaid payments allowed for all hospitals was reduced to permit extra payments to hospitals with high Medicaid volume). Where allowances are limited to a fixed pool, competition is likely to be quite strong, particularly between public and private hospitals. Allowing Cook County Hospital to qualify for distressed hospital aid from the state of Illinois, for example, substantially diminished funds available for private institutions. That action generated cries of outrage from private hospitals, who argued that the public hospitals could and should rely on local taxpayers for necessary support, rather than use up what to them was a last resort for funds. Similar arguments led New York to adopt different rules for public than for private hospitals in allocating its fund for bad debt and charity care.

Shifting Costs to the Federal Government. As these examples suggest, public hospitals' efforts to gain extra funds are essentially attempts to shift responsibility for financing care for the poor from one level of government to another. Sometimes the shift is accomplished simply by taking advantage of program rules—for example, New York public hospitals' assuring that Medicaid pays the maximum share of overhead; or Boston City Hospital's brief use of a loop-hole in payment rules to charge Medicaid more than $300 per outpatient visit. Sometimes local pressure produces new rules—for example, inclusion of public hospitals in the pool for distressed hospitals in Illinois and New York, or having state-employed workers make on-site determinations of Medicaid eligibility (an action by the private corporation that took over Detroit's public hospital, which doubled the hospital's Medicaid eligibility rates).

Both state and local participants recognize the trade-off between Medicaid and local financing, and both sides try to limit their liabilities. As in other city-state exchanges, who wins or loses depends on how well the governor and the mayor get along, how the legislature feels toward state aid to the city, and—where the city has few allies—how much harm city discontent can cause. Explaining why recession-ravaged Michigan expanded rather than contracted Medicaid eligibility, a hospital official said: "It was simple. They didn't want to see Detroit burn."

State responses to individual hospitals may be the least costly way for states to control their costs and still maintain service for the poor. If, as many states believe (and much analysis supports), reimbursement methods have been too generous, cutbacks are in order. But it is impossible to know all the effects of cutbacks in advance or to assure that those effects will be desirable. Squeezing the overall system, and then identifying and helping institutions perceived as hit too hard, allows a state to pursue its cost-containment objectives while avoiding untoward effects.

The institution-by-institution approach, however, does not give hospitals much security. If aid funds are limited, a given institution cannot know in advance whether it will qualify for aid, and if so, for how much. To provide more predictability and control, some city hospitals have begun to band together, negotiating with the state for new approaches to reimbursement. In Boston, Chicago, and Philadelphia, for example, hospitals are promoting new approaches to Medicaid financing (typically involving capitation payment for an enrolled poor population) that have the potential to stabilize hospitals' funding while saving money through more efficient service delivery.

Major teaching hospitals, which provide a substantial share of care to the poor (53 percent) in big cities,[19] have often been the prime movers behind these Medicaid demonstrations. Medicaid cuts that threaten the revenues and teaching capacity of these politically influential hospitals may be difficult to sustain. Although the new financing arrangements these hospitals propose may produce greater efficiency, their attractiveness to the state may rest less on that potential than on the legitimacy they give to a negotiated settlement on total state spending.

Rate Setting. Whether institution-specific or involving a group of hospitals, the political action discussed thus far involves only hospitals serving the poor. Another type of political action involves the entire hospital industry, basically redistributing resources from hospitals that do not serve the poor to hospitals that do. This redistribution operates through rate setting for all payers, which constrains the rates of increase in private payments (primarily affecting hospitals with predominantly private patients) while increasing individual hospitals' rates by a factor that reflects the volume of care they provide to the poor or uninsured—basically, giving some financial recognition to all hospitals' bad-debt and charity care.

---

19. Jack Hadley, Judith Feder, and Ross Mullner, "Hospitals' Financial Status and Care to the Poor in 1980," Working Paper (Washington, D.C.: Urban Institute, October 1983), table III-2.

Four states have such systems (Maryland, Massachusets, New Jersey, and New York). Although they vary in the constraints they impose on private rates, the degree to which they equalize different payers' rates, and the proportion of charity costs they recognize, all four systems enhance the resources of hospitals that serve predominantly poor patients while restraining the resources of hospitals that serve the more affluent.

Because rate setting can increase resources for one segment (a minority) of the hospital industry at the expense of another (the majority), the hospital industry does not perceive it as a desirable means of financing care for the poor. Not surprisingly, hospitals are generally opposed to regulations that constrain their private revenues, and their opposition appears to increase rather than decline with reductions in public revenues. In Illinois, where rate setting was enacted but never implemented, the hospital industry made its retraction a primary objective in their negotiations with the state over Medicaid cutbacks. Where public programs are cut back, hospitals with private as well as public patients become more dependent on private charges to maintain their revenues and, consequently, more opposed to charge constraints.

In Massachusetts and New York, however, the hospital industry supported (and the state adopted) new all-payer rate-setting systems, in which enhanced financing to hospitals serving the poor was a major issue. If most hospitals have more to lose than to gain from rate setting and redistribution, why did this come about? In both states, the answer seems to be that hospitals *not* serving the poor already faced significant revenue constraints and that the new system therefore looked better than the status quo. Adopting a system that seemed likely to enhance most hospitals' revenues became an opportunity to offer some specific benefits to hospitals serving the poor.

In both these two states the pressure on the industry to make a change came, in large part, from the existing rate-setting system. In Massachusetts the pressure was more potential than real; some action was necessary to forestall implementation of rate-setting regulations that would impose severe limits on private charges in many of the state's major institutions. In New York the rate setting in effect had so significantly constrained hospitals' revenues that most hospitals were already running deficits and drawing down assets.

These problems probably would not have been sufficient to bring about industry agreement to change had it not been for another source of fiscal pressure: the Medicare payment changes enacted in 1982, effective in fiscal 1983. Adopting an all-payer rate system allowed hospitals to seek a federal waiver from Medicare's new rules. Although the waiver included limits on Medicare's obligations, theoretically preventing hospitals from doing better than they otherwise would have done, the alternative system nevertheless had several advantages. Measuring what Medicare would have spent is difficult, leaving room for gains in spite of limits. Furthermore, the new system re-distributed Medicare's penalties, improving the position of many hospitals. Given these factors, for most hospitals, having Medicare play according to state rules that hospitals had helped develop was preferable to accepting Medicare's own new rules.

Finally, in both states the new systems were attractive for the protection they offered from the ups and downs of state budgets. Acquiring some pre-dictability for Medicaid in particular, and rate levels in general, was appealing to hospitals that felt themselves prey to somewhat arbitrary state action.

In Massachusetts these factors allowed hospitals to go along with a totally new payment system that primarily aimed to constrain rates and reduce the differential between the charges paid by private commercial insurers and the rates paid by Blue Cross and government programs. Secondarily, adoption of a new system brought new recognition of free care—both through Med-icare's agreement to pay its share of that care and through extra Medicaid payments to public hospitals (the latter a condition for the Boston legislative delegation's support for the bill).

Recognition of bad-debt and free care was a primary concern in New York. The poor tend to absorb a larger proportion of care in New York City hospitals than they do in Massachusetts hospitals, and, given past rate setting, fewer New York hospitals had access to relatively unconstrained private revenues. In New York a major advantage to the new system was the new revenue it brought from Medicaid and Medicare to finance bad-debt and charity care.

In both states a number of hospitals gave up some autonomy and revenues with passage of the new rules. Leadership in industry believed that benefits to the industry as a whole outweighed these costs. But even in these states, where hospitals were in serious trouble (New York) or faced serious payment constraints (Massachusetts), the hospital association's official position created substantial conflict among its members.

The experiences of New York and Massachusetts basically confirm the point of view that hospitals serving the poor and wanting to continue that service will not easily acquire support from hospitals that do not provide similar service. Unless pressures independent of care for the poor force the affluent institutions to accept rate setting, hospitals serving the poor are likely to be on their own in the quest for financial assistance.

Public Policy and Hospitals' Care for the Poor

The evidence presented in this chapter suggests that public financing is essential to maintaining the volume of hospital care received by the poor.

Under current conditions it appears that most private hospitals either cannot or will not use private resources to expand the amount of care they provide to the poor if public financing is reduced.

Broadening health insurance coverage may be the best way to maintain patient access and hospital funding but such expansion seems inconsistent with government efforts to limit spending.[20] Two alternative approaches remain: (1) directing additional public payments to institutions that serve large numbers of the poor (as with special Medicaid adjustments, funding pools for distressed hospitals, and special deals with influential institutions) or (2) redistributing funds from hospitals with large populations of persons who can pay for care to hospitals serving the poor.

The first approach keeps the hospitals providing the most care to the poor afloat, leaves the rest of the industry unconstrained, and makes it increasingly likely that the poor in need of care will be concentrated in specific hospitals. The second solution constrains all hospitals' opportunities to generate large financial surpluses, recognizes any hospital's care for the poor, and reduces the pressure for rationing and concentration.

Identifying the pros and cons of alternative approaches to increase financing for care for the poor, while important, was not our main objective. Our goal was to identify the financing problem—namely, that the public sector cannot cut back its financial support and expect private institutions to satisfy the demand for free care.

If policymakers believe that much of the care that hospitals provide to the poor is unnecessary, the combination of broad government cutbacks and constraints on hospitals' private revenues may achieve the desired results. Neither public nor private hospitals that limit care do so indiscriminately; they appear to treat the worst cases first. To determine whether the people who are deterred or deferred by hospital rationing actually suffer lower health status as a result requires much better data than are currently available.

If, alternatively, policymakers believe that the poor should have the same access to care as those who are better off, policymakers must find a way to pay for it.

---

20. For contrary evidence indicating that expanded insurance can be compatible with cost containment, see Jack Hadley, John Holahan, and William Scanlon, "Can Fee-for-Service Reimbursement Coexist with Demand Creation?" *Inquiry*, vol. 16, no. 3 (1979), pp. 247–58.

DO BUDGET REDUCTIONS STIMULATE PUBLIC SECTOR PRODUCTIVITY? EVIDENCE FROM PROPOSITION 2½ IN MASSACHUSETTS

John M. Greiner and George E. Peterson

One contention central to the Reagan critique of government holds that the public sector is an inefficient, ineffective provider of services. From this it follows that budget cutting has virtues that transcend the political goal of reducing taxpayer burdens, the objective usually invoked to justify spending cuts. According to the Reagan analysis, one can reduce government waste simply by reducing the magnitude of public expenditures. Moreover, fiscal stringency may prompt the public sector to reorganize its service delivery along more imaginative and more efficient lines. It may even persuade the public sector to retire from service responsibilities better performed by the private sector.

At the federal level, the Reagan administration has applied this line of reasoning not only to justify domestic budget cuts but also to advocate limitations on future revenues. The indexing of personal income taxes as well as the proposed constitutional amendment to curtail deficit spending and limit spending growth seek to force greater efficiency on the part of the federal government through the simple strategem of cutting the amount of money available. The Grace Commission, in a controversial analysis, promised that $424 billion could be squeezed out of federal spending in three years, with little adverse impact on service levels.[1]

The research on which this chapter is based was supported by a grant from the U.S. Department of Housing and Urban Development's Office of Policy Development and Research, Governmental Capacity Sharing Division. Staff from the Impact: 2½ project headquartered at the Massachusetts Institute of Technology and directed by Professor Larry Susskind also played a central role in the field work and other data collection efforts associated with this study.

1. *President's Private Sector Survey on Cost Control: A Report to the President*, vol. 1 (January 15, 1984).

The federal aid reductions implemented thus far have not been deep enough and abrupt enough to test the hypothesis that cuts in federal assistance, on their own, can cause *local* governments to operate more productively. More intergovernmental fiscal stringency lies ahead, however, in both the grants-in-aid side of the budget and—possibly—the tax side (if federal deductibility of state and local taxes is eliminated). In the meantime, some states have already adopted revenue limitation measures of their own that affect municipal finances profoundly. In this chapter, we examine one of these— Massachusetts' Proposition 2½—with a special eye to determining whether this revenue limitation has promoted productivity and innovation in the provision of municipal services. Although it is risky to generalize from one state's experience, this analysis does begin to establish an empirical base for deciding whether productivity gains are likely to offset some of the impacts of budget cuts on service provision.

Background

On November 4, 1980, Massachusetts voters approved Proposition 2½ by a resounding 59-to-41 percent margin. It was the most significant and most severe revenue limitation measure to be approved since California's Proposition 13.

Proposition 2½ required each of the 351 municipalities in Massachusetts to reduce property taxes by up to 15 percent annually until the tax rate was no more than 2½ percent of the full market value of taxable property. The measure also included drastic reductions in the motor vehicle excise tax (the second-largest source of municipal revenues in Massachusetts) and various modifications to the authority granted to local government officials to raise taxes in the future.

Most provisions of Proposition 2½ took effect July 1, 1981 (that is, for fiscal 1982). The property tax is the only general tax available to Massachusetts cities and towns, and Massachusetts' effective tax notes had become among the highest in the nation. Therefore, the expected loss of revenue from the restrictions of Proposition 2½ was steep. For instance, compliance with the proposition was expected to produce a 78 percent fall in property tax receipts in Boston, a 76 percent drop in Chelsea, a 64 percent reduction in Cambridge, and a 62 percent decline in Worcester. These revenue losses came at a time of reductions in federal assistance and a general worsening in the fiscal condition of many cities. Although the revenue effects were offset to some extent by boosts in state aid to localities, most communities found their total revenues reduced in the first year of Proposition 2½, and virtually all made their budgetary plans on the assumption that total revenues would fall.

Proponents of Proposition 2½ predicted that the measure would stimulate local governments in Massachusetts to experiment with innovative strategies for coping with reduced revenues, such as productivity improvements, contractual arrangements with the private sector for the performance of previously public responsibilities, greater use of volunteers, and initiation or expansion of user fees to raise revenues and regulate demand. It was predicted that these efforts would compensate for the revenue loss, resulting in little if any deterioration in the quality of services.

Opponents of the legislation, however, believed that the revenue reductions would lead to serious service deterioration. In the words of Gerald W. McEntee, president of the American Federation of State, County, and Municipal Employees, the average family soon would begin to wonder

> why they have to wait longer for a dirty, crowded bus to get to work; why their kids' school has to hold fundraisers; why the library isn't open at nights or on weekends; why their parks and public buildings are shabbier; why their trash isn't picked up as often; why the street in front of their home has so many pits and cracks; and why when they make that urgent call for help it takes so long for the police car or the fire truck or the ambulance to show up—if it shows up at all.[2]

The debate over the costs and benefits of voter-imposed limits on government spending has not been restricted to Massachusetts. A number of studies have been made of the impacts of revenue or spending limitations. Most of these studies have been limited to the effects on overall tax and expenditure levels; few have examined impacts on the way individual services are provided, and fewer still have attempted to measure changes in the quality or level of services. Despite this, there have been several illuminating examinations of the responses to and impacts of local government expenditure limits.

In their report on responses to fiscal stress in four local governments, Levine, Rubin, and Wolohojian included several examples of agency-level responses to general fiscal pressure and assessed changes in service quality.[3] A team of researchers from the Rand Corporation examined the effects of fiscal restraint on ten cities in three states.[4] In each city they considered,

---

2. Quoted in the *LMRS Newsletter*, U.S. Conference of Mayors, vol. 14 (February–March 1983), p. 2.

3. Charles Levine, Irene Rubin, and George Wolohojian, *The Politics of Retrenchment: How Local Governments Manage Fiscal Stress* (Beverly Hills, California: Sage Publications, 1981).

4. Mark Menchik, Judith Fernandez, and Michael Caggiano, *How Fiscal Restraint Affects Spending and Services in Cities*, Report no. R-2644-FF/RC (Santa Monica, California: Rand Corporation, January 1982).

whenever possible, changes in service quality, service levels, and the efficiency of service delivery for three types of services: police protection, libraries, and parks and recreation. The Assembly Office of Research (an arm of the California State Assembly) examined post-Proposition 13 changes in expenditure and service levels for five service areas: police, fire, streets, parks and recreation, and libraries.[5] In their assessment of service-level changes, which was based on responses to a mail survey, the researchers compared post-Proposition 13 (fiscal 1980) to pre-Proposition 13 (fiscal 1978) service levels and examined several quality-of-service indicators such as police and fire response times and library service hours.

Like Proposition 13, Massachusetts' Proposition 2½ has stimulated considerable research. Some has involved extensive case studies of the experiences of individual jurisdictions[6] or services.[7] Only a few researchers have focused explicitly on the impact of Proposition 2½ on municipal service quality. Polls of citizens (by the University of Massachusetts) and of local government officials (by the Massachusetts Municipal Association) have provided some indications of the early effects of Proposition 2½ on service quality.[8] And Bradbury, Ladd, and Christopherson have examined service level disparities in public education in the wake of Proposition 2½.[9]

5. Kevin M. Bacon with Diane R. Thomas, "City and County Finances in the Post-Proposition 13 Era: An Analysis of Changes in the Fiscal Condition of Cities and Counties during the 1977–78 and 1979–80 Fiscal Years," Assembly Office of Research, State of California (Sacramento, California: June 1982).

6. See, for instance, the case studies for Amesbury, Arlington, Bridgewater, Burlington, Cambridge, Chelsea, Framingham, Marshfield, Quincy, Salem, Sandwich, Springfield, and Wayland reported in Lawrence E. Susskind and Jane Fountain Serio, eds., *Proposition 2½: Its Impact on Massachusetts* (Cambridge, Massachusetts: Oelgeschlager, Gunn, and Hain, 1983).

7. Edward P. Morgan, "The Effects of Proposition 2½ in Massachusetts," *Phi Delta Kappan* (December 1982), pp. 252–258 (impacts on public education); Carmen Buell and Joan McCallion, "Cutback Management: Its Application to Financially Strained Urban Delivery Systems," unpublished master's thesis, Department of Landscape Architecture and Regional Planning, University of Massachusetts (December 1983) (impacts on parks and recreation departments); and Langley Keyes, "Monitoring the Effects of Municipal, State and Federal Budget Cuts on Human Services," in Lawrence Susskind, ed., "Status Report: The Impacts of Proposition 2½" proceedings of a symposium at the Massachusetts State House, Boston, June 1983, pp. 49–52.

8. "University of Massachusetts Poll on State Taxes and Spending," Center for Studies in Policy and the Public Interest, University of Massachusetts (Boston, Massachusetts, October 1981); "Report on the Impact of Proposition 2½," Massachusetts Municipal Association (Boston, Massachusetts, January 1982); and Dan Soyer, "The Quality of Public Services," in Susskind "Status Report," pp. 53–59.

9. Katherine L. Bradbury and Helen F. Ladd, with Claire Christopherson, "Proposition 2½: Initial Impacts," Project Report no. 82-A12, Institute for Research on Educational Finance and Governance, Stanford University (Palo Alto, California, June 1982).

Many of these researchers have concluded that fiscal constraints and fiscal contractions are more likely to dampen efforts at government innovation than to promote them.[10] In particular, governments have often been found to cope with resource limitations by trying to avoid major service cuts and major realignments of service delivery. Instead, they resort to "such tactics as across-the-board budget reductions, hiring freezes, reduction-by-attrition, deferred maintenance, and freezing and rationing operating expenses," short-run expedients that have been thought to weaken the effectiveness of government organizations.[11]

Still, analytical studies have shown that most communities do not operate efficiently when providing local public services. Moreover, an abundance of resources—at least in the form of external governmental aid—seems to make them *less* efficient in service provision.[12] Thus it appears to be a reasonable inference, if not a logically necessary one, that actions to reduce resource availability should make local governments run a tighter ship.

Organization of the Chapter

This chapter is organized around four sets of questions. First, which service expenditures are cut back most when municipal spending is reduced? That is, which services do municipal officials (and the citizens for whom they act) view as "marginal" items to be adjusted downward when revenues are constrained? Second, do spending reductions at the agency level translate into declines in service levels and service quality? Or, as critics of public spending have sometimes maintained, is public service delivery so inefficiently organized that spending cutbacks have no discernible impact on the quality of services delivered? Third, did the revenue constraints resulting from Proposition 2½ cause significant changes in the way local public services were delivered or managed? Did they, in particular, promote innovation? Finally, is there evidence that innovations in local public service delivery can compensate for spending reductions? Or, to ask the question another way,

10. See, for instance, Warren E. Walker and Jan M. Chaiken, "The Effects of Fiscal Contraction on Innovation in the Public Sector," paper prepared for the National Institute on Education's Program on Research and Educational Practices (April 1981).

11. Charles H. Levine, "Retrenchment, Human Resource Erosion, and the Role of the Personnel Manager," paper prepared for the 19th Congress of the International Institute of Administrative Services (West Berlin, Germany: September 19–23, 1983), p. 16.

12. Richard H. Silkman and Dennis R. Young, *Subsidizing Inefficiency: A Study of State Aid and Local Government Productivity* (New York: Praeger, 1985).

can municipalities substitute innovation, management skill, and productivity improvements to preserve service quality in the face of budget reductions?

A crucial requirement in examining these questions is the ability to measure service quality and service levels—and the changes in each—independently of expenditures. For this purpose, we used two special techniques, in addition to examining information from state and local records on selected municipal services: surveys to determine citizen assessments of service quality and measurements of selected service quality characteristics by trained observers. Seventeen cities and towns representing a cross section of Massachusetts municipalities were chosen for detailed study; they ranged in population from Wayland's 12,170 to Worcester's 161,799. The results for sixteen of these sites are reported here (consistent expenditure data were not available from the seventeenth site).

In fourteen of the communities studied, we surveyed a sample of households regarding their perceptions of service quality and changes in service quality over the previous year. One survey was conducted in the summer of 1982 (at the beginning of the second year of Proposition 2½); a second survey was administered in the summer of 1983 (at the beginning of the third year of Proposition 2½). While it would have been preferable to employ a true baseline survey conducted before Proposition 2½ was implemented, this was not possible.

The surveys focused on citizen experiences with several everyday government services over the previous twelve months. The questions were adapted from similar surveys conducted by Urban Institute and government staffs in a number of cities and urban counties over the past ten years.[13] Thus, the clarity and validity of most of the relevant questions had already been established.

The questionnaire focused on citizen usage and perceptions of the following services:

Parks and recreation—adequacy and use of parks and recreation facilities;
Libraries—adequacy and use of library services and facilities;
Police—crime victimization, feeling of security, adequacy of police patrols and response times;
Sanitation—cleanliness of the streets, overall adequacy of waste collection services; and

---

13. See, for example, Harry Hatry et al., *How Effective Are Your Community Services: Procedures for Monitoring the Effectiveness of Municipal Services* (Washington, D.C.: Urban Institute and International City Management Association, 1977).

Streets—roughness and rideability, effectiveness of snow and ice removal, adequacy of street lighting, physical condition of the sidewalks.

Questions on the quality of fire services were excluded because of the low probability that a given household had had direct experience with a fire or fire inspection during the previous twelve months.

The two surveys employed essentially the same questionnaire. The interviews were conducted by telephone by professional survey firms and averaged twelve minutes in length. Respondents were stratified by site, with a goal of thirty-five male and thirty-five female respondents (seventy households) per municipality. Respondents had to be eighteen years or older and a resident of the town for at least twelve months. The July 1982 sample covered fourteen sites and 985 respondents; the August 1983 sample covered ten sites and 701 respondents.

The second major technique used to gather information on service quality involved measurements by trained observers—persons who make and record visual ratings of various conditions using prespecified scales. Such ratings are based on photographic standards and detailed written definitions that enable the observers to accurately assign discrete numerical grades to the conditions observed. Experience with the use of trained observers in a number of cities has shown that when properly trained and managed, such observers exhibit a high degree of interrater and intertemporal consistency.[14] Trained-observer ratings were obtained for pavement conditions, street cleanliness, and park and playground conditions in the various sites for three consecutive years, beginning in November 1981.[15]

Changes in the Availability of Local Resources

Initial predictions of the property tax reductions that would be required under Proposition 2½ ranged from 35 percent cuts in Wayland and Marshfield to a 76 percent drop in Chelsea. As it turned out, these estimates considerably overestimated the revenue losses that the municipalities actually had to absorb. The property tax rate ceiling established by Proposition 2½ was to be applied

---

14. See, for instance, Hatry et al., *How Effective Are Your Community Services*, Chapter 13, and Frederick O'R. Hayes et al., "Helping City Government Improve Productivity: An Evaluation of the Productivity Projects of the Fund for the City of New York," Frederick O'R. Hayes Associates (New York, May 1980), pp. 32–36.

15. For details on these and other measurement procedures used, see John M. Greiner, *The Impacts of Massachusetts' Proposition 2½ on the Delivery and Quality of Municipal Services* (Washington, D.C.: Urban Institute, September 1984).

to the full market value of taxable property. Where towns had been assessing property at less than full market value, they were able to avoid some of the revenue loss by reassessing their property base at full valuation. Nearly all jurisdictions adopted this strategy, although the slowness of the reassessment process delayed relief for several years in some cases.

Table 16 shows the reductions in property taxes that ultimately proved necessary to comply with Proposition 2½. Burlington and Wayland did not have to cut property taxes at all, whereas Chelsea, New Bedford, Pittsfield, and Quincy had to reduce property taxes in each of the three years examined. (Since much of Chelsea's taxable property was old and had not appreciated in market value, the city could achieve little relief by means of reassessment.) Cambridge was able to avoid reductions after the first year only because two-thirds of its voters approved an override of the levy reduction requirement, as provided under the terms of Proposition 2½.

TABLE 16

PERCENTAGE REDUCTIONS IN PROPERTY TAXES IN SIXTEEN MASSACHUSETTS MUNICIPALITIES AFTER THE INTRODUCTION OF PROPOSITION 2½, FISCAL YEARS 1982–84[a]

Municipality	1980 Population	Property Tax Reduction		
		1982	1983	1984
Amesbury	13,961	6	1	0
Arlington	48,219	15	0	0
Bridgewater	17,202	15	5	0
Burlington	23,486	0	0	0
Cambridge	95,322	15	0	0
Chelsea	25,431	15	15	15
Everett	37,195	15	0	0
Marshfield	20,916	1	0	0
New Bedford	98,478	15.5	5	1
Pittsfield	51,974	15	15	10
Quincy	84,743	15	15	5
Salem	38,220	15	0	0
Springfield	152,319	16	3	0
Watertown	34,384	15	0	0
Wayland	12,170	0	0	0
Worcester	161,799	15	15	0

SOURCES: Based on personal communication with municipal finance offices and other material reported in John M. Greiner, ''The Impacts of Massachusetts' Proposition 2½ on the Delivery and Quality of Municipal Services'' (Washington, D.C.: Urban Institute, September 28, 1984).

a.   The figures shown are the percentage reductions relative to the previous year's property tax levy. A zero entry denotes that no reductions were made; there might have been a tax increase in such a case, however.

During the first year of Proposition 2½, twelve of the sixteen sites had to cut property tax revenues by the maximum required amount (15 percent), and two of these chose to cut even more deeply; two made small reductions (1 to 6 percent); and two sites did not have to reduce their property tax levies at all. However, by fiscal 1983, the pressure on revenues had weakened substantially; only four sites had to reduce their property taxes by the maximum percentage, while four others made only small reductions, and eight municipalities made none at all. By fiscal 1984 only four jurisdictions had to make any further cuts to comply with Proposition 2½. Thus, the fiscal pressure from Proposition 2½ apparently peaked in fiscal 1982 and abated rather quickly thereafter. The varied pattern of property tax reductions, plus the uneven effects of state aid, federal assistance, and state "Chapter 90" funds for repair of municipal streets, produced a great variation in the total revenue loss to which different municipalities were exposed in any given year.

The Pattern of Budget Adjustments

A clear pattern of budget adjustments has emerged from the experience with Proposition 2½ (see table 17). A "marginal" set of public services—consisting of parks and recreation, libraries, and street maintenance—has been sharply affected by the budget adjustments.[16] On the other hand, a "core" set of services, consisting of police and fire protection plus sanitation, has been preserved at or near their former levels of expenditure in spite of revenue limitations. The same pattern of budget adjustments has been found by other investigators in a variety of communities.[17]

If the municipalities in our sample that were exposed to the maximum property tax reduction are separated from the rest, the pattern of budget adjustments becomes especially pronounced. The twelve communities falling into this category in the first year of Proposition 2½ cut parks and recreation

---

16. These are not necessarily the only public services to be sharply affected by the budget adjustments triggered under Proposition 2½. The work reported here focused only on police, fire, library, parks and recreation, and various public works services (especially street maintenance, street sweeping, and solid waste collection and disposal), omitting such potentially important areas as public education and social services. Indeed, other results suggest that school districts in Massachusetts also experienced substantial funding reductions in the wake of Proposition 2½. See Thomas Collins, "The Effect of Proposition 2½ on Massachusetts School Districts," in Susskind, "Status Report," pp. 39–48.

17. For example, Harold L. Wolman, "Local Government Strategies to Cope with Fiscal Pressure," in Charles H. Levine and Irene Rubin, eds., *Fiscal Stress and Public Policy* (Beverly Hills, California: Sage Publications, 1983); Harold L. Wolman and George E. Peterson, "State and Local Government Strategies for Responding to Fiscal Pressure," *Tulane Law Review* (April 1981).

TABLE 17

PERCENTAGE CHANGES IN EXPENDITURES FOR SELECTED MUNICIPAL SERVICES IN THE FIRST YEAR AFTER THE INTRODUCTION OF PROPOSITION 2½, FISCAL 1982 VERSUS FISCAL 1981

Municipality	Police	Fire	Libraries	Parks and Recreation	Sanitation	Street Maintenance	Public Works
Amesbury	5.0	11.6	−9.7	29.5	14.5	24.1	39.1
Arlington	−1.3	−7.1	−12.4	−11.5	3.5	−20.5	−3.6
Bridgewater	1.6	−0.2	−10.3	−7.7	−2.8	−8.3	−7.7
Burlington	−2.8	11.7	−4.5	−11.4	10.1	n.a.	2.2
Cambridge	0.5	4.9	−6.7	−17.9	−7.0	−32.5	−12.9
Chelsea	8.6	5.8	−12.6	3.2	23.2	−1.3	−2.5
Everett[a]	−16.2	−17.5	−18.8	−16.6	0.0	n.a.	−10.6
Marshfield	−8.4	−2.3	−0.4	−24.1	6.0	−19.3	−4.9
New Bedford	2.1	0.5	8.0	−17.1	−2.5	5.2	−0.2
Pittsfield	1.9	17.5	−6.5	−23.2	−26.8	12.4	−6.7
Quincy	−7.5	−6.9	−25.5	−17.2	3.1	−0.6	5.2
Salem	1.2	−3.1	−9.9	−25.4	6.4	−26.9	−3.2
Springfield	5.6	4.6	−0.2	−2.3	n.a.	n.a.	6.8
Watertown	3.0	12.9	−12.1	−37.3	−1.6	n.a.	6.0
Wayland	5.0	−0.7	3.7	−12.4	−80.0	94.4	−6.9
Worcester	−6.3	−7.1	−6.4	−10.2	−12.7	−14.6	−8.9
Median, all sixteen sites	1.4	0.2	−8.2	−14.5	0.0	−4.8	−3.4
Median, twelve sites with maximum property tax reduction	1.4	2.5	−10.0	−17.2	−1.6	−11.4	−3.4

SOURCES: Same as table 16.

n.a.   Not available.

a.   Changes based on budgeted fiscal 1981 figures. Expenditures for Everett were unavailable.

spending by a median rate of 17.2 percent, street maintenance by 11.4 percent, and libraries by 10.0 percent. Meanwhile, the median sanitation expenditure for these municipalities went down only slightly (1.6 percent). Police and fire protection were the only two service categories to experience expenditure increases, although even these were well below the rate of inflation.

The "marginal" nature of spending on parks and recreation, libraries, and street maintenance is further confirmed by the budget allocations made after the resource constraints began to stabilize or were relaxed. For the sample as a whole, spending on libraries and on parks and recreation bounced back vigorously in the second and third years of Proposition 2½; street maintenance expenditures also began to turn around, although somewhat less sharply. But for the few cities remaining under the pressure of maximum second-year tax reductions, the pattern of budget adjustments in the second year generally paralleled the pattern of the first year (see table 18). Thus, parks and recreation spending in the second year fell by a median 12.1 percent in the four municipalities subject to maximum property tax reductions, but rose by a median 7.3 percent in other towns; street maintenance spending fell a median 11.3 percent in the towns with maximum revenue reductions but rose 11.7 percent elsewhere. Library expenditures exhibited a similar pattern. Note that public works spending might have shared more fully in local budget reductions had it not been for the presence of preexisting state aid programs designed to bolster expenditures on highways and other infrastructure systems.

By the third year of Proposition 2½ (see table 19), spending growth had resumed its previous course in almost all locations. Not only was total spending growth much higher, but libraries, parks and recreation, and street maintenance (the service categories hardest hit by revenue restrictions) were often at the forefront of expenditure increases as revenue limitations were relaxed in individual municipalities. Expenditures on these services, in other words, were especially sensitive to the municipal revenue position.

The Effects on Service Levels and Service Quality

Some critics of public sector inefficiency have gone so far as to maintain that taxpayer incomes are so unproductively spent through the public sector that there is *no* relation between spending levels and service quality. For example, the director of planning and evaluation of the U.S. Department of Education, in releasing the annual comparison between pupil test scores and state per pupil spending on education, described the results as showing that "there is not a correlation" between spending and school performance. Such a view implies that substantial cutbacks in public spending could be made without having any systematic impact on service levels.

TABLE 18

PERCENTAGE CHANGES IN EXPENDITURES FOR SELECTED MUNICIPAL SERVICES IN THE SECOND YEAR AFTER THE INTRODUCTION OF PROPOSITION 2½, FISCAL 1983 VERSUS FISCAL 1982

Municipality	Police	Fire	Libraries	Parks and Recreation	Sanitation	Street Maintenance	Public Works
Amesbury	21.4	1.6	22.7	7.3	-1.7	-3.7	26.8
Arlington	2.8	12.9	6.0	18.0	5.5	1.9	14.2
Bridgewater	8.8	8.0	20.7	22.3	-45.4	21.5	-0.7
Burlington	7.9	5.9	7.3	26.8	10.8	n.a.	19.4
Cambridge	2.1	0.9	-11.0	7.3	25.8	-16.3	-6.1
Chelsea	-3.8	6.8	9.5	18.3	3.9	3.4	6.9
Everett[a]	-3.5	-5.2	-0.8	-8.0	11.0	n.a.	-9.5
Marshfield	3.2	5.8	2.1	-9.7	9.4	35.8	15.7
New Bedford	2.9	11.3	10.6	-4.0	-17.6	45.3	16.7
Pittsfield	0.7	-6.9	-6.8	-9.3	23.0	-11.9	-0.4
Quincy	-1.5	-2.3	-8.4	-14.9	0.7	-12.3	2.6
Salem	-7.1	-1.0	0.6	-1.2	1.1	43.5	7.5
Springfield	9.5	3.4	4.2	7.4	n.a.	n.a.	4.5
Watertown	8.0	13.8	17.5	6.0	39.1	n.a.	5.0
Wayland	9.5	6.9	3.5	7.3	141.4	-7.7	1.3
Worcester	2.2	16.6	0.4	-5.6	3.5	-10.7	-10.2
Median, all sixteen sites	2.9	5.9	3.9	6.7	3.9	-0.9	4.8
Median, four sites with maximum property tax reduction	-0.4	2.2	-3.2	-12.1	3.7	-11.3	1.1

SOURCES: Same as table 16.

n.a. Not available.

a. Fiscal 1983 figures exclude a 6 percent salary increase paid retroactively in fiscal 1984.

TABLE 19

PERCENTAGE CHANGES IN EXPENDITURES FOR SELECTED MUNICIPAL SERVICES IN THE THIRD YEAR AFTER THE INTRODUCTION OF PROPOSITION 2½, FISCAL 1984 VERSUS FISCAL 1983

Municipality	Police	Fire	Libraries	Parks and Recreation	Sanitation	Street Maintenance	Public Works
Amesbury[a]	1.6	6.9	2.2	1.1	-4.2	0.1	28.7
Arlington	8.3	10.9	17.8	1.5	16.6	-8.8	3.5
Bridgewater[a]	2.0	-1.7	25.8	2.6	22.3	16.6	16.8
Burlington	6.1	5.3	10.5	26.3	2.3	n.a.	-0.3
Cambridge	2.5	11.4	26.4	26.6	-24.2	72.7	6.2
Chelsea	6.2	4.2	2.1	5.6	-4.6	17.1	9.4
Everett[a,b]	4.4	1.5	1.4	2.5	5.1	n.a.	5.5
Marshfield[a,b]	15.9	20.3	11.2	45.6	13.4	40.3	0.7
New Bedford	4.6	0.0	13.2	4.2	7.4	-6.2	-2.4
Pittsfield	22.6	9.7	-2.3	9.0	-16.3	3.5	4.4
Quincy[a]	6.5	6.0	12.0	5.1	9.0	6.4	1.3
Salem	12.7	3.3	7.0	5.2	5.6	-11.6	-5.9
Springfield	6.3	-1.8	15.8	5.2	n.a.	n.a.	11.6
Watertown	8.2	2.3	5.9	4.6	53.3	n.a.	16.2
Wayland[a]	9.4	10.0	6.8	-3.5	6.0	-4.3	3.3
Worcester[a,c]	1.8	-9.6	-2.6	-4.5	-1.1	-8.6	6.3
Mean	7.2	4.9	9.6	9.1	6.0	9.8	6.6
Median	6.3	3.8	8.8	4.9	5.1	1.8	5.0

SOURCES: Same as table 16.

n.a. Not available.
a. Budgeted (or mixture of budgeted plus actual) expenditures used for fiscal 1984.
b. Includes 6 percent wage increase paid in fiscal 1984 retroactive to fiscal 1983.
c. Excludes cost of retroactive 8 to 10 percent wage increase negotiated after the end of the fiscal year.

The ultimate arbiters of service quality, of course, are the people who consume the services and pay taxes for their provision. Their reactions to Proposition 2½ suggest that, on the average, changes in agency spending were associated with changes in service quality as perceived by the consumer. The Massachusetts citizens we polled reported diminished service quality, by and large, where local budgets had been cut. Across communities, residents of the municipalities that made the largest budget reductions generally reported the greatest deterioration in services.

Police Services

The service-quality measure that is probably linked most closely with police department responses to Proposition 2½ is citizen perception of the adequacy of police patrolling. Our survey asked respondents whether they thought that police patrolling in their neighborhoods had gotten better, gotten worse, or remained about the same over the previous twelve months. Here, as elsewhere in this chapter, we emphasize the results of the survey conducted after the first year of Proposition 2½, when budget restrictions were most severe.

The survey revealed a widespread conviction that police patrolling had deteriorated. On the average, about 11 percent more respondents believed that police patrolling had gotten worse than believed that it had gotten better (table 20). Citizens in every site except one (Springfield) reported a deterioration along this dimension of police services. Although the typical police budget in the first year of Proposition 2½ was essentially unchanged from the previous year, it declined significantly in real terms and generally lagged far behind the budget adjustments of earlier years. Half of the sites reported at least some curtailment of patrol activities in response to Proposition 2½.[18] The survey results suggest that such efforts to cut costs in order to cope with budgetary stringency was associated with a decline in service quality, as perceived by local citizens.

Perceptions of the adequacy of police patrolling deteriorated most in those towns where budget cutbacks were most severe (see table 20). The correlation between changes in police expenditures and changes in the perceived adequacy of police patrolling was very high ($r = 0.68$, significant at the 99.5 percent level). Everett and Worcester, for example, were two of the

---

18. These and other first-year responses to Proposition 2½ are catalogued in "Coping with Cutbacks: Initial Agency-Level Responses in 17 Local Governments to Massachusetts' Proposition 2½," by John M. Greiner and Harry P. Hatry, Project Report (Washington, DC: Urban Institute, October 1982). Reprinted in Susskind and Serio, *Proposition 2½*, Chapter 27. See also the appendix to this chapter.

departments facing the largest budget cuts (Everett lost 29 funded positions); according to table 20, these two municipalities also exhibited some of the largest declines in the perceived adequacy of police patrols.

A more general measure of police protection and the quality of police services is the "feeling of security" among local residents when walking alone in their neighborhood at night. This is obviously affected by factors other than the efforts of police officers (for example, the actions of criminals and media publicity concerning specific criminal incidents); nevertheless, it is probably the most important index of police protection for the average citizen. The "feeling of security" declined sharply after Proposition 2½ (see table 20), and changes in this measure exhibited the expected (positive) correlation with changes in police expenditures, although the correlation was not quite significant at the 90 percent level.

The correlations between police department spending changes and citizen satisfaction were supported by an important direct measure of service quality—total arrests. On the average, arrests fell 8 percent in the year after Proposition 2½, and changes in total arrests were significantly correlated (at the 90 percent level) with local changes in police spending: the less spent, the fewer arrests.

On the other hand, the rate of serious (Part I) crimes *fell* in Massachusetts communities after Proposition 2½, as it did in the rest of the country. This may partly account for the decline in arrests noted above. The anticipated correlation between the growth of police expenditures in different communities and the changes in reported Part I crime rates was not found.

All this suggests that there is generally a close connection between police inputs and local safety, especially as perceived by the public. When budgets are cut or patrol activities reduced, citizens feel the difference, even though the impact on actual crime rates may be less clear.

Library Services

The general reductions in library budgets translated directly into declines in the total circulation of library materials (table 21). Circulation fell in thirteen of the sixteen sites during the first year of Proposition 2½, and by as much as 24 percent. Detailed site-by-site analysis indicated that the change in circulation levels was traceable, in large part, to reductions in library hours and, in a few cases, branch closings. The correlation between changes in library circulation (fiscal 1982 versus fiscal 1981) and changes in library expenditures was significant at the 95 percent confidence level.

The connection between library spending and citizen satisfaction with the libraries was considerably less firm. Reductions in library spending were

TABLE 20

PERCENTAGE CHANGES IN THE QUALITY AND EFFECTIVENESS OF POLICE SERVICES IN
THE FIRST YEAR AFTER THE INTRODUCTION OF PROPOSITION 2½, FISCAL 1982
VERSUS FISCAL 1981[a]

Municipality	Expenditures	Reported Serious (Part I) Crimes	Total Arrests	Feeling of Security[b]	Adequacy of Police Patrols[c]
Amesbury	5.0	6.0	2.7	n.a.	n.a.
Arlington	-1.3	-7.8	-14.9	1.4	-7.1
Bridgewater	1.6	-8.3	-2.3	-8.6	-2.9
Burlington	-2.8	-7.3	-17.4	n.a.	n.a.
Cambridge	0.5	-5.8	-2.7	-4.3	-10.0
Chelsea	-8.6	-4.8	-8.4	-31.4	-22.9
Everett	-16.2	-9.0	-25.6	-47.1	-48.6
Marshfield	-8.4	-16.0	11.0	-4.3	-7.1
New Bedford	2.1	0.6	-7.9	-13.5	-14.9
Pittsfield	1.9	-3.4	-8.8	-24.3	-11.4
Quincy	-7.5	-0.6	-6.5	-10.0	-22.9
Salem	1.2	-0.5	-13.1	-14.3	-12.9
Springfield	5.6	-3.9	-5.3	-15.7	5.7
Watertown	3.0	-11.1	-17.9	-11.3	-5.6
Wayland	5.0	28.7	32.0	3.0	-1.4
Worcester	-6.3	-1.0	n.a.	-32.9	-32.9
Median change	1.4	-5.3	-7.9	-12.5	-10.7

SOURCES: Same as table 16.

    n.a. Not available.

    a. The last two columns show percentage-point changes.

    b. Net proportion of July 1982 citizen survey respondents who reported that their feeling of safety walking alone in their neighborhood at night had improved over the previous twelve months (percentage of respondents reporting improvements minus percentage reporting worsening).

    c. Net proportion of July 1982 citizen survey respondents who reported that the amount of police patrolling in their neighborhood had improved over the previous twelve months (percentage reporting improvements minus percentage reporting worsening).

not systematically related to reductions in citizen use of the libraries, to a perceived worsening of the hours of operation, to perceived changes in the availability of library materials, or—when all is said and done—to citizen perceptions of the change in *overall* adequacy of library service.

    These results suggest that while budget cuts have forced libraries to take economy measures that resulted in a deterioration of service levels and service quality in terms of some of the traditional dimensions of library activity (circulation and hours of operation), libraries have generally been successful

TABLE 21

PERCENTAGE CHANGES IN THE QUALITY AND EFFECTIVENESS OF LIBRARY SERVICES IN THE FIRST YEAR AFTER THE INTRODUCTION OF PROPOSITION 2½, FISCAL 1982 VERSUS FISCAL 1981

Municipality	Expenditures	Total Circulation[a]	Hours of Operation[a]	Use of Library[b]	Availability of Materials[c]	Overall Adequacy[d]
Amesbury	−9.7	6.6	n.a.	n.a.	n.a.	n.a.
Arlington	−12.4	−7.1	23.9	14.3	8.7	4.3
Bridgewater	−10.3	−11.9	15.6	−1.4	4.4	14.3
Burlington	−4.5	−1.7	n.a.	n.a.	n.a.	n.a.
Cambridge	−6.7	3.6	−9.1	2.9	9.1	1.4
Chelsea	−12.6	−24.2	−7.4	1.4	11.1	4.3
Everett	−18.8	−6.0	−3.4	−1.4	−3.4	−14.3
Marshfield	−0.4	−2.6	−10.9	7.1	4.3	−2.9
New Bedford	8.0	−10.7	−32.0	−8.1	−4.0	−5.4
Pittsfield	−6.5	−15.7	−33.3	−1.4	−5.9	−7.1
Quincy	−25.5	−22.7	−19.2	−4.2	−7.7	−10.0
Salem	−9.9	−4.9	−8.6	10.0	−5.7	−1.4
Springfield	−0.2	9.1	8.8	−5.7	14.7	8.6
Watertown	−12.1	−15.1	−21.2	4.2	3.0	−8.5
Wayland	3.7	−0.8	−8.2	2.9	4.1	5.7
Worcester	−6.4	−2.1	0.0	0.0	0.0	2.9
Median change	−8.2	−5.5	−8.4	0.7	3.6	0.0

SOURCES: Same as table 16. The last four columns show percentage point changes.

n.a. Not available.

a. Net proportion of library users among the July 1982 citizen survey respondents who reported that the hours of operation improved over the previous twelve months (percentage reporting improvements minus percentage reporting worsening).

b. Net proportion of July 1982 citizen survey respondents who reported that their household had used public libraries to a greater extent over the previous twelve months (percentage reporting "used to greater extent" minus percentage reporting "used to a lesser extent").

c. Net proportion of library users among the July 1982 citizen survey respondents who reported that the availability of the reading materials they wanted improved over the previous twelve months (percentage reporting improvement minus percentage reporting worsening).

d. Net proportion of July 1982 citizen survey respondents who reported that the overall adequacy of public libraries improved over the previous twelve months (percentage reporting improvements minus percentage reporting worsening).

in avoiding declines in citizen satisfaction with library services. Many of the libraries in the sample towns were able to take steps to help compensate for funding reductions. Moreover, librarians appear to have more flexibility than police departments in deciding how they will serve the local citizenry. Efforts to improve productivity, increase the use of volunteers, solicit contributions, and have the public shoulder more of the burden for providing certain library services appear to have produced outputs that, in the eyes of the public, offset the declines in traditional measures of library service quality such as circulation rates and hours of operation. Overall, citizen perceptions of the quality of library services were fairly upbeat; there was little evidence of the pattern found for police services where cuts in spending usually led to poorer service quality in the eyes of the public.

Parks and Recreation Services

This category of service suffered more than any other from the budget reductions necessitated by Proposition 2½. In our sample, the median fiscal 1982 expenditure on parks and recreation from general municipal resources fell 14.5 percent. Only two sites showed increases in parks and recreation expenditures.

Table 22 summarizes the results for several indicators of the quality of parks and recreation services. All these measures were obtained from the July 1982 citizen survey. Although most focused only on the perceptions of *users* of parks and recreation programs, two measures (use of facilities, overall program adequacy) drew upon all survey respondents, users and nonusers alike.

All but one of the eight quality measures examined (including three more not shown in table 22—park safety conditions, physical attractiveness, and program variety) exhibited a net decline in service quality in the year following Proposition 2½. In general, more citizens reported that they had decreased their use of park and recreation facilities than reported increasing use. Reports of worsening conditions exceeded reports of improvements with regard to the condition of the equipment, safety conditions and perceived security, physical attractiveness of the facilities, the variety of recreational offerings, hours of operation, and the overall adequacy of the parks and recreation program.

Ratings of park and recreation service quality varied greatly from site to site. In general, however, the first-year changes in the various quality measures tracked changes in total parks and recreation expenditures (the correlations were in the expected directions). Reductions in park and recreation expenditures were especially closely associated with perceived declines in

TABLE 22

PERCENTAGE CHANGES IN THE QUALITY AND EFFECTIVENESS
OF PARKS AND RECREATION SERVICES IN THE FIRST YEAR AFTER THE INTRODUCTION OF PROPOSITION 2½,
FISCAL 1982 VERSUS FISCAL 1981

Municipality	Expenditure	Use of Facilities[a]	Cleanliness of Facilities[b]	Condition of Equipment[c]	Hours of Operation[d]	Overall Adequacy[e]
Amesbury	29.5	n.a.	n.a.	n.a.	n.a.	n.a.
Arlington	−11.5	1.4	3.6	−7.1	0.0	10.0
Bridgewater	−7.7	2.9	0.0	−4.5	−4.5	1.4
Burlington	−11.4	n.a.	n.a.	n.a.	n.a.	n.a.
Cambridge	−17.9	20.0	3.1	6.3	−3.1	7.1
Chelsea	3.2	2.9	21.4	0.0	−0.0	−1.4
Everett	−16.6	5.7	−20.0	−40.0	−26.7	−17.1
Marshfield	−24.1	−2.9	−8.0	−12.0	−8.0	−15.7
New Bedford	−17.1	−5.4	3.8	−7.7	0.0	−1.4
Pittsfield	−23.2	−11.4	−21.1	−36.8	−21.1	−20.0
Quincy	−17.2	−5.7	−16.7	−11.1	−11.1	−2.9
Salem	−25.4	−1.4	0.0	−3.2	−3.2	−2.9

TABLE 22 (Continued)

Municipality	Expenditure	Use of Facilities[a]	Cleanliness of Facilities[b]	Condition of Equipment[c]	Hours of Operation[d]	Overall Adequacy[e]
Springfield	-2.3	-12.9	-6.5	-16.1	3.2	2.9
Watertown	-37.3	1.4	-12.1	-12.1	-12.1	-4.2
Wayland	-12.4	-1.4	31.0	24.1	20.7	14.3
Worchester	-10.2	-5.7	3.7	3.7	3.7	-10.0
Median change	-14.5	-1.4	0.0	-7.4	-3.2	-2.2

SOURCES: Same as table 16. All columns except the first report percentage point changes.

n.a. Not available.

a. Net proportion of July 1982 citizen survey respondents who reported that their household had used recreation programs, playgrounds, or park facilities to a greater extent over the previous twelve months (percentage reporting greater extent minus percentage reporting lesser extent).

b. Net proportion of parks and recreation users among the July 1982 citizen survey respondents who reported that the cleanliness of the facilities had improved over the previous twelve months (percentage reporting improvement minus percentage reporting worsening).

c. Net proportion of parks and recreation users among the July 1982 citizen survey respondents who reported that the condition of the equipment had improved over the previous twelve months (percent reporting improvements minus percentage reporting worsening).

d. Net proportion of parks and recreation users among the July 1982 citizen survey respondents who reported that the hours of operation had improved over the previous twelve months (percentage reporting improvements minus percentage reporting worsening).

e. Net proportion of the July 1982 citizen survey respondents who judged the overall adequacy of the city's park and recreation program to have improved over the previous twelve months (percentage reporting improvement minus percentage reporting worsening).

satisfactoriness with facility cleanliness and hours of operation, where the correlations were significant at the 90 to 95 percent confidence level.

Three sites—Wayland, Cambridge, and Arlington—stood out from the sample by showing large first-year *improvements* in most of the quality-of-service measures, despite budget reductions. These sites were marked by strong efforts to increase or initiate fees and charges for recreation programs and, whenever possible, to make such programs self-supporting. These efforts appear to have been successful in preserving and improving service quality, despite sharp decreases in recreation spending from the general municipal budget.

Streets and Sanitation

Assessments of the change in quality of local street and sanitation services suggest some divergences between ratings by trained observers and perceptions by citizens. Trained observers, using standardized measuring scales, found that street pavement surfaces (table 23) and neighborhood cleanliness (table 24) *improved* in the typical community after Proposition 2½. In particular, measurements of the worst conditions—the percentage of street segments classified as "very bumpy" and the percentage of neighborhood blocks classified as "very dirty"—improved (for example, the percentage decreased) on the whole after the introduction of Proposition 2½. Moreover, these changes in local conditions were significantly correlated with changes in agency expenditures: the greater the increase (or the smaller the decrease) in expenditures, the greater the improvement in rideability or cleanliness.

These results suggest that street maintenance and sanitation expenditures were not usually reduced enough to produce declines in service quality as seen by trained observers. Indeed, expenditures on these areas often increased, with corresponding improvements in service quality. Such increases were due in large part to (1) the presence of special federal and state aid programs that protected street maintenance from extreme cutbacks, (2) the high budget priority that local governments gave to the preservation of sanitation services, and (3) contractually required spending increases under preexisting multiyear contracts in cases where municipal waste collection services were contracted to private firms.

The findings from citizen surveys on sidewalk maintenance were consistent with the results that trained observers obtained. Thus on the average slightly more persons reported improvements in sidewalk conditions than reported worsening conditions in the twelve months after Proposition 2½. Moreover, the perceived changes in sidewalk conditions were positively cor-

TABLE 23

PERCENTAGE CHANGES IN THE QUALITY AND EFFECTIVENESS OF STREET
MAINTENANCE AND RELATED SERVICES IN THE FIRST YEAR AFTER THE
INTRODUCTION OF PROPOSITION 2½, FISCAL 1982 VERSUS FISCAL 1981

Municipality	Expenditure	Percentage of Blocks Rated as Very Bumpy[a]	Condition of Streets and Roads[b]	Condition of Sidewalk[c]
Amesbury	24.1	−9.4	n.a.	n.a.
Arlington	−20.5	−1.5	10.0	12.9
Bridgewater	−8.3	−1.1	21.4	7.1
Burlington	n.a.	−5.0	n.a.	n.a.
Cambridge	−32.5	4.5	1.4	−2.9
Chelsea	−1.3	−8.1	−11.4	8.6
Everett	n.a.	−1.1	−32.9	−17.1
Marshfield	−19.3	0.2	−14.3	−7.1
New Bedford	5.2	−1.0	2.7	5.4
Pittsfield	12.4	−15.7	−10.0	−2.9
Quincy	−0.6	−0.4	−20.0	−11.4
Salem	−26.9	5.8	−11.4	−20.0
Springfield	n.a.	0.7	−18.6	5.7
Watertown	n.a.	6.6	−1.4	4.2
Wayland	94.4	−3.0	−12.9	17.1
Worcester	−14.6	−1.5	−34.3	−17.1
Median change	1.0	−1.7	−9.4	−1.3

SOURCES: Same as table 16. The last three columns show percentage point changes.

n.a. Not available.

a. Percentage-point change in proportion of blocks where the pavement was rated 2.5 or worse (very bumpy) by trained observers in rideability tests: 1982–83 proportion minus 1981–82 proportion.

b. Net proportion of July 1982 citizen survey respondents who reported that the condition of streets and roads in their neighborhood had improved over the previous twelve months (percentage reporting improvement minus percentage reporting worsening).

c. Net proportion of July 1982 citizen survey respondents who reported that the condition of sidewalks in their neighborhood had improved over the previous twelve months (percentage reporting improvement minus percentage reporting worsening).

related with changes in street and sidewalk maintenance expenditures (significant at the 95 percent level).

However, citizens responding to the July 1982 survey generally reported a worsening in their perceptions of both street maintenance and neighborhood cleanliness, although correlations between changes in these *perceived* conditions and changes in spending levels were not statistically significant. In part, these apparent discrepancies can be explained by differences in the timing of the citizen surveys and the trained observer ratings: the changes derived

TABLE 24

Percentage Changes in the Quality and Effectiveness of Sanitation and and Litter Control Services in the First Year after the Introduction of Proposition 2½, Fiscal 1982 versus Fiscal 1981

Municipality	Expenditure	Percentage of Blocks Rated as Very Dirty[a]	Cleanliness of Neighborhood[b]	Adequacy of Trash and Garbage Collections[c]
Amesbury	14.5	−2.2	n.a.	n.a.
Arlington	3.5	−1.0	−1.4	−1.7
Bridgewater	−2.8	0.0	4.3	−21.8
Burlington	10.1	−1.2	n.a.	n.a.
Cambridge	−7.0	−2.7	−12.9	−20.0
Chelsea	23.2	−16.6	−14.3	−4.1
Everett	0.0	−2.8	−30.0	−33.9
Marshfield	6.0	−1.8	0.0	−2.9
New Bedford	−2.5	−2.9	1.4	−19.6
Pittsfield	−26.8	−1.8	1.4	54.1
Quincy	3.1	−3.7	−15.7	−2.0
Salem	6.4	0.9	−12.9	−5.4
Springfield	n.a.	−2.9	−2.9	−11.7
Watertown	−1.6	−0.7	−9.9	13.1
Wayland	−80.0	0.0	−5.7	12.3
Worcester	−12.7	−0.9	7.1	−7.1
Median change	0.0	−1.8	−4.3	−4.8

Sources: Same as table 16. The last three columns show percentage point changes.

n.a.　Not available.

a.　Percentage-point change in proportion of blocks where the pavement was rated 2.5 or worse (very dirty) by trained observers: 1982–83 proportion minus 1981–82 proportion.

b.　Net proportion of July 1982 citizen survey respondents who reported that the cleanliness of their neighborhood had improved over the previous twelve months (percentage reporting improvements minus percentage reporting worsening).

c.　Net proportion of persons living in a house or duplex and responding to the July 1982 citizen survey who reported that the adequacy of trash and garbage collections had improved over the previous twelve months (percentage reporting improvements minus percentage reporting worsening).

from trained observer ratings covered a somewhat later period (relative to the introduction of Proposition 2½) than did the citizen survey results.[19]

---

19. Citizens were interviewed in July 1982 and August 1983 and were asked for their perceptions of changes in service quality over the previous twelve months. Most of the trained observer measurements were conducted between the fall and spring, so that the first comparison covered the period fall 1981–spring 1982 versus fall 1982–spring 1983.

In the case of street maintenance, which typically requires some time for its effects to become perceptible, the later evaluations (that is, the comparisons of trained observer ratings) probably give more reliable information on the (delayed) effects of street maintenance spending. Indeed, the *second-year* citizen survey revealed local perceptions of changes in street conditions that conformed much more closely with the trained observer ratings given in table 23, as citizens reported widespread net improvements in street conditions during the preceding twelve-month period (which overlapped that used for the first round of trained observer measurements).

Direct comparisons between citizen perceptions and trained observer ratings of neighborhood cleanliness are hampered by the fact that citizens were interviewed in the summer, when litter conditions are especially bad, whereas the trained observer ratings occurred for the most part in the late fall and early spring, when seasonal littering is less. Citizens were asked to make their assessments of changes in cleanliness for the year as a whole, but to the extent that their time horizon was foreshortened, citizen ratings would tend to be biased toward a perceived worsening of litter conditions. This would render comparisons with the trained-observer results problematic.

A much more dramatic discrepancy arises between citizen perceptions of the adequacy of trash and garbage collection and government expenditures on solid waste collection. This correlation was statistically significant (at the 90 percent level), but in the opposite direction from that which was expected! In other words, higher expenditures were associated with decreased citizen satisfaction. This anomaly appears to reflect a longstanding trend toward higher trash collection costs and less service in several of the sites. Dissatisfaction with service, plus the fiscal pressure of Proposition 2½, prompted some sites to make major changes in sanitation service delivery arrangements. Such changes often, but not always, led to lower costs *and* improved citizen satisfaction. (This phenomenon is discussed further in later sections.)

Innovation

Although the predominant response by local agencies to Proposition 2½ was straightforward cost cutting and service reductions, a number of innovative responses were stimulated or accelerated (see the appendix to this chapter). These responses included initiation or expansion of such alternative service-delivery arrangements as contracts with private service providers, imposition of fees and charges, greater reliance on private funding and private contributions, greater use of volunteers, and requirements that the public itself bear greater responsibility for service delivery. These responses do not exhaust the range of municipal reactions that have been predicted or urged by some.

Some types of responses were rarely found, including service shedding (complete elimination of a service), attempts to limit service demand through stricter eligibility requirements, and the use of vouchers to encourage use of the competitive private marketplace. Many of these latter options were probably too complex or long term to have been of interest to municipal officials faced with surviving the first year of Proposition 2½. Others appear to have been philosophically unacceptable to some local government officials.

It is difficult to compare the intensity or breadth of innovation across communities, but the degree of change appears to have been directly related to the amount of pressure that Proposition 2½ placed on agency resources. The greatest amount of innovation and restructuring occurred during the first year of Proposition 2½, when the fiscal pressures were most severe. Innovation abated thereafter, although most of the practices introduced in the first year were maintained.

Officials of several cities observed that the changes had led to a "new mentality" in city hall. Agencies and programs found themselves focusing on ways to become self-sufficient. Elected officials as well as department heads reported paying greater attention to the need for good management per se. In one site that was hard hit by Proposition 2½ during the first year, an official observed that local administrators now viewed their role primarily as one of organizing community members to provide services for *themselves* and of finding new sources of community involvement to draw upon. Although this attitude was not endorsed by officials at all sites, it did appear relatively widespread. Whether it will survive the continuing decline in fiscal stress remains to be seen.

Can Innovation Compensate for Budget Reductions?

One cannot expect a study of sixteen Massachusetts municipalities to provide a definitive answer to the question of whether innovation in service delivery can compensate for budget reductions. Aside from the difficulty of measuring service quality along the many dimensions that consumers find relevant, controlling for external factors, and the even greater difficulty of measuring "innovation" in service delivery, it is evident that the success of any particular strategy for increasing productivity will depend on "internal" local conditions. A department already operating efficiently and exercising imagination in service organization will find it harder to absorb budget cuts without adverse service impacts than an agency that has many inefficiencies to excise. Generalizations about the workability of management strategies are likely to break down in the face of local reality.

Nonetheless, it helps tie together the threads of this chapter to consider which strategies seem to have worked, and under which circumstances, in counteracting the effects of budget cuts.

Fees and Charges

It is perhaps stretching matters to characterize fees and charges as an "innovative" management strategy. The entire state and local sector has been shifting its revenue mix toward fees and charges in the past several years. This was overwhelmingly the preferred response of California localities in coping with the tax limitations contained in Proposition 13.

One objective—usually, the foremost goal—of raising fees and charges is to generate additional local revenues. At the same time a policy of charging for services helps establish the self-sufficiency of a program, because revenues collected in this manner typically are dedicated to program purposes and kept separate from the rest of the municipal budget. Charging for services also is a means of allocating scarce public resources—like playgrounds, recreation facilities, and staff time—among competing demands. Only people willing to pay the prescribed charges gain access to the facilities. On the other hand, the use of fees and charges has been criticized from the standpoint of equity: such costs can be a special burden for the poor, families with perhaps the greatest need for access to low-cost recreation services.

It appears from our surveys and our interviews of municipal officials that consumers have accepted fees and charges as necessary for preserving services—at least in parks and recreation, where the strategy has been used most extensively in Massachusetts. Not one respondent to our July 1982 or August 1983 surveys cited excessive costs as a reason for *not* using local parks and recreation programs more often. It was primarily because of the fees and charges policy that many Massachusetts communities were able to sustain the level of parks and recreation services to the extent that they did, despite the steepest budget cuts of any service area. In most cases, however, the net result was still a modest decline in the perceived quality of parks and recreation services (see table 22), and some sites (for example, Quincy and Watertown) that shifted toward greater reliance on fees and charges still exhibited above-average declines in perceived service quality. On the other hand, three of the communities that made the most pronounced commitment to fees and charges—Wayland, Cambridge, and Arlington—managed to substantially increase overall consumer satisfaction with parks and recreation services, despite first-year municipal budget reductions in this area of 12.4, 17.9, and 11.5 percent, respectively.

Increased Reliance on the Private Sector and the Individual Citizen

A strategy adopted by many towns was to contract with private providers for services ranging from park maintenance to ambulance calls. Others adopted policies designed to encourage taxpayers to take on a greater role in the provision of the services they need. The net result tended to be less reliance on city employees for the provision of municipal services. These options— and their implications—were well illustrated by the case of trash and garbage collection services.

Two municipalities in our sample, Pittsfield and Wayland, were able to *reduce* solid waste expenditures substantially while greatly increasing consumer satisfaction with trash and garbage collection. These two communities, in fact, were largely responsible for the negative correlation between spending and consumer perception of service adequacy for the sample as a whole. Both communities reorganized their trash collection services to virtually eliminate the use of municipal employees while encouraging much greater use of private providers, citizen initiative, or both. Pittsfield contracted out for its entire trash collection service. Wayland simply discontinued all municipal garbage collection services (services reportedly utilized by a relatively small number of households) and left it up to each household to arrange for the disposal of its own garbage, either through its own efforts or by paying a private collection firm to do it.

These efforts at reorganization appear to have been successful. Pittsfield citizens reported a 54.1 percent net *increase* in consumer satisfaction (the largest gain for any site in any service area), despite a 26.8 percent decrease in municipal expenditures. Wayland citizens reported a net 12.3 percent increase in consumer satisfaction in the face of an 80 percent cut in expenditures (a percentage somewhat exaggerated by the relatively small amounts involved in this, the smallest town in our sample).

The success in shifting away from public provision of sanitation services contrasts with the reactions encountered by communities that attempted to cut back on traditional trash collection activities. In New Bedford, local authorities reduced trash collection from twice to once a week, and citizen satisfaction fell sharply (19.6 percent). Worcester reduced its public works staff (including sanitation) by a total of 108 positions, achieving a 12.7 percent reduction in sanitation expenditures; however, citizen satisfaction with the adequacy of overall sanitation services declined. Bridgewater discontinued its contract with a private refuse collection firm in favor of requiring citizens to haul their trash to a new transfer station. This move was prompted by widespread resentment over the rising costs and declining service quality being provided by the private firm. However, a major concern on the part of local officials was that this change might lead to more litter because some citizens would not take their trash all the way to the transfer station. This fear apparently was justified. The trained-observer ratings showed a major degradation in overall neighborhood cleanliness, and Bridgewater was one of only three sites not to exhibit improvements in the incidence of very dirty blocks.[20]

Perhaps paradoxically, it appears that many of the communities making use of private contracting *before* Proposition 2½ actually possessed less flexibility in responding to Proposition 2½ than did communities with traditional service-delivery arrangements. Seven of the sixteen sites already had private contracts for trash collection, and they probably had the least flexibility for making budget adjustments. Long-term contracts and contractor resistance made it impossible to quickly reduce sanitation expenses in these towns. Indeed, it was the possibility of *shifting* service arrangements (from public employees to private firms or, in the case of Bridgewater, from a private firm to individual citizens), that created the opportunity to redefine service responsibilities to produce both significant financial savings and greater consumer satisfaction. This appears to support earlier research suggesting that the reality or threat of a major *change* in service delivery arrangements— whether from public to private or vice versa—that is associated with improvements in service delivery.[21] Once in place, however, no particular service delivery approach is necessarily more flexible or productive in the long run.

Volunteers

A third strategy that showed promise, at least in delivering library services (and, of course, in parks and recreation), was greater use of volunteers. Arlington and Bridgewater both managed to increase consumer satisfaction with many aspects of library services, despite expenditure cuts of 12.4 percent and 10.3 percent, respectively. Their principal response strategy, though by no means the only one they relied on, was greatly increased use of volunteers in staffing libraries and library programs.

---

20. These changes in service arrangements were implemented in late fiscal 1982 and early fiscal 1983. Thus, the changes were too late to be fully captured by the July 1982 citizen survey (which did, however, register the extent of citizen displeasure with the old contractual arrangement, see table 23). However, the trained observer ratings were late enough to reflect some of the impacts of the new arrangements.

21. Donald Fisk, Herbert Kiesling, and Thomas Muller, *Private Provision of Public Services: An Overview*, Report 2702-2-1 (Washington, D.C.: Urban Institute, May 1978).

Police Services

None of the productivity improvement strategies and other innovations employed by local police departments gave evidence of being able to break the linkage between changes in police budgets and changes in citizen perceptions of the adequacy of police services. Police productivity improvement efforts included the establishment of priority rules for allocating police resources in solving crimes or in responding to police calls, changes in the size or deployment of police patrols, and greater use of (volunteer) police auxiliaries. None of these measures gave rise to systematic improvement in citizen perceptions of service quality. Perhaps this was because most police departments were not squeezed hard enough by Proposition 2½ to go much beyond the first-level response to fiscal stress—cost cutting. Thus the departments were not prodded into making major innovations in productivity and service delivery. Moreover, the cost-cutting responses adopted by many policy departments—the most visible one being cutbacks in patrols—tended to impinge sharply on the public's fixed ideas about how police work contributes to neighborhood safety. Because the management innovations that were adopted were often visible to the public, such innovations were apparently unable to compensate, in the eyes of citizens, for reductions in traditional (visible) indications of service levels and service quality—such as how often one sees a patrol car.

Conclusions

At the beginning of this paper we set out to test the proposition that revenue limitations enhance government efficiency. Advocates of this position have put forward two versions of the argument.

The more extreme argument contends that inefficiency is so rife in the public sector that the only certain way to increase output per dollar is to reduce spending. The linkage between service quality and spending levels, it is claimed, is so tenuous that expenditure cuts can be made without *any* systematic impact on services.

The evidence found in our study stands as a rebuttal to this version of the argument. In four of the five services examined (police protection, library services, street maintenance, parks and recreation), there was a clear correlation between changes in municipal spending, in the wake of Proposition 2½, and changes in one or more major indicators of service quality. In service areas and towns where spending was cut back, citizens generally perceived a decline in service quality. Given the unavoidable ambiguities of measurement, the correlations between spending change and changes in service quality are quite impressive. Even in the fifth service area, sanitation, the trained observer measurements showed a significant positive correlation between neighborhood cleanliness and changes in the sanitation budget. Consumer perceptions of changes in cleanliness did not support this correlation, however, and there was actually an *inverse* correlation between citizen perceptions of the change in overall adequacy of trash collection and changes in municipal spending for this purpose—reflecting a pre-existing situation of rising costs and declining service quality that—with Proposition 2½ as a catalyst—triggered some major service realignments.

The second, less extreme argument for the beneficial impacts of revenue limitations holds that, in the face of revenue constraints, local authorities will try new methods of service delivery in order to sustain citizen satisfaction with services. Given the inefficiency that marks many public service delivery arrangements, the opportunity for successful innovation is great.

This version of the argument received considerably more support from our study. Attempts to restructure service delivery did accelerate with Proposition 2½. The impact was greatest in the first year, when fiscal stress was greatest; subsequently the impact subsided as the revenue constraint was relaxed. Most of the innovations introduced in the first year remained in effect during succeeding years, however, and local communities continued to adjust some service-delivery arrangements.

At least some of these efforts were successful in breaking the linkage between decreased expenditure levels and worsening consumer perceptions of service quality. Some towns were able to reorganize their trash collection to rely more on private providers or the efforts of individual citizens in a way that both reduced spending and increased consumer satisfaction. Greater use of volunteers and dedicated fees and charges were other strategies that sometimes seemed able to sever the connection between general budget levels and consumer satisfaction. Indeed, libraries that adopted a *mix* of responses (increased use of volunteers, productivity improvements, solicitation of private contributions, and greater self-help on the part of library users) were especially successful in sustaining citizen satisfaction in the face of sharp spending cuts.

Clearly, such innovations were not always applicable or used effectively. In most cases agency innovations were unable to avoid or counteract the effects of widespread cost cutting on service quality. On the whole, the quality of police, parks and recreation and—to some extent—library services appears to have declined in the sixteen cities in the year following Proposition 2½.

Although fiscal stringency may indeed have forced greater efficiency, the concomitant decline in service quality in at least three major public services makes clear that, on balance, Proposition 2½ and the innovations it spawned did *not* enhance productivity sufficiently to offset budget reductions.

APPENDIX

Examples of Alternative Service Delivery Innovations Adopted by Massachusetts Local Governments[22] in Response to Proposition 2½

Increased Reliance on or Assistance from the Private Sector for Service Delivery

Pittsfield began to contract with a private provider for trash collection.

Cambridge and Watertown contracted maintenance of several parks to private landscaping firms.

Everett eliminated emergency medical services; the city now sends a police car and calls a private ambulance.

Increased Reliance on or Assistance from Individual Citizens

Cambridge enacted new ordinances requiring (1) that persons renovating a house also repair any substandard sidewalks and (2) that users of private security systems pay a fee for each false alarm (to encourage citizens to make their equipment less susceptible to such alarms).

Quincy's public works department no longer widens private driveways—the city now merely grants a permit to the homeowner.

New Bedford police require citizens to come to the station to file a minor complaint (instead of sending a patrol car).

Bridgewater citizens are now required to haul their own trash to a dumping site.

Arlington and Bridgewater greatly increased the use of volunteers in public libraries.

---

22. For more details on these and other local responses to Proposition 2½, see Greiner and Hatry, "Coping with Cutbacks."

Acquisition of Additional Revenues/Financial Assistance

Worcester police now charge for providing parade protection and for conducting weapons training classes.

Quincy police have sought community funding of police vehicles; private firms and organizations have donated funds and equipment to help support patrolling of the waterfront area.

New Bedford has successfully sought private donations for recreation programs. The Polaroid Foundation has donated playground equipment, film, and "camperships."

Most towns increased their use of fees and charges for parks and recreation services.

Many towns introduced or raised fees for ambulance services, fire inspections, or both.

Productivity Measures

Bridgewater provided off-duty firefighters with personal pagers to better match recalls of reserves to need.

Arlington, Quincy, and New Bedford allocated police resources in investigating crimes according to "solvability;" Amesbury established priority rules according to seriousness of incidents, for responding to police calls.

Springfield initiated a "task force" approach at one fire station: six firefighters and one officer were assigned to staff two companies.

Worcester replaced watchmen at public works facilities with electronic surveillance.

Arlington, Everett, and Pittsfield established priorities for maintenance for parks and recreation.

ENTERPRISE ZONES AND INNER-CITY ECONOMIC REVITALIZATION

Marc Bendick, Jr., and David W. Rasmussen

Within the boundaries of virtually all the major cities of the United States lie sprawling islands of urban blight. As large areas of underutilized, centrally located real estate, they undermine the tax base and fiscal viability of their cities. As a source of "negative externalities" such as visual ugliness, crime, and declining property values, they threaten to spread decay to adjacent areas. And as the home of concentrated numbers of the nation's minorities, recent immigrants, low-income elderly, public assistance recipients, and other economically distressed groups, they symbolize many problems of poverty and disadvantage. Small wonder that for more than thirty years, successive waves of public programs have been aimed at the social and economic regeneration of these distressed areas.

In this long history of public efforts, enterprise zones as advocated by Ronald Reagan represent both a continuation of certain lines of thinking and a sharp break with other long-held concepts. Continuity is evident in the notion that initiatives should be targeted spatially—at distressed local areas within a city—as a way to aid distressed persons who live there and to benefit the city as a whole. Discontinuity is manifest in how economic growth in the area is to be enhanced. Previous programs have poured public monies into distressed areas, to clear and prepare building sites for private developers, to improve public infrastructure and services, and to provide special benefits and opportunities to area residents.

The authors gratefully acknowledge helpful comments by Mary Lou Egan and Phyllis M. Levinson.

In contrast, the Reagan administration's concept of enterprise zones is that *reduction* of the public presence within the area should be used to make it a fertile seedbed for indigenous enterpreneurial activity. This reduced public presence is to be achieved by tax and regulatory relief, in combination with avoidance of the increased public expenditures and planning typical of past programs.

In this chapter, we examine enterprise zones as a strategy for the development of these distressed areas within cities.[1] We discuss, in turn, the nature of the urban redevelopment process, the theoretical underpinnings of the enterprise zone approach, specific zone programs proposed at both the federal and state levels, and the lessons of the zone approach for future urban redevelopment policy. Central to this discussion is the contrast between theory and practice. Our general conclusion is that enterprise zones can help revitalize distressed inner-city areas, but they do so largely through state-initiated programs that bear little resemblance to the original concept endorsed by the Reagan administration.

The Conventional Wisdom Concerning the Recycling of Urban Land

In developing this paradoxical conclusion, we must begin by setting forth the conventional view of the process of urban growth and decline that has developed over the past thirty years, based both on research and on practical experience. This view is rejected by advocates of the enterprise zone approach, but we find that ultimately the reality embodied in it has ensnared even enterprise zone programs.

The first tenet of this view is that there is a very strong "zero sum" ("I can win only if you lose") aspect to the development of distressed localities within a metropolitan area. To be sure, it is clear that when the entire nation prospers or the entire region grows, some of this prosperity "trickles down" to even the poorest neighborhoods; and conversely, when the nation is in recession or the entire region is in decline, it is difficult for any neighborhood-specific effort to generate new jobs or prosperity in the face of the general trend. But this having been said, it must be recognized that there are inevitable competitive aspects of local area development: If a company locates in area A, that means that it has not located in area B; if area B rebounds from distress to prosperity, the low-income residents who once resided in B are

---

1. Equally serious, although often less visible, pockets of poverty and distress are to be found in rural areas. They, and the application of enterprise zones to them, are not directly addressed in this chapter, but much of what is said here applies to them as well.

displaced into area C. Spatially targeted local area development activities are thus primarily a means of making the target area a more attractive locale for economic activity that will exist somewhere, rather than generating jobs and income that would not otherwise exist.

Considerable historical and analytical evidence supports this view. Typically, the very areas within cities that are the objects of public concern in the 1980s were prosperous industrial or commercial areas or fashionable residential sections perhaps sixty years before. Prosperity fled with the development of newer areas—usually further away from the city center—which offered a newer generation of buildings and infrastructure, more space for expansion, and escape from problems such as crime, low-income neighbors, overburdened facilities, and inadequate public services. This shift in the locus of prosperity has occurred on a major scale. For example, between 1970 and 1977, although total employment grew nearly 26 percent in the suburban fringe of major U.S. metropolitan areas, it fell a fraction of 1 percent in the central cities of these areas; the distressed subareas of the central cities bore the brunt of the loss.[2]

The same competitive process that generates the decline of an area in one era can lead to its regeneration later. Inner-city locations retain their advantages of central location and access to urban facilities. Eventually, suburban areas may find their own stock of housing, business facilities, and infrastructure aging and their own public services overburdened. If, in the meantime, the buildings in the older areas have dropped sufficiently in value and occupancy that they can be replaced or rehabilitated and the area opened for new uses, then the balance of attractiveness can shift back and growth recur in formerly distressed areas.

The private real estate market has moved urban areas through this cycle of decay and renewal in a number of places. Lowell, Massachusetts, now a booming center of electronics manufacturing after decades as a decayed, abandoned former milltown, is one example. The renaissance of central city commercial areas such as those around Faneuil Hall in Boston or Harbor Place in Baltimore is a parallel phenomenon, as is the reemergence of "gentrified" in-city residential areas in former slum neighborhoods such as Georgetown or Capitol Hill in Washington, D.C.

However, a number of these "showcase" examples were substantially aided by various forms of public sector support. The experiences of most distressed areas suggest that government programs are required at the least

---

2. U.S. Bureau of the Census, *Social and Economic Characteristics of the Metropolitan and Non-Metropolitan Population, 1970–1977* (Washington, D.C.: U.S. Bureau of the Census, 1980), report 75, p. 23.

to speed the often-glacial pace at which the private recycling of land might occur. They also suggest that the "externalities" or "neighborhood effects" in area development are so strong that public agencies must play a role in facilitating efficient land use.[3] And finally, this experience typically indicates that government action is necessary to ensure that the benefits of revitalization are shared with the low-income residents of the area rather than simply leading to their displacement.

From such considerations have emerged federal programs such as Urban Renewal during the 1950s, Model Cities during the 1960s, Urban Development Action Grants (UDAG) and community development block grants during the 1970s, and Economic Development Administration programs over several decades. These programs financed such activities as public land assembly to speed the process of sweeping away old land uses to make way for new uses; public investment in the area, in public infrastructure such as streets and sewers and in private infrastructure such as industrial parks; publicly subsidized financing for private investment through below-market-rate loans or loan guarantees; public expenditures such as special job training or employment programs targeted toward residents of distressed locales; and public planning for the directions of urban growth. Federal outlays on such programs started at a modest $200 million in 1960; and in fiscal 1981, the last year before the Reagan administration took office, they stood at $9.4 billion.[4] These expenditures never grew to more than a modest scale in relation to the total level of investment in the nation; at their peak they amounted to only 3 percent of private fixed investment. Nevertheless, they represented a large proportion of the investment that was occurring in these distresssed areas.

The Dissenting Theory of Enterprise Zones

Nothing is more of an anathema to the original proponents of the enterprise zone approach than this conventional view of the urban development

---

3. Economists use the term *externalities* to refer to the fact that most of the decisions concerning a piece of property in a crowded urban environment have important effects—either positive or negative—on adjacent properties. For example, the failure of one landlord to maintain his property may reduce the value of a neighbor's property. In such circumstances, private decisions made only in light of private benefits and costs may be incompatible with maximizing the public welfare, and government control is often said to be necessary to represent the public interest.

4. These figures refer to outlays in function code 450 (community development, area and regional development, and disaster relief and insurance) in *Budget of the United States Government, Fiscal Year 1983* (Washington, D.C.: Executive Office of the President, 1983), pp. 5–93. They therefore somewhat overstate the funding for economic development activities narrowly defined.

process and the programs it spawned. These thinkers do not see urban development as a competitive process of city versus suburb, or as one of displacement of local residents as part of the process of growth, or as one in which government's role is either necessary or productive. It was with deliberation that one of President Reagan's early domestic policy advisers, Martin Anderson, had in a book some years before damned the urban renewal program as a counterproductive "federal bulldozer."[5]

Prototypes of what the advocates of enterprise zones envisaged as an alternative approach to urban development are Hong Kong and similar success stories from newly industrialized third world nations.[6] They reasoned that rapid growth in such low-income nations was associated with an absence of government regulations, a low level of taxation, and a high level of individual work effort and entrepreneurial initiative. If this environment were recreated in distressed areas of America's inner cities, they argued, similar increases in income would result. Conversely, they reasoned, the pervasive intrusion of government into the economic life of these inner cities is largely to blame for the distress of these areas: heavy taxation has reduced the financial returns to work and to investment, government planning has made cities incapable of adapting flexibly to changing circumstances, welfare payments have reduced incentives to work, and government regulation has stifled business initiative. In this view, individual entrepreneurial zeal and business opportunities would be found in ample supply in the urban ghetto if only they were allowed to flourish unburdened by government. Then new income would be created by and for local residents, and neighborhoods would revitalize without displacement and without "stealing" economic activity from neighboring areas.

The role of indigenous small-business and individual enterpreneurism is central in this scenario for enterprise zones; and findings from studies by researcher David Birch and his colleagues seemed to confirm the sensibleness of this focus.[7] According to this work, small businesses (defined as those having twenty or fewer employees) are responsible for generating two-thirds of all new job opportunities in the United States, a proportion far higher than

5. Martin Anderson, *The Federal Bulldozer: A Critical Analysis of Urban Renewal, 1949–1962* (Cambridge, Massachusetts: M.I.T. Press, 1964).

6. See Stuart M. Butler, *Enterprise Zones: Greenlining the Inner Cities* (New York: Universe Books, 1981); *Enterprise Zones—The Concept*, Hearings before the Joint Economic Committee, 97th Cong., 1st sess., October 23, 1981; and Andrew Garoogian, *Urban Enterprise Zones: A Selected Review of the Literature with Annotations*. Bibliography 102 (Chicago: Council of Planning Libraries, 1983).

7. See David L. Birch, "Who Creates Jobs?" *The Public Interest*, vol. 65 (Fall 1981), pp. 3–14.

their share of total employment. The focus on small firms was also consistent with another of Birch's findings—that very little of the difference in job opportunity between prosperous areas and declining areas is due to the migration of existing firms, fleeing from a distressed area to the suburbs or to the Sun Belt. Rather, the distinguishing characteristic of an area of rapid economic growth was a high birthrate of new, small firms.

Given such evidence, it seemed clear that if a shortage of employment opportunities in distressed neighborhoods is the problem, actions to foster the development and survival of small business should be central to the solution. Small wonder, then, that advocates of enterprise zones viewed with horror much of the record of federal urban renewal programs, where large-scale slum clearance and land recycling were seen as destroying indigenous small enterprises. A case study of the large urban renewal project in the Hyde Park-Kenwood community in Chicago in the 1960s, for example, found that 641 small businesses were uprooted by the project; of these, only 233 survived the disruption. At the same time, the project reduced the number of potential sites in the community for such enterprises from 2,200 to 700.[8]

Equally unappealing to advocates of enterprise zones was the record of federal economic development programs in terms of their expense and cost-effectiveness. In 1980, the federal outlays required to generate one net new job in a distressed locale were estimated to range from $11,570 in the Urban Development Action Grant program, through $13,000 per job in the Business Loan program of the Economic Development Administration, to $60,000 per job in the local Public Works program of the Economic Development Administration.[9] Critics attributed such high costs to the tendencies of such programs to move jobs rather than to create new ones, to the mistake of repeatedly clearing and preparing land for which there was no commercial market, and to the failure of programs to provide inputs that were effective in promoting business growth. This last criticism was lodged against the local Public Works program in particular, which often invested its resources in infrastructure, such as residential sewer systems, that bore little direct relationship to industrial development.

The enterprise zone policies suggested to improve on this record have one element in common with traditional federal urban revitalization initiatives:

---

8. See Brian J. L. Berry, Sandra J. Parsons, and Rutherford H. Platt, *The Impact of Urban Renewal on Small Business, The Hyde Park-Kenwood Case* (Chicago: Center for Urban Studies, University of Chicago, 1968), p. xiv.

9. See Marc Bendick, Jr., "Employment, Training, and Economic Development," in John L. Palmer and Isabel V. Sawhill, eds., *The Reagan Experiment* (Washington, D.C.: Urban Institute Press, 1981), pp. 263–65.

spatial targeting to a distressed subarea within a metropolitan area. In all other respects, the two approaches are mirror opposites. The presence of government was to be minimized in the area, both in the sense of removing regulatory constraints on business activity and in the sense of minimizing public planning and special public expenditures on infrastructure, workers training, or benefits and services to residents. At the same time, tax burdens were to be sharply reduced—not as part of a competition among localities to lure firms to locate in one area rather than another on the basis of differences in tax rates but rather to increase the net financial returns to work effort and entrepreneurial risk-taking. Thus unhindered by government plans and controls, allowed to keep the rewards of their labor, and freed from competing for workers against government projects or welfare schemes, the natural seeds of business initiative already present in the distressed areas would at last achieve their natural flowering.

From Theory to Federal Proposal

When Ronald Reagan was campaigning for the presidency in 1980, such ideas concerning enterprise zones were already in the air, in the writings of advocates at several conservative think tanks (most prominently, Stuart Butler at the Heritage Foundation), in federal legislation proposed by New York Congressmen Jack F. Kemp and Robert Garcia, and in a program operating in Britain, which was an initiative of Thatcher's Conservative government. President Reagan mentioned the approach favorably in his campaign, most notably in a speech against the dramatic backdrop of the South Bronx slums in New York City. Once in office, a working group was established, led by Department of Housing and Urban Development officials, to develop a specific initiative. The idea was intellectually appealing to the administration because it was a local-area analogue of the "supply-side economics" approach to economic policy that the administration was advocating for the nation as a whole—that is, an approach emphasizing tax reductions, deregulation, and private business growth rather than government redistribution. The idea also was politically appealing because it offered the administration an opportunity to present a "positive" approach to urban and poverty problems, to blunt the criticism that its only actions on those subjects had been to cut the budgets of existing federal programs. In his State of the Union message in January 1982, the president announced his commitment to a federal enterprise zone program, and he sent a legislative proposal to Congress on March 23, 1982.

By mid-1985, the president's proposal still had not passed Congress. It was approved by the Senate as part of the 1984 tax revision bill but failed to

survive reconciliation with the House. The president has said he will continue
to press vigorously for legislation in his second term.

Appendix A to this chapter summarizes the major components of the
administration's proposal for a federal enterprise zone program, as embodied
in the initial bill considered by the House.

As the appendix indicates, the approach envisages a modest, experimental scale of operation, involving designation of seventy-five zones, one-
third in rural areas, over a three-year period. This scale allows coverage of
about 4 percent of the approximately 2,000 urban locales eligible under the
program's proposed eligibility criteria, which restrict zones to areas of pervasive poverty, unemployment, and general economic distress. Because of
the limited scale, the approach cannot be thought of at this time as a true
"urban policy" in any sense substituting for more traditional federal programs
because it provides no resources to deal with 96 percent of the distressed
locales. Nevertheless, the proposal can be examined from the point of view
of whether it would work in that role should it be expanded to a larger scale.
Three aspects of the proposal are crucial in that analysis: the role of deregulation, the role of tax incentives, and rules for program targeting.

The Role of Deregulation

In the theory of enterprise zones, designation as a zone is supposed to
trigger extensive deregulation as a major stimulus to new business activity.
In practice, however, the administration's proposal is surprisingly meager on
this score. Left intact are the minimum wage, equal employment opportunity,
occupational safety and health, and environmental restrictions, and all other
regulations mandated by federal law. Deregulation can therefore consist only
of actions taken by states and localities, plus some possible federal deregulation from among more discretionarily imposed regulations.

This particular version of deregulation—one exempting most prominent
federal regulations—probably reflects a realistic assessment by the administration that any proposal weakening employment protections, civil rights,
or environmental and health laws would not be politically acceptable to the
Congress, or constitutionally acceptable as pertains to civil rights. Similar
political pressure is likely to apply at the state and local levels, severely
restricting deregulation there as well. It is difficult to imagine a locality
allowing lower standards of health inspection for restaurants within a zone,
for example, or less rigid standards for building construction. Most government regulations have arisen in response to public concerns about the welfare
of citizens, and, once imposed, the regulations have become part of what
citizens perceive as necessary protections. The first life-taking collapse of a

below-standard building within a zone, or the first case of food poisoning in an uninspected restaurant, or the first case of consumer fraud perpetrated by an unsupervised business headquartered within a zone, and deregulation would prove impossible to pursue very far.

Given that deregulation, either federal or state and local, is unlikely to be a major component of enterprise zones, the question becomes moot whether deregulation, were it to occur, would in fact make an important contribution to business success. Nevertheless, the question is worth addressing because it allows examination of a central tenet of the theory of enterprise zones. Empirical evidence suggests that, however much the business community may rail against red tape and government interference, the actual burdens of regulation are seldom crucial in business survival or prosperity. For example, a recent survey conducted by the National Federation of Independent Business found that local inspection, the ease of obtaining licenses and permits, and local zoning were ranked near the bottom of a list of twenty-five problems faced by urban small business;[10] a survey of Cleveland area businessmen revealed that only 16 percent thought that building codes were a detriment to their expansion.[11] A recent series of interviews conducted among business executives in four cities across the country found a widespread indifference to most deregulation issues as major factors affecting their businesses.[12] And when the state of Connecticut, in conjunction with its own enterprise zone program, set up a special commission on regulatory relief, the group concluded that they had virtually no changes to recommend.[13] Such evidence clearly suggests that an emphasis on regulatory relief would be misplaced in terms of effectively promoting inner-city business growth and employment opportunities.

Tax Incentives in the Reagan Administration's Proposal

Under the administration's proposal, designation as a zone would also trigger twenty-four years of eligibility for a package of federal tax incentives. The most dramatic of these is elimination of all taxation on capital gains on businesses located in the zones. On top of that, about 75 percent of corporate income taxation in the zone would be eliminated through a variety of tax

---

10. *Enterprise Zones—1982*, Hearings before the U.S. Senate, Committee on Finance, 97th Cong., 2 sess., April 21, 1982, p. 212.

11. *Ibid.*, p. 433.

12. See Phyllis M. Levinson and Marc Bendick, Jr., *How's Business in the Reagan Era? The Perceived Impact of Federal Policies* (Washington, D.C.: Urban Institute, 1983), chap. 3.

13. See Steven D. Gold, *State Urban Enterprise Zones: A Policy Overview* (Denver, Colorado: National Conference of State Legislatures, 1982), p. 26.

credits for investment and for wages paid. And employees' earnings within the zone would be subject to a special 5 percent credit against their personal income tax liability. By the administration's estimates, these tax reductions would cost the federal Treasury about $1,240 annually per employee in the zone.[14]

These tax incentives suffer from a number of design flaws that would hamper their effectiveness as tools for promoting business development, particularly small-business development. A crucial shortcoming is that only firms that are showing a profit in the current year can make use of the proposed credits. New firms, small firms, and firms struggling to get established obviously need help most but are the least likely to experience a profit. The proposal offers a carry-forward provision, so that credits could be claimed in future years, but the value of such future use is modest indeed. The provision would be no help to firms in their early years, when cash flow is typically extremely tight; the value of postponed benefits diminishes very rapidly over time; and many new-start firms in fact never survive long enough to turn a profit and claim the offset. This last effect is important in a world in which some 60 percent or more of small businesses do not survive beyond their fourth year.

Even for the firms able to take advantage of the tax benefits, however, the experience with earlier tax credit programs is that such incentives typically engender only modest changes in business behavior, particularly with respect to hiring disadvantaged workers. The records of the Targeted Jobs Tax Credit program, Work Incentive Program (WIN) tax credit, and the National Alliance of Businesses NAB-JOBS program, among others, suggest that even fairly generous tax credits are used by very few firms. When the credits are used, they are often claimed largely for hires that would have been made even in the absence of the credit. To the extent that the latter is the case, most of the revenue loss to the federal Treasury represents a windfall gain to firms, with little new employment generated. To the extent that the former is the case, the revenue losses are small, but no employment is generated. Particularly dramatic experience on this point is provided by the Youth Incentive Entitlement Pilot Project, an experiment of the Carter administration. In this effort the federal government offered a 100 percent wage subsidy, but fewer than one private firm in five was willing to hire disadvantaged youths. Similarly

---

14. *The Administration's Enterprise Zone Proposal Fact Sheet* (Washington, D.C.: Office of the White House Press Secretary, March 23, 1982), p. 4. This estimate is based on the administration's March 1982 proposal. No updated estimate has been provided for the current version embodied in H.R. 1955, but the figure is likely to be of the same order of magnitude.

modest levels of use have been experienced in the Targeted Jobs Tax Credit program.[15]

Finally, the type of business behavior that the tax breaks are most likely to induce is not the creation and growth of firms indigenous to the zones; on that score, the evidence is ambiguous indeed that lower taxation would induce more starts or survivals of entrepreneurial firms. To rely again on the National Federation of Independent Businesses survey cited earlier concerning the key problems of survival for small businesses, taxes were near the bottom of the list.[16] To the extent that the incentives do increase the level of business activity within the zone, they are most likely to do so by inducing in-migration of firms, the very effect that enterprise zone theorists criticize in previous urban revitalization programs.

The reasons this might be true are straightforward. The major determinants of where firms locate are not taxes but considerations of business efficiency such as local labor costs and proximity to markets or raw material. But within a metropolitan area, these factors are largely equalized, so that in selecting among sites all within a few miles of each other, tax incentives can become very important. Although taxes may represent only a small proportion of total costs, they can be substantial relative to profits. For example, in a typical manufacturing firm with profits amounting to 5 percent of sales, the offer of a property tax differential of 1 percent of sales amounts to a potential 20 percent increase in profit. Various empirical studies in New York, Philadelphia, and other cities have borne out this predicted willingness of firms to move locally in response to tax incentives.[17]

To some extent, of course, an important public purpose might be served by the relocation into enterprise zones of firms that would have existed elsewhere but located within the same metropolitan area. If the firms locate within

15. See Richard McGahey, "Whatever Happened to Enterprise Zones?" *New York Affairs*, vol. 7, no. 4 (1983) p. 52.

16. *Enterprise Zones-1982*, There is also evidence that the average effective tax rate on small businesses is lower than the rate on larger ones; see Rosapepe Fuchs and Associates, "Review of Federal Business Tax Incentives and an Analysis by Business Size" (Washington, D.C.: paper prepared for the Small Business Administration), 1980.

17. See W. Warren McHone, "Supply-Side Considerations in the Location of Industry in Suburban Communities, Empirical Evidence from the Philadelphia SMSA," unpublished paper (Philadelphia, Pennsylvania: 1983); Ronald Greison, "The Effect of Business Taxation on the Location of Industry," *Journal of Urban Economics*, vol. 8 (September 1977), pp. 21–35; William Oakland, "Local Taxes and Intra-Urban Location: A Survey," in George F. Break, ed., *Metropolitan Financing and Growth Management Policies* (Madison: University of Wisconsin Press, 1978); and Kenneth A. Small, *Geographically Differentiated Taxes and the Location of Firms*, (Princeton, New Jersey: Princeton Urban and Regional Research Center, 1982). The Reagan proposal guards against quick exits by calling for zone designation to continue for twenty-four years.

the boundaries of the central city rather than in the surrounding suburban jurisdictions, then the often-weak tax base of the central city will be enhanced and jobs may be somewhat more accessible to disadvantaged inner-city residents. But the magnitude of such benefits would almost certainly be modest. The firms most likely to move into the zone in response to tax incentives are those for whom all factors other than taxes are most similar before and after the move—that is, firms that are likely to have located near the zone in any case, not far away in the suburbs. Because the gains in tax base and in job accessibility may be small, the ratio of tax loss to real benefits may be high. The extreme scenario—that of a firm relocating across the street because one block is part of an enterprise zone and the next block is not—is not completely unrealistic.

Finally, questions need to be raised about the types of firms that would migrate into zones in response to tax incentives. Are they likely to be good generators of employment opportunities for local residents? Some would be, of course. But many might be less than ideal in this regard. The experience of some localities using local tax relief to attract firms is that such firms tend to move out of the area as soon as the tax relief expires.[18] Furthermore, the heavy emphasis on capital gains exemptions in the administration's enterprise zone proposal would probably mean that many "paper firms" would tend to locate there—for example, firms consisting of a solo venture capitalist or commodity trader, or pharamaceutical firms whose major basis for income is not the wages paid to manufacturing employees but the return to intangible assets such as product research and development. In such cases, heavy revenue losses might be experienced by the federal Treasury with relatively few jobs created within the zones.

Program Targeting: Jobs in Neighborhoods or in Industrial Areas?

Consistent with its emphasis on individual entrepreneurs and new and small businesses, the provisions in the administration's proposal governing eligible areas emphasize the incorporation of residential neighborhoods within zones. This appears to be appropriate for two reasons: first, residential neighborhoods are seen as likely locales for small retail firms serving local residents or "garage or basement" enterprises started on a financial shoestring. Second, having jobs in neighborhoods, it is argued, will ensure the hiring of local

---

18. For the experience of Puerto Rico in this regard, see Eric Bond, "Tax Holidays and Industry Behavior," *Review of Economics and Statistics*, vol. 63 (November 1981), pp. 503–12.

residents. However, experience suggests major difficulties with both of these presumptions and argues for an alternative approach that focuses more on large-scale industrial and office developments outside residential areas.

This latter approach is important because economic development of distressed inner-city areas must ultimately involve meeting the needs of medium-size and large-scale firms as well as those of small enterprises. Earlier in this chapter, we mentioned research by David Birch on which advocates of enterprise zones have relied to argue that small businesses are the source of most new job opportunities in the nation. Subsequent work by other investigators has found several methodological errors in this analysis. Researchers at The Brookings Institution, reanalyzing the data used in Birch's earlier studies, have concluded that in fact small businesses (in this case, defined as those with one hundred or fewer employees) generate only about 40 percent of all job openings in the economy, a proportion corresponding quite closely to their proportion of all employment in the economy.[19] Small businesses are not an extraordinary, unique answer to problems of unemployment. Rather, they are just part, and a minority at that, of a broad spectrum of firms of different sizes, all of which generate job opportunities. Thus there is little basis for putting all one's eggs in the small-business basket, in terms of generating a new employment base for distressed inner-city areas.

The modest number of jobs that small businesses generate is only one reason to look beyond them, however. Small businesses tend to offer lower wages, fewer fringe benefits, and fewer opportunities for skill training and for occupational advancement than larger firms do.[20] Also, small businesses experience a high bankruptcy rate; consequently, jobs in small businesses tend to be unstable and of short duration. Earlier in this chapter we cited figures describing a high rate of failure of small businesses in the Kenwood-Hyde Park area of Chicago in the wake of a major federal urban renewal program. In fact, however, the failure rate in the urban renewal area was no higher than the failure rate in adjacent, nonrenewed areas.[21] For small businesses struggling to survive in the inner city, life is often nasty, brutish, and short; what critics of federal urban renewal thought they had observed as business destruction by federal action was at least in part only the public face of that harsh fact.

---

19. See Catherine Armington and Marjorie Odle, "Small Business—How Many Jobs?" *The Brookings Review*, vol. 1 (Winter 1982), pp. 14–17.

20. See Harvey A. Garn and Larry C. Ledebur, *The Role of Small Business Enterprise in Economic Development*. Joint Economic Committee, U.S. Congress, 97th Cong., 1st sess., September 1981.

21. Berry, Parsons, and Platt, *The Impact of Urban Renewal*, p. xiv.

Some small businesses, of course, do survive and grow in distressed inner-city areas. But that fact provides by far the strongest rationale for being concerned about the needs of medium-size and larger firms as well as the needs of small businesses. If the inner-city environment does not provide for the needs of these larger firms, then when small firms begin to prosper and to grow—at precisely the moment when their job generation potential is at its maximum—they will move out of the inner-city area that served as their incubator and seek room for expansion elsewhere. One of the basic principles of local area economic development is that it is easier to retain an existing firm in an area than to find a firm from outside willing to replace it. A sensible strategy for local area economic redevelopment must therefore address the needs of firms as they grow, and that means addressing the needs of firms of all sizes—small, medium, and large.

Related to this notion of looking beyond small business alone for economic revitalization is the notion of looking beyond locally oriented retail or service establishments. Enterprises serving their local neighborhoods account for almost 70 percent of all small businesses, largely because their start-up costs are relatively low, they are labor intensive, and in many cases they require only modestly skilled employees. Unfortunately, the prototypical enterprise zone locale is, by definition, a distressed locale that will be hard-pressed to provide a market for new, locally oriented firms.

Thus, improving the economic activity of the distressed enterprise zone areas first requires an increase in its "export base," so that sales to outside the zone will bring in new wages and profits. Such export activities are likely to be in the manufacturing sector or in the large-scale business services sector, where the prerequisites of significant initial investment requirements, large-area space requirements, and sophisticated expertise typically preclude many minority, low-income entrepreneurs and "garage" or "cottage industry" start-ups. When cast in the mold of neighborhood enterprise and indigenous entrepreneurs, the zones are designed to serve and foster precisely the kinds of enterprises that can neither survive in the zones nor provide the needed economic opportunities to its residents.

The appropriate environment for attracting and fostering the larger-scale enterprises needed to provide economic opportunity is not residential neighborhoods themselves but rather industrial and office park settings. Such sites, however, may be developed fairly near the home neighborhoods of the disadvantaged, reducing the problem of the physical accessibility of jobs for this group. In any case, major studies of employment among the residents of distressed inner-city locales have determined that the physical proximity of jobs to the homes of disadvantaged workers is generally not the most serious barrier to their employment. If these workers can offer appropriate job skills and other credentials to quality for jobs, then commuting a moderate distance to the job site is generally not difficult to arrange.[22] Disadvantaged workers do not require jobs literally at their doorsteps, any more than the rest of the working population does.

How Government Can Aid Inner-City Business Development

Two conclusions seem evident from the foregoing discussion of the Reagan administration's enterprise zone proposal: (1) for a variety of political and fiscal reasons, it is a pale version of the bold concept of zones as islands of unfettered free enterprise; rather, the proposed zones are merely fairly traditional islands of tax incentives; (2) the amount of new employment opportunities to be generated within zones for disadvantaged members of society is likely to be modest at best.

What, then, should government be doing to enhance inner-city business development and consequent employment and tax opportunities? What alternative approach is likely to be more successful? The answer is to be found by reference to the so-called conventional wisdom concerning urban development set forth at the beginning of this chapter. In brief, that answer is that the federal government—and its state and local partners—should be engaged in efforts to serve the needs of medium-size and large firms, particularly "export base" types of business, as well as the small firms so central to the enterprise zone approach. To do so effectively requires a panoply of simultaneous government actions, pairing tax incentives with government expenditures and active public planning, rather than relying on tax incentives plus a reduction in the public role.

A considerable body of research has been gathered concerning the constraints that businesses face in seeking to survive and to grow, the factors that determine where businesses choose to locate, and the forms of government assistance that are most valuable to businesses. The answers are quite different for small businesses—for whom the critical question is survival—and for medium-to-large firms, for whom the critical question usually is location.

---

22. Alan Altschuler, *The Urban Transportation System: Politics and Policy Innovation*, chap. 8 (Cambridge, Massasusetts: M.I.T. Press, 1979); Arthur Saltzman, "Providing for the Transportation Disadvantaged," in George E. Gray and Lester A. Hoel, eds., *Public Transportation: Planning, Operations, and Management* (Englewood Cliffs, New Jersey: Prentice Hall, 1980), pp. 573–74.

For small businesses, the key problems in survival are:[23] (1) lack of access to financing at affordable interest rates; (2) lack of training and experience in running a business; and (3) lack of predictable demand for the goods or services they produce. For larger firms, the key determinants of business location, particularly with respect to potentially locating in distressed inner-city areas, are:[24] physical security of the plant site, including absence of threats to personnel, plant and equipment, and goods; adequate space to construct a modern single-story plant and related storage and parking; access to transportation modes, particularly railroads and highways; and facilities within the site, including water and sewage hookups, local roads, and other infrastructure.

What forms should government actions take to address these business concerns? Loan subsidies, loan guarantees, technical assistance/management training programs, and public sector purchase agreements would directly address the problems that constrain the growth of small businesses. Federal programs like those administered by the Small Business Administration and Minority Business Development Agency have been involved in such activities for many years, and local programs to encourage small business are now being launched in many cities. Larger firms need government help in land assembly, investment in infrastructure, and upgrading of inner-city facilities and services. Through the use of public planning, the exercise of the power of eminent domain, and public expenditures, the government can help to create secure, modern, large-scale, nonresidential industrial and office parks in the city that offer the same sorts of security, space, and facilities found in suburban locations.[25] And the most direct and cost-effective way the government can help inner-city residents seeking

---

23. See U.S. Small Business Administration, *The State of Small Business* (Washington, D.C.: U.S. Government Printing Office, 1980), p. 12; and Michael Kieschnick, *Venture Capital and Urban Development* (Washington, D.C.: National Council of State Planning Agencies, 1979), p. 25.

24. See Roger W. Schmenner, *Making Business Location Decisions* (Englewood Cliffs, New Jersey: Prentice Hall, 1982), pp. 250–55.

25. See Marc Bendick, Jr., and David W. Rasmussen, "Enterprise Zones: A Land Banking Approach," *Enterprise Zones—1982*, pp. 477–86. Land assembly and preparation are particularly effective forms of government assistance because they are the actions most difficult for firms to undertake themselves and because they are least subject to offsetting losses of tax deductibility. See David W. Rasmussen, Marc Bendick, Jr., and Larry C. Ledebur, "Evaluating State Economic Development Incentives from a Firm's Perspective," *Business Economics*, vol. 10 (May 1982), pp. 23–29.

Another offsetting effect might further diminish the power of tax incentives unless government action is taken to increase the supply of commercial sites in the zone. The local real estate market is likely to react to any substantial inflow of firms into a zone by raising the price of property within the zone. This rise in price—a capitalization of the tax incentives into the value of the land—tends to reduce the net value of the incentives to the firm locating in the zone. The owners of real estate within the zone would be better off than before the program, but neither

employment seems to be to finance training to equip these people with occupational skills in demand by private firms.[26]

What might an enterprise zone program look like if it were designed to take these considerations into account? It would start by seeking an area for zone designation that is generally suitable for industrial sites or large-scale office development, not a residential area. The area would have to be large enough to provide adequate opportunities for firm growth in modern, single-story plants, surrounded by adequate parking. It would have to be well prepared in terms of having vacant building sites (or buildings suitable for rehabilitation), access to transportation linkages, and infrastructure. It would have to offer security from crime. Then, when the pot is sweetened by financial incentives through special tax provisions, when special training programs make inner-city residents attractive candidates for new job opportunities, and when special capital funds and technical assistance are made available to struggling businesses, some dramatic results might be achieved.

The reason that it is feasible to think of assembling large industrial or office acreage in the city is, of course, that the inner cities of many major metropolitan areas are rapidly losing population. Many vacant properties are coming into the possession of city governments through abandonment and default of taxes. Of course, the acquired properties are typically scattered among other properties still in private hands. In some cases the process of large-scale land assembly therefore would require deliberate selection of certain neighborhoods for preservation and others for recycling, with the remaining occupants of redevelopment areas to be relocated over time. In other cases, cities already possess large vacant areas, resulting from past urban renewal projects; under the industrial park approach, these vacant areas change from liabilities to valuable assets because they involve no additional displacement.[27]

---

firms nor local job seekers would be. Indeed, the rise in land prices might even have an effect on firms opposite to the favorable effect intended: small, struggling firms might be forced to close or to move out of the zone because they could not afford the higher rents. If the tax breaks were generous enough to create substantial incentives and the supply of commercial and industrial sites within the zone were small in relation to demand, a zone might experience a dramatic in-migration of firms able to use the tax incentive (incorporated ones with substantial profits to shelter) and a forced out-migration of firms unable to utilize the benefits (unincorporated firms or firms showing no profits). This reshuffling might make it appear that a zone is a booming economic success, but the net gains in tax base or job opportunities might be almost zero.

26. See Marc Bendick, Jr., "Employment, Training, and Economic Development," in *The Reagan Experiment*, pp. 258–61.

27. See U.S. Congress, House, Committee on Housing, Banking, and Urban Affairs, report prepared by Wilbur Thompson, "Land Management Strategies for Central City Depopulation," in *How Cities Can Grow Old Gracefully*, 95th Cong., 1st sess., December 1977; and James Heilbrun, "On the Theory and Policy of Neighborhood Consolidation," *American Planning Association Journal*, vol. 45 (October 1979), pp. 417–27.

Some States Prove More Enterprising

Many of the federal assistance programs mentioned in the previous section are not directly implemented by the federal government itself but operate through grants to states and cities. The Reagan administration's enterprise zone proposal continues in this tradition by envisaging a program in which federal designation as zones is awarded to proposals that are put forward by state and local governments and operated nonfederally as well.

As events have unfolded, the nonfederal role has proved even more central to the zone idea, for while federal legislation has been stalled in Congress, some twenty-one states have passed zone laws of their own. Many of these laws were initially conceived of as preparing the state to compete for federal zones. By the time the bills were passed, however, many had been transformed into state programs intended to operate largely without federal assistance; most state programs envisage perhaps one or two of their zones being designated as both a federal and a state zone, with consequently greater benefits to offer, but most of their zones having to operate solely on incentives provided by the state and local levels of government.

Appendix B (table 25) to this chapter summarizes the major characteristics of zone programs in fifteen of the twenty-one states that had passed laws as of early 1984. The programs vary greatly but some general patterns can be described. Chief among these is that, for reasons discussed earlier in this chapter and in parallel with the experience of proposed federal legislation, the programs are essentially tax incentive efforts with little more than symbolic nods in the direction of deregulation. Furthermore, most of the tax incentives are straightforward reductions of *total tax* designed to make the tax burdens within the zone competitive against tax rates offered elsewhere; they are not designed around notions of increased work effort or entrepreneurial initiative through reduced *marginal* tax rates.

Most states supplement these tax incentives with extensive government activity within the zones. In some states, the resources available under existing public programs are being targeted toward zones at the expense of other locales; in other states, new public efforts are being initiated in addition to preexisting levels of expenditure. But in either case, far from creating an environment of "no government" and "unfettered free enterprise," state enterprise zones typically are areas of concentrated public effort—in land use planning, infrastructure investment, public service improvement (especially in arson and other crime control), business loan funds, business technical assistance, training of disadvantaged workers, and similar efforts.

In view of the discussion earlier about the ways that government programs can meet the real constraints to survival and the growth that inner-city firms may face, this government activism may in fact end up being associated with some impressive growth within these zones. This is likely to be particularly true where area selection also conforms to the principles discussed in this chapter rather than to "neighborhood" rhetoric associated with the original enterprise zone theory. To see how this may be so, let us briefly examine two state-sponsored enterprise zones already in operation, those in Louisville, Kentucky, and New London, Connecticut.

The enterprise zone in Louisville covers a very large strip of land (2,400 acres) west of the city's downtown and stretching south from the Ohio River. The majority of the nine census tracts involved are industrial; some of the area is now vacant, some of it is occupied by old industrial buildings suitable for rehabilitation, and some of it is occupied by ongoing businesses (including a new plant of the Brown and Williamson Tobacco Company). Easy access to three railroad lines and two interstate highways complete the picture of an area offering attractive locations for firms of a variety of sizes, including very large ones, seeking to operate extensive manufacturing, warehousing, shipping, or office operations. Although 12,000 residents reside within the zone, they do so largely in three concentrated pockets separate from the industrial areas; and the zone is surrounded by extensive low-income residential areas. Thus, the focus is on development of employment opportunities in traditional enterprises geographically accessible to residential areas, not on indigenous entrepreneurial opportunities in the residential neighborhoods themselves.

Consistent with this emphasis, the city of Louisville has spent or committed more than $57 million in physical rehabilitation, land clearance and assembly, and infrastructure development in the zone, aimed primarily at upgrading the industrial areas to meet the needs of firms. Working with the local financial community and with public participation to reduce private financial risk, the city is developing a pool of $30 million in long-term financing to be made available to firms located within the zone. The city is offering financial incentives to zone firms in the form of virtual elimination of a city business inventory tax and reduction of water and sewer fees and connection charges. These local incentives are in addition to state-provided benefits, which include exemption from state taxes for interest paid on mortgages or loans to zone firms and exemptions from state sales taxes and motor vehicle taxes.

These forms of assistance are designed to address many of the highest-priority constraints on business survival and expansion identified earlier in this chapter, including adequate physical space and access to financing, as well as offering immediate reduction of operating costs important to ongoing industrial firms. The tax incentives focus on tax liabilities that are incurred whether or not a firm enjoys a taxable profit. Regulatory relief, reductions in taxation on long-term capital gains, or other exotic incentives represent only minor aspects of the program. To be eligible for full zone benefits, a firm within the zone must draw 25 percent of its employees from a disadvantaged background (defined as persons residing within the zone or having received public assistance for more than one year or being unemployed for more than one year). Given the high unemployment rate in the Louisville area, such constraints should not unduly burden most firms or deter them from participating in the zone program.

To make available the $57 million for infrastructure development within the zone, Louisville will probably be forced to reduce or postpone physical investment in other neighborhoods of the city. The same pattern of diversion from other use is probably true for most of the $30 million in private financing targeted on the zone. The city's stated strategy for the zone is explicit in viewing the program as a means of retaining firms now located within Louisville that will, in the absence of special efforts, move out of the city in search of expansion space, lower taxes, and lower operating costs. Thus, the Louisville enterprise zone program is one that, if successful, will largely relocate economic activity rather than create additional activity. Given the distressed condition of inner-city Louisville, and the unemployment and social and economic distress of its inner-city residents, however, this will be no mean feat in itself. Because Louisville has selected an appropriate site and a well-designed package of assistance, that success is a real possibility.

The experience in Louisville, with a population of 300,000 and a 2,400-acre zone, contrasts sharply in scale with the experience in New London, which has a population of 29,000 and a 125-acre zone. However, the smaller city shares with the larger one the same skill in shaping the enterprise zone approach to match business realities. The heart of the New London site consists of a 19-acre parcel of vacant land formerly occupied by a public housing project, plus a 200,000-square-foot vacant, brick, former mill building suitable for renovation. A small section of low- and moderate-income residential housing (with 800 total residents) is also included because the program's legislation mandates inclusion of some residents, but city officials see the program as primarily commercial and industrial. The city itself is so small that employment opportunities anywhere in the city are readily accessible to persons throughout the area.

The industrial site has excellent development potential, even in the absence of special zone incentives. Infrastructure such as streets and sewers are all in place, having been built earlier when the area was redeveloped as a housing project. The land is flat, vacant, and ready for building. It abuts the U.S. Naval Underwater Systems Center and is located immediately across the Thames River from the General Dynamics Electric Boat Company, both of which offer a ready market for the products of small electronic, computer, or machining firms. Rail lines, an interstate highway, and river access are all present, and the commercial area of downtown New London is within walking distance. Partially fueled by extensive and rapidly expanding military production in the area, the general economy is growing, and the local unemployment rate is well below the national average. Small wonder then that, soon after its designation as a zone, the New London project had attracted a number of proposals for business development in the site, including one from a developer interested in constructing seven small factory buildings for Navy-related high-technology companies, a retail outlet store seeking to locate in the vacant mill building, and a large seafood market/restaurant complex. As in Louisville, the enterprises are typically existing and growing ones, not small start-ups from local entrepreneurs, and represent a relocation of economic activity that would have otherwise existed elsewhere.

The state of Connecticut offers a substantial package of incentives to further enhance the attractiveness of the site. An 80 percent reduction in local property taxes for new or renovated manufacturing facilities, a cash grant of $1,000 per job for each additional employment slot created within the zone, and a sales tax exemption for spare parts for manufacturing equipment are benefits particularly well designed to help businesses of all sizes and states of current profitability. Access to a special pool of small-business loan funds, technical assistance and counseling to small business, and free training of workers are other benefits aimed at priority business needs. As in Louisville, deregulation, incentives for residential rehabilitation, and other forms of assistance not directly related to the most important needs of businesses play only a minor role in the program. At the same time, program rules do not impose heavy operational costs or handicaps on firms as a condition of enjoying zone benefits. In Connecticut, to be eligible for full zone benefits, a firm need draw only 30 percent of its work force from zone residents or from persons eligible for services under federal employment and training assistance. Of course, the firm must locate within a zone. But, in the case of New London, the zone is a clean, quiet section of a tranquil small city, not a site surrounded by miles of smouldering, crime-ridden ghetto. These burdens are not heavy.

Neither the enterprise zone program in Kentucky nor that in Connecticut is without flaws. At other sites in the same states, less appropriate sites may be selected, and the balance of benefits offered to costs imposed may be far different. Moreover, in zone programs in states other than these two, many more serious problems of program design and administration can be observed;[28] a number of states are planning to seek major revisions of their initial state legislation soon. Thus, the point in discussing these two examples is not to suggest that they are typical of all state and local efforts now being started. Rather, the point is that when, among the set of existing state and local programs, we examine examples likely to "succeed," these examples display a consistent pattern. It is by following this pattern that the promised potential in the enterprise zone approach can be realized.

Toward the Next Generation of Urban Revitalization Programs

The irony of this promise is that these potentially successful urban revitalization initiatives derive little more than their name from the original enterprise zone theory. They focus on attracting in-migrant firms, rather than indigenous ones, and serve firms of a variety of sizes, rather than exclusively small ones. They use increased public expenditures as part of their package of attractions, rather than avoiding such outlays. They offer tax reductions primarily as a means of competition against adjacent areas rather than as a means of reducing tax burdens alleged to stifle work effort and investment. They embody little effort to reduce public regulations or planning but instead use government power to collect and allocate land. Thus, whatever they may be called, they derive far more of their spirit from the conventional approach to urban redevelopment than from the enterprise zone dissent from that approach.[29]

In light of everything we know about urban growth, business decisions, and the workings of the markets for labor and for land, this evolution is a favorable development. In its pure form, as originally conceived by theorists

---

28. Among the many weaknesses in state programs, the following are among the most prominent: offering inadequate incentives to firms by reducing tax liabilities that were already low; offering to firms that locate outside of zones economic development incentives that are nearly as generous as the incentives available within the zones; designating large proportions of a state's total area as zones, thereby failing to target on areas in distress; failing to coordinate zone incentives with other relevant state programs, such as those involving worker training, infrastructure development, or business finance; requiring zone businesses to deal with multiple government agencies and work their way through extensive red tape before receiving benefits; selecting zone areas exclusively on the basis of need rather than also considering the development potential of the area; imposing excessively burdensome operating conditions on firms as a condition of receiving benefits; and offering benefits in inappropriate forms (such as nonrefundable tax credits).

29. The enterprise program in Britain has also moved toward traditional industrial area development approaches. See David Hardison, *From Ideology to Incrementalism: The Concept of Urban Enterprise Zones in the United States and Great Britain* (Princeton, New Jersey: The Woodrow Wilson School of Public Affairs, Princeton University, 1982).

and as rhetorically supported by the Reagan administration, the enterprise zone approach envisaged a process and projected an outcome unlikely to come to pass. It does not offer a workable alternative to the traditional approach to urban revitalization.

Nevertheless, the nation's encounter with enterprise zones may leave some useful heritage. Future public programs may be structured more in terms of using public programs to encourage and assist private enterprise in the inner city than in relying on public programs alone. The programs may reflect a greater awareness of the need to help firms of many sizes, not simply large firms, and existing and indigenous firms, not simply in-migrants. They may become increasingly sensitive to criteria of economic growth, in addition to their traditional concerns with equity. They may be more skillfully designed to respond to the most important constraints on firms' success in distressed urban areas. In short, they may offer more sophisticated and effective combinations of public and private efforts than could either previous government-centered programs or the dissenting "pure theory" enterprise zones.[30]

If such lessons are incorporated in the next generation of public initiatives for urban revitalization, the nation's experimentation with enterprise zones may prove to have been worth the effort. But only if we recognize that "successful" enterprise zones demonstrate the potential of traditional urban revitalization approaches more than a radical return to unfettered free enterprise will we understand the meaning of this experience.

---

30. For other analyses of enterprise zones that advocate such future directions synthesizing the best of both approaches, see Charles M. Haar, "The Joint Venture Approach to Urban Renewal: From Model Cities to Urban Enterprise Zones," in Harvey Brooks, Lance Liebman, and Corinne S. Schelling, ed., *Public-Private Partnership* (Boston, Massachusetts: Ballinger, 1984), pp. 63–88; and Susan S. Jacobs and Michael Wasylenko, "Government Policy to Stimulate Economic Development: Enterprise Zones," in Norman Walzer and David L. Chicoine, eds., *Financing State and Local Government in the 1980s* (Cambridge, Massachusetts: Oelgeschlager, Gunn, and Hain, 1981), pp. 175–201.

APPENDIX A

The Reagan Administration's Proposal for a Federal
Enterprise Zone Program[31]

Eligibility Criteria—A total of seventy-five zones are to be designated over a three-year period. Eligibility is limited to areas of pervasive poverty, unemployment, and general distress. Zone proposals will compete against one another for federal designation on the quality and strength of the incentives offered by their sponsoring states and localities.

Tax Incentives—The federal government shall offer nonrefundable credit against: (1) federal corporate income tax liabilities equal to 10 percent of the increase in wages paid to employees within the zone compared with wages paid before the zone was designated; (2) federal corporate income tax liabilities for a portion of wages paid to disadvantaged employees during their first seven years of employment; (3) federal personal income tax liabilities equal to 5 percent of earnings for zone employees; and (4) federal income tax liabilities for capital investment in buildings or equipment within the zone (10 percent for buildings, 3 or 5 percent for personal property). Federal taxation on capital gains income earned within the zone is to be eliminated. States and localities shall offer additional incentives as part of their competitive proposal.

Regulatory Relief—Federal relief will be provided in response to state and local request but cannot affect occupational health or safety, equal employment opportunity, minimum wage, or other regulations mandated by federal law. States and localities shall offer additional regulatory relief as part of their competitive proposal.

---

31. Based on provisions of H.R. 1955, The Enterprise Zone Employment and Development Act of 1983, as scheduled for hearings before the Committee on Ways and Means, House of Representatives, November 17, 1983.

Other Provisions — Low-interest industrial development shall continue to be available for small business within zones when their availability is terminated elsewhere. States and localities may offer other inducements to zone development, including improved local services and increased involvement of neighborhood associations.

APPENDIX B

State Enterprise Zone Programs

TABLE 25

MAJOR CHARACTERISTICS OF STATE ENTERPRISE ZONE PROGRAMS
IN FIFTEEN STATES, AS OF 1983

State[a]	Eligibility Criteria	Incentives for Qualified Business	Number of Zones
Arkansas	Tentative criteria: percentage of households using public assistance; and percentage of households below poverty level.	Discount on sales tax for construction materials; $2,000 discount on corporate income tax for each job created.	No more than 25 percent of the state may be designated.
Connecticut	One of the following: 25 percent or more of the population below poverty level; or 25 percent or more of the population on welfare; or an unemployment rate twice the state average.	$1 million available in venture capital loans to small businesses; 50 percent state corporate tax reduction for ten years for firms employing 30 percent of their new hires from disadvantaged workers or zone residents; assessments phased over a seven-year period for new commercial construction; $1,000 provided to manufacturers for each new job created for disadvantaged workers or zone residents; purchases of spare or replacement parts exempt from sales tax; 80 percent property tax abatement on machinery, land, and buildings for five years; and employment training vouchers for disadvantaged workers or zone residents.	Three in cities over 80,000; three in cities under 80,000.

TABLE 25 (Continued)

State[a]	Eligibility Criteria	Incentives for Qualified Business	Number of Zones
Florida	Considerations: housing conditions, per capita income, unemployment, per capita local taxes, and percentage of elderly and young people.	Tax credits for: new or expanded business; contributions to community development projects; businesses that employ zone residents whose salaries are less than $18,000 per year; loans and grants to zone community development corporations; tax-free industrial revenue bonds, to be issued only for projects within zones; and tax increment financing.	Unlimited (120 already designated)
Illinois	Depressed area; low-income area; 10 percent decrease in population between 1970 and 1980; and unemployment rate 120 percent of state average for a six-month period.	Loan institutions allowed to deduct certain interest income from taxable income; state investment tax credit of 0.5 percent of new investment; state and local sales tax exemption on building materials used in the zone; $100 million in industrial revenue bonds for zone enterprises; and dividends from corporations conducting business solely in zone exempt from state income tax.	Eight zones per year for six years
Indiana	25 percent of households below poverty level or unemployment 150 percent of the state average; population between 2,000 and 8,000; area with continuous boundary between 0.75 square miles and 3 square miles; area suitable for	A 5 percent tax credit on interest from loans to firms in the zone; a 10 percent tax credit on employer income tax for employee wages; property tax credits; investment by Small Business Investment Corporation, Minority Business	Maximum of six

	Criteria	Incentives	Number
	development of a mix of commercial, industrial, and residential use; an urban enterprise association; specified economic development incentives in the area.	Investment Corporation, and Corporation for Innovation Development for zone businesses; tax increment financing; and priority for neighborhood assistance funds.	Unlimited (one designated so far)
Kansas	Location within a city; maximum of 25 percent of land area or population of jurisdiction; widespread unemployment, poverty, and general distress; eligible for federal Urban Development Action Grants or one of the following: (1) loss of 10 percent of the population between 1970 and 1980; (2) 70 percent of the residents with income less than 80 percent of median income; or (3) unemployment at 1½ times the state average for the previous eighteen months; at least one local incentive.	Sales tax refund for the cost of machinery, equipment, construction or modernization; tax credits for the first ten years to businesses with new employees or investment in the zone; tax increment financing; and job tax credit: $350 for each employee and $500 for each disadvantaged employee.	
Kentucky	Areas of pervasive poverty, unemployment, and economic distress; decrease in population; a continuous boundary; and local government participation.	Exemptions from sales tax on qualified property and sales and use tax for building materials. Neighborhood enterprise associations can lease for ninety-nine years, at not more than $1, all state and local property not in use.	Two zones per year for three years and one zone for the fourth year
Louisiana	Considerations: unemployment, per capita income, migration, and residents receiving public assistance; local governments provide additional incentives.	Exemption from state sales tax for purchase of equipment; exemption for urban-zone-qualified businesses from state income and corporate franchise tax; $2,500 tax credit per net new employee for rural-zone-qualified businesses.	25 percent of the state (411 zones already selected)

TABLE 25 (Continued)

State[a]	Eligibility Criteria	Incentives for Qualified Business	Number of Zones
Maryland	Unemployment at least 50 percent above state or national rate; low-income poverty area; 70 percent of the residents have income less than 80 percent of median income; 10 percent decrease in population between 1970 and 1980; and zone limited to 160 acres unless exception is specifically justified.	Tax credits for local property taxes and wages paid to employees; $2 million in loan guarantees from the Venture Capital Guarantee Fund; and larger loans from Maryland's existing loan programs for qualified businesses.	Six zones in any twelve-month period.
Minnesota	Commitment from locality to promote economic development; any area adversely affected by the closing of a military facility; population of at least 4,000 in metropolitan areas and 2,500 in other areas; housing before 1950; 20 percent of households below poverty level; and 10 percent population decrease in the past ten years.	50 percent tax abatement for new capital improvements for the first twelve years.	Unlimited.
Mississippi	Level of migration, manufacturing activity, per capita income, unemployment, and distribution of income. Creation of community appearance committee, existing industries committee, industrial site committee, and community data committee. Zone can be an entire county or a jurisdiction within the county.	For manufacturing operations: exemption from sales and use tax on materials for construction of buildings and equipment, and tax credit of $1,000 on state income tax per new employee.	Five zones first year, one in each congressional district; no more than five zones in one year, and no more than twenty-five at one time.

Missouri	Population: areas of 4,000 to 30,000 in a metropolitan area, and areas of 2,500 to 10,000 outside a metropolitan area. Cooperation from the localities; areas of pervasive poverty, unemployment, and general distress; eligibility for federal Urban Development Action Grants. One of the following: unemployment 50 percent above state average; decrease of population of at least 20 percent between 1970 and 1980; or 70 percent of the population below 80 percent of the median income for the state.	Tax credits: 10 percent for the first $10,000 in investment, 5 percent for the remainder; $400 for each new employee; a maximum of $400 for each employee trained; $100 credit every three months for each employee who lives in the zone; $100 credit every three months for each person disadvantaged at the time of employment. Ten-year state income tax exemption on half of earned income; unused tax credit to be refunded at a rate of 50 percent or $50,000 the first year and 25 percent or $25,000 the second; 50 percent exemption from property taxes for first ten years; and infrastructure improvements.	Unlimited.
Ohio	An area of continuous boundary with a population of at least 4,000; eligibility for federal Urban Development Action Grants; expenditures for public assistance programs at least 1.25 percent of the state average by the county in which a municipality is located; and the most populous municipal corporation in the county or within 20,000 population of the county's largest municipal corporation. In addition, one of four requirements must be met: unemployment 150 percent of the national average, low-	Cities or counties are responsible for providing incentives; they may include: abatement for a period of up to ten years and up to 100 percent of taxes on real property and tangible personal property; if the zone is designated by the county, the maximum abatement of such taxes is ten years and up to 50 percent; an exemption for up to ten years for any optional services or assistance authorized for the project site. State sales tax exemption for purchases for up to five years; business income tax credit; and unemployment tax credit.	Unlimited.

TABLE 25   (Continued)

State[a]	Eligibility Criteria	Incentives for Qualified Business	Number of Zones
	income or poverty population, population loss of 10 percent since 1970, abandoned structures or a number of structures with delinquent taxes.		
Pennsylvania	Areas of distressed populations and distressed businesses are eligible if at least one of following criteria is present: Population: In municipalities of less than 5,000, the zone may include the entire population. In municipalities of less than 50,000, the zone may have up to 8,000 in population. In municipalities of more than 50,000 or central cities, the zone may include one or two census tracts. Eligibility for federal Urban Development Action Grants on the basis of two of the following characteristics: 20 percent or more of the population with income below poverty level; 15 percent or more of the labor force unemployed; loss of population between 1970 and 1980. Working partnership between local government, state government, and the private sector. Must have one of the following characteristics: 25 percent or more of	Targeting of all available state programs such as capital for small business, infrastructure improvements, and low-interest loans for industrial land.	Six zones fully designated in 1983; fifteen zones preliminarily designated.

the population below poverty level; 25 percent or more of the population dependent on welfare; or an unemployment rate twice the state average.		
Virginia	At least 25 percent of the population with income below 80 percent of the median income for the jurisdiction; and unemployment rate 1½ times the state average. Localities are asked to cooperate in reducing tax and regulatory burdens.	State sales tax exemption for purchases for up to five years; business income tax credit; and credit equal to what the employer would pay in state unemployment taxes.	Maximum of six zones.

SOURCE: Adapted from *State Enterprise Zone Roundup* (Washington, D.C.: National Association of State Development Agencies, June 1983).

a. Since this table was compiled, enterprise zone legislation (or an administrative enterprise zone initiative) has been adopted in Alabama, Georgia, Nevada, New Jersey, Oklahoma, Rhode Island, and Texas.

THE EFFECTS OF REAGAN ADMINISTRATION BUDGET CUTS ON HUMAN SERVICES IN ROCHESTER, NEW YORK

Sarah F. Liebschutz and Alan J. Taddiken

> Our values as a free and caring people and the lessons of recent decades suggest . . . that our urban policy should be broad enough to encompass the diversity of our cities [and] that States and cities, properly unfettered, can manage themselves more wisely than the federal government can. . . .[1]

Congressional enactment of the Omnibus Budget Reconciliation Act of 1981—the Reagan administration's key initiative to "unfetter" states and localities—enables us to test those propositions. What have been the effects on American cities of the cuts in grants-in-aid and the merger of categorical programs into block grants administered by the states?

In this chapter we consider the effects of federal funding reductions and program changes on the politics and residents of one city—Rochester, New York. Although Rochester's history and culture make it unique, contributing to the basically diverse condition of urban America, its public service arrangements and demography are not atypical of cities in the northeastern and midwestern regions of the country. Thus an examination of the responses of public and nonprofit institutions and residents in Rochester may aid in understanding the ability of other cities to manage with less federal aid and fewer fetters, if indeed that is the case.

In the sections that follow, we describe the dependence of the Rochester city government on other governments and the dependence of one subpopulation, the working poor, on federal aid. Analyses of the local effects of cuts and changes in the social services block grant and Aid to Families with

---

1. U. S. Department of Housing and Urban Development, *The President's National Urban Policy Report* (Washington, D.C.: U.S. Government Printing Office, 1982), p. 1.

Dependent Children (AFDC) are presented. In these analyses we use interview data generated in a local survey of former beneficiaries of these federal grants.

Rochester's Dual Dependence

Rochester, the third-largest city in New York State, projects a mixed image. On one hand, it is the home of prominent national and multinational corporations, including the Eastman Kodak Company and Bausch and Lomb; the administrative, legal, and financial center of its five-country metropolitan area; and the center of such highly regarded cultural, educational, and health facilities as the Eastman School of Music, the medical center of the University of Rochester, and the International Museum of Photography. Moreover, the city's government—the council-manager form from 1925 to 1985—is widely viewed as professional and efficient; since the mid-1970s, the level of co-operation between the city's numerous neighborhood associations and city hall has been extensive. The slogan, "Our Spirit Shows," captured well Rochester's mood of civic pride as it celebrated its sesquicentennial in 1984.

Yet Rochester shares characteristics common to many northeastern and midwestern cities: declining population; abandoned housing; deteriorating roads, sidewalks, sewers, and houses; and a stagnant property tax base. Rochester's population in 1980—241,741—was 27 percent smaller than in 1950. This decline was accompanied by changes in the composition of the city's population: in 1980, considerably more residents of the city—34 percent of the total Monroe County population—were economically disadvantaged and nonwhite than was true of residents of the overlying county and in the metropolitan area. Declining jobs in manufacturing—the city's dominant economic sector—accompanied the population loss. The resulting squeeze on the property tax base, the largest single source of revenues for city operations, has generated a condition of fiscal and service dependence.[2]

Rochester's dependence takes two forms: (1) reliance on other local governments and state government for provision of services to city residents and (2) reliance of the local governments on both the federal and state governments for revenues. In addition, of course, the state relies on federal aid. The focus here is on Rochester's reliance on service provision from other local governments and on aid from the federal government.

---

2. See Sarah F. Liebschutz, *Federal Aid to Rochester* (Washington, D.C.: Brookings Institution, 1984), for an elaboration of these points.

Rochester is typical of New York's central cities, towns, and villages (except for New York City)[3] in its dependence on other areawide local governments and the state government for delivery of services to city residents. The city government provides fire and police protection, public works (except for certain highways and bridges and the sewer-storm water system), and community development, and shares with Monroe County the task of providing other functions such as parks, recreation, and library service.

Monroe County assumes sole local responsibility for income maintenance, many social services, and public health services. Three special districts—the fiscally dependent city school district, Rochester Housing Authority, and Rochester-Genesee Regional Transportation Authority, provide public education, public housing, and public transportation, respectively, to Rochester residents (as well as to other county and regional residents). State agencies provide a variety of services for mentally ill and physically and developmentally disabled people, as well as employment services, educational programs, and economic development activities.

The dependence of Rochester residents on these other local governments and state agencies is especially great in the case of the city's poor and near-poor residents, as they are the greatest targets and users of publicly subsidized income, health, housing, transportation, and education programs. In June 1983, 91 percent of the persons receiving public assistance (AFDC) administered by the county government were city residents. Various surveys indicate that lower-income city residents are substantially more dependent on public transit than are middle- and upper-income residents. Eighty percent of the lunches served by the city school district are free for low-income students. All the people living in public housing units administered by the Rochester Housing Authority qualify as poor or near-poor. State agencies serve a somewhat wider public with special needs, but one that includes many poor city residents.

The reliance of the five local governments on federal aid encompasses entitlement assistance to Rochester's needy residents and grants for operating programs and capital projects. As shown in table 26, Monroe County, because of its central role in administering AFDC, food stamps, Medicaid, energy, health, and social services, accounted for two-thirds of all aid allocated in 1981 from Washington to these Rochester area governments under the pro-

---

3. New York City, like other city-county combinations but unlike most cities in the state and in the nation, directly administers and assumes the local costs for a wide range of welfare, health, social, and education services. For an analysis of the contribution of these responsibilities to the New York City fiscal crisis in 1974–75, see Peter D. McClelland and Alan L. Magdovitz, *Crisis in the Making* (Cambridge, England: Cambridge University Press, 1981).

grams analyzed. In contrast, the city government in 1981 received only 14 percent of the grants listed in table 26.

These facts about Rochester's dual dependence on other local governments and on Washington suggest that although the largest users of federal aid are city residents, city hall itself has been largely bypassed in the local politics and policies concerning these grants. Hence, a case study of the effects of the Reagan domestic program on Rochester city residents, especially low-income residents, must focus on institutions outside of the city government.

Trends in Federal Aid: Specific Grants

For Rochester residents, the changes enacted in the omnibus budget act of 1981 created varied effects, according to the nature of the federal grants. Entitlement funds for income, medical, and food assistance in Rochester increased after 1981—a reflection of the growing numbers of local residents affected by the recession. The increases in AFDC, food stamps, and Medicaid

TABLE 26

FEDERAL FUNDS BENEFITING LOWER-INCOME RESIDENTS OF
ROCHESTER, NEW YORK, FISCAL YEARS 1981–84
(*Thousands of Dollars*)

Category	1981	1982	1983	1984
Rochester city government				
Comprehensive Employment and Training Act (CETA) and Job Training Partnership Act[a]	5,142	3,940	3,586	3,072[b]
Community development block grant[a]	12,972	12,512	12,921[c]	10,870
Monroe County				
Aid to families with dependent children (AFDC)[d]	20,504	24,342	23,917	22,163
Medicaid[d]	47,278	66,616	67,776	77,256
Food stamps[d]	17,529	17,304	22,692	NA
Low-income energy assistance block grant[d]	3,096	3,796	5,393	6,156
Health care block grants Alcohol, drug abuse, mental health[a]	488[e]	252[e]	NA	NA
Preventive health[d]	99	210	178	160
Maternal and child health[a]	326	212	202	167
Social services block grant[f]	5,944	5,602	5,710	6,105[c]

TABLE 26 (*Continued*)

Category	1981	1982	1983	1984
City school district				
Education block grant[f]	3,650	3,260	910	710
Compensatory education[f]	5,330	4,170	4,710	5,270
Rochester Housing Authority				
Public housing[a]	3,925[g]	5,744[g]	3,459[g]	2,350[h]
Section 8[a]	4,578	4,527	4,697	5,035
Rochester-Genesee Regional Transportation Authority				
Mass transit, operating[i]	4,756	4,313	2,169	2,979
Mass transit, capital[i]	2,715	6,205	2,738	3,200

SOURCES: Documents and interviews with staff from Rochester City Government, Monroe County, City school district, Rochester Housing Authority, and Rochester-Genesee Regional Transportation Authority.

These data are federal revenues (actual or estimated) to the recipient governments for selected programs; they have not been apportioned to Rochester residents but reflect total revenues to the listed governmental units.

a. October 1 through September 30.

b. Transition year, October 1 through June 30.

c. Includes emergency jobs bill supplement: community development block grant, $2,366,000; community services block grant $30,000; social services block grant, $395,000.

d. Calendar year.

e. Drug abuse grant only received.

f. School year, September 1 through August 31.

g. Operating subsidy and community improvement assistance funds.

h. Operating subsidy only.

i. Authority fiscal year, April 1 through March 31.

funds in Rochester would have been even larger, however, if the federal budget changes had not made large numbers of near-poor Rochester residents ineligible for these entitlement grants. Federal aid for operating job training, education, health, and social service programs generally decreased after 1981; cuts in the Comprehensive Employment and Training Act (CETA) and education aid were particularly steep. Grants for community development also declined between 1981 and 1984.

Among the local governments, the effects varied as well. The city school district was most severely affected by the federal changes; its block grant entitlement in 1984 amounted to only 20 percent of the categorical aid it had received in 1981. The transportation authority also experienced a decrease in its federal operating subsidy.

For selected programs, Monroe County actually administered more federal aid in 1984 than in 1981. The major increase occurred in Medicaid (see table 24); this increase reflected the federal government's share of escalating costs associated with New York's generous coverage of benefits and clients, which remained unchanged following the omnibus budget act. However, as counties are mandated by New York to share with the state the nonfederal costs of Medicaid and AFDC, county spending also increased for these entitlement programs.

For the Rochester city government, the omnibus budget act changes resulted in $2 million less for job training in 1984 (from the Job Training Partnership Act) than in 1981 (under CETA), and a similar decline in funds for community development (funds from both of these federal programs have been declining since the late 1970s). An analysis of the city of Rochester's total revenue situation (excluding the fiscally dependent city school district), showed significant shifts in federal revenues (as a percentage of total revenues) from 1977 to 1982. In 1977, the city received 19.3 percent of its revenues from the federal government; by 1982, this proportion had declined to 12.4 percent. This decline in federal revenues had actually started in 1981; the four previous years were relatively stable at the 1977 level (both in terms of proportion of federal revenues and absolute amount in current dollars). State source revenues had remained stable, whereas the local share had increased from 71.8 to 79.7 percent.[4]

The Working Poor

For the most part these estimated budgetary effects of federal grant reductions do not present an accurate perspective of the effects on individuals and households. The 1981 omnibus budget act represented not only a reduced funding but also a different social philosophy from that of previous administrations.

Nathan Glazer has characterized the Reagan administration's social policies as follows:

> Their underlying force was provided by a vision of how societies grew economically and what makes them strong. Individual action, unhampered by government, spurs an economy. Consideration for the poor, in the form of special programs, tends to undermine the incentives that move the poor into economic

---

4. Center for Governmental Research, "Trends in Local Government Revenues," working paper (Rochester, New York: Monroe County Human Services Data Sharing Project, December 17, 1982).

action and out of poverty. If only government gets out of people's way, they can make their own way.[5]

Thus the Reagan administration pressed forward the federal policy under which "welfare would become basic charitable support, with a sufficient degree of harshness in administration and in limitation of benefits that people who could work would be happy to get off, and those who did work would try to stay off—even if working provided less than welfare." Glazer has further indicated the Reagan administration's rejection of "social engineering": "programs based on discrete and sophisticated interventions . . . have been cut and further cuts are in store."[6] All the Reagan administration's budget proposals have attempted to advance these themes—in many cases, successfully (especially, of course, in the omnibus budget act of 1981).

It is generally conceded that the major effects of these various Reagan policies have fallen on the working poor, as the quotations indicate:

> Through the actions taken at the president's request in 1981, Congress moved away from the notion that low-income people are to be encouraged to work through positive financial incentives. . . . Benefit cuts were greatest for those low-income people who work.[7]
> According to the 1980 Census, half of the over six million families below poverty worked at least part of the year. . . . It is these low-income families who are trying to work themselves out of poverty who are hit hardest by the FY 1982 changes and FY 1983 budget provisions. . . . the incomes of AFDC families with average earnings were reduced from an average of 101 percent of the poverty standard in 1981 to 81 percent in 1982 as the result of the provisions in The Budget Reconciliation Act.[8]
> Richard P. Nathan . . . said the research confirmed a tentative conclusion last year that the cuts hit the working poor hardest and were not so damaging as expected to local governments . . . the cuts were affecting poor people receiving transfer payments and services from programs more than they were affecting state government treasuries. Those on the margin of eligibility for assistance were most affected.[9]

Reflecting concerns similar to these, Rochester area officials, service providers, and public interest advocates began a cooperative research project in

---

5. Nathan Glazer, "The Social Policy of the Reagan Administration: A Review," *The Public Interest*, no. 75 (Spring 1984), p. 78.

6. Ibid., pp. 85, 88, 98.

7. James R. Storey, "Income Security," in John L. Palmer and Isabel V. Sawhill, eds., *The Reagan Experiment* (Washington, D.C.: Urban Institute Press, 1982), pp. 384, 391.

8. Tom Joe, "Profiles of Families in Poverty: Effects of the FY 1983 Budget Proposals on the Poor," working paper (Washington, D.C.: Center for the Study of Social Policy, February 25, 1982), pp. 13–14.

9. John Herbers, "Study Tells How 14 States Countered U.S. Aid Cuts," *New York Times*, May 8, 1983.

June 1981 to monitor objectively the local impacts of Reagan's social policy shifts. The project sponsors had different views on the value of the policies, but they generally agreed that the effects of the Reagan administration's changes should be objectively evaluated. The findings were intended to be used in local policy debates concerning social equity issues and public and private budget allocations.

The concern in Rochester for the effects on individuals and households was based partly on the large number of federal changes targeted at eligibility, level of services, and cost of services. There was a general fear that such changes might interact in many instances—creating major burdens for certain persons and households. Both the fairness of such burdens and the possible subsequent costs to correct problems caused by excessive stress or inadequate preventive services stimulated interest.

The targeting of federal funds intended for lower-income people has long been recognized as a major problem. Do the poor persons and households eligible for special benefits actually get them? How can "indirect" benefits to the poor—that is, community development grants used for infrastructure improvements or economic development—be measured? How much of a federal grant targeted to the poor should go for local administrative expenses? To what extent do federal funds targeted toward the poor result in displacement of other local, state, and private funds previously allocated to the same people?

Given the reduction in available federal funds and eligibility levels, there was concern in Rochester that targeting benefits toward the poor would become still more difficult. Not only would many poor households lose eligibility for the rather tightly targeted programs such as AFDC and Medicaid, but these households would also become less successful competitors for subsidized housing, transportation, social services, and educational services—all services involving ambiguously targeted federal grants.

Furthermore, there was concern that, because of rural migration into the county and an unusually tight local economy because of job loss, Monroe County was adding poor people at a higher rate than either the state or nation. The number of persons below the poverty line in the county increased 22 percent between 1969 and 1979, compared with an increase for the state of 15.8 percent and a decrease for the nation of nearly 10 percent over the same period.

Between 1969 and 1979, the number of poor people in Monroe County grew by 10,000, bringing the total number of poor persons there to 60,000. Most of these people lived within the city of Rochester. An additional 43,000 people in the county were living on incomes between the poverty level and 150 percent of poverty in 1979. This group was known to include an increasing proportion of families headed by single women—many with preschool or school-age children. It is well recognized that many such families headed by single women have daily problems providing for the basic necessities such as food, housing, clothing, and child care. In contrast, the vast majority (over 75 percent) of the county's residents had incomes at least twice the poverty level.

Thus, given the federal cutbacks, local government responses, and the local perceptions of an increasing population of poor, local interest became focused on a group of households that lost subsidized day care and another group that lost eligibility for AFDC. The sections that follow describe the changes in federal programs (Social Services Block Grant and AFDC), the local and state institutional reactions to those changes, and, most important, the consequences to and adjustments by the families losing benefits.

Social Services

The social services block grant (Title XX) was originally intended to help low-income families and individuals achieve or maintain economic self-support. Recipients of public assistance are a major target group. Title XX goals stress the prevention, reduction, or elimination of dependency on government social welfare services. Additional goals are the prevention or remedying of neglect, abuse, or exploitation of children and adults unable to protect their own interests.

As the major funding source for state and local provision of services intended to achieve the above goals, Title XX was typically used to support a variety of services: foster care; adoption; child and adult protective programs; day care; counseling; homemaker, housekeeper/chore services; information and referral; and family planning services. In New York State, Title XX involved a 12.5 percent state and 12.5 percent local match of federal aid.

In 1981, under the budget reconciliation act, a social services block grant was established to replace Title XX. The major change was an initial cut in funding from $2.9 billion (fiscal 1981) to $2.4 billion (fiscal 1982), although funding recovered to $2.7 billion in fiscal 1983. The budget act changes also allowed states discretion to determine types of services, removed state matching requirements, eliminated the requirement that a specific portion of funds go to welfare recipients, and removed the requirement limiting services to families with incomes below 115 percent of the state's median income.

General Institutional Reactions to the Changes

The passage of the omnibus budget act was widely hailed in New York state as a disaster for social services and social services recipients.[10] In fact, allocations to New York were reduced by $59 million (25 percent) between fiscal 1981 and fiscal 1982. Yet, although this reduction was a shock to the social services system in New York, the state was able to cushion the effects of the federal cuts so that, with a few exceptions, the full range of services was maintained at the local level.

New York has a longstanding tradition of maintaining comprehensive social services with generous benefit levels, broad eligibility, and high program standards. State law, predating the Reagan administration, mandates considerable state and county fiscal support of social services regardless of federal participation. The most significant piece of legislation in this regard is the New York State Child Welfare Reform Act of 1979, which reimburses counties for mandated services when Title XX (now the social services block grant) funds are exhausted. These mandated services include those that support families to prevent placement of children in out-of-home care, protect children and adults from harmful situations, promote adoption, and provide for foster care.

From a state fiscal standpoint, the open-ended state match for mandated services, ranging between 50 and 75 percent, opens the door for an expanding commitment of state funds no matter how much is recovered from federal sources. From the local standpoint, New York's 58 social service districts (57 counties plus New York City) realize significant benefits because of the large state share for mandated services. At the same time, however, they lose flexibility, because mandated services much be provided regardless of other fiscal pressures on local program priorities.

Elimination of Subsidized Day Care

Day care is especially vulnerable to cuts because it is the largest non-mandated expenditure of all former Title XX services. One analysis characterizes day care services within the state as follows:

> Outside New York City, day care accounts for only 12 percent of Title XX expenditures, but 51 percent of optional services. In New York City day care consumes 45 percent of all Title XX funds and 83 percent of Title XX optional services. The differential reimbursement rates between Title XX (12.5 percent local) and state streams (25–50 percent local) available for certain mandated services when a district exceeds its Title XX ceiling encourage counties to use Title XX funds for mandated services and reduce optional services, particularly day care. Reductions are made by entirely eliminating day care for the working

---

10. See New York State, Governor's Task Force on the Federal Human Services Budget, *Impact Report of the Governor's Task Force on the Federal Human Services Budget* (Albany, New York: August 1981).

poor funded out of Title XX or by reducing eligibility levels. In FFY [federal fiscal year] 1983, 34 out of 58 social services districts no longer offer[ed] income eligible day care.[11]

Monroe County's cuts in Title XX day care predated the omnibus budget act. "Beginning in the spring of 1980 . . . in anticipation of a County Department of Social Services deficit of $2 million . . . DSS income eligibility for non-mandated (that is, not protective or preventive) day care was reduced from 70 to 62 percent of the state median income."[12] The 200 families affected at that time became eligible for partial day-care subsidies from the United Way, which, since 1974, had provided such subsidies on a sliding scale for group day care for low- and moderate-income families.

In July 1981, in anticipation of both continuing Title XX shortfalls and a federal and state funding decrease of $800,000 for 1982, the Monroe County legislature approved a recommendation from Department of Social Services officials that all "income-eligible" day care be discontinued. An income-eligible family of four at that time, for example, was defined as a non-AFDC household with annual earnings up to $15,000.

The 293 families cut included 642 children, 430 of whom were using some form of county-subsidized day care. The United Way, in turn, tightened its eligibility levels, and 198 of the families became eligible for partial United Way group day care subsidies. The remaining families using family day care were eliminated completely from service.

Monroe County was not alone in choosing to eliminate day-care subsidies for income-eligible families: eight other New York counties took the same step between fiscal 1980 and fiscal 1983. In fact, with the exception of the Long Island counties of Nassau and Suffolk and New York City, all of New York's urban counties cut their own spending for day-care subsidies by reducing income eligibility limits, raising parents' fees, or eliminating the program altogether.[13]

Monroe County's decision, however, lasted a relatively short time. A coalition of groups led by Statewide Youth Advocacy, Inc., a children's lobby based in Rochester that includes local day-care center directors, formed in response to the cuts. The coalition argued that "many poor women [would be] forced to choose between jobs or child-care arrangements—or to com-

---

11. Statewide Youth Advocacy, Inc., *Where Have All the Children Gone?* (Rochester, New York: SYA, 1983), p. viii.

12. Center for Governmental Research, "Effects of Cutting Day Care Subsidies to Low Income Families," working paper (Rochester, New York: Monroe County Human Services Data Sharing Project, 1983), p. 2.

13. Statewide Youth Advocacy, *Where Have All the Children Gone?* pp. 35–46.

promise both.''[14] Television and newspaper stores in 1983 raised questions about the county's cost overrun rationale—the Title XX cut (federal and state funds) turned out to be not $800,000 but $520,000 for fiscal 1982—and the deference of county legislators to DSS explanations. The county legislature established a special committee in late 1983 to investigate county services for children—a committee that proved to be sympathetic to restoration of the subsidies. A local survey of the effects of the day-care cuts, discussed in the next section, also influenced the decision to restore the subsidies. Partially in response to stronger lobbying efforts, the availability of new federal emergency jobs funds, and the first election for a county executive, the county manager (who was the Republican candidate for executive) proposed reinstating the income-eligible day-care program.

And so, Monroe County in September 1983—two years after their termination—reinstated the day-care subsidies to employed families with incomes at or below 58 percent of the state median. In January 1984, eligibility was expanded to families with incomes up to 65 percent of the median (hence, a family of four with income up to $15,395 became eligible). Total spending in 1984 for subsidies to about 500 income-eligible children was budgeted to increase by $1.3 million over the 1983 amount; $400,000 was to come from federal emergency jobs aid, and the remainder, equally from the state and county governments.

Effects of the Cuts on Families, 1981–83

As part of an effort to develop better data on the effects of federal government cutbacks on families and individuals, a detailed survey was conducted of the 293 families who lost income-eligible day-care subsidies in June 1981. The survey was conducted by telephone, using volunteer interviewers, in March and April 1983. The interviewers asked questions about how families had adjusted their child-care arrangements after losing county subsidies.

As may be seen from the following summary, the survey findings offer compelling reasons to be concerned about the provision of day-care subsidies to certain lower-income families.[15] Not only had these subsidies enhanced the quality of life of many hundreds of children and their parents, they had also provided an effective tool in reinforcing individual work efforts.

Characteristics of Survey Respondents. As previously mentioned, the 293 families cut included 642 children, 430 of whom were using some form

---

14. Carol Eisenberg, "Study Backs Day Care Aid," *Rochester Times Union*, January 17, 1984.
15. See generally, Center for Governmental Research, "Effects of Cutting Day Care."

of county-subsidized care at the time of termination (either family care or day-care center). These families had an average of two children. The average age of the 642 children at termination was approximately seven years; 48 percent were preschoolers. In addition, 74 percent of families had at least one child of school age who could be expected to need supplemental care. The average of the 430 children receiving subsidized care at time of termination was approximately five years; their ages ranged from less than twelve months to thirteen years.

Nearly all survey respondents were women. Most were between twenty-two and twenty-nine years old. Eighty-three percent were women who either were unmarried or were not living with their husbands at the time of program termination. Sixty-six percent of the families' last known addresses were concentrated in the central and northeastern sectors of the city of Rochester. Only 9 percent lived in the Rochester suburbs. Since the time of the income-eligible subsidy cut, 39 percent of the families had, at one time or another, received a partial United Way day-care subsidy.

Household composition of survey families remained substantially unchanged from 1981 to 1983; in both years, approximately two-thirds of the respondents had no adult living with them who could help with child care.

Child Care Arrangements. Families adjusted to the termination of federal day care in part by making more ad hoc child care arrangements. The average number of different arrangements used each week per child increased from 1.5 immediately before the subsidy cut to 1.7 at the time of the interview. The percentage of children in one child-care arrangement per week decreased from 59 percent before the subsidy cut to 48.4 percent at time of the interview, while the percentage in three or more arrangements per week increased from 8.9 percent to 17.9 percent. Structured methods of care (day-care centers and certified family-care providers) made up 46 percent of all methods used before the subsidy cut but only 14 percent of methods used at time of interview.

A recent study by the Community Service Society of New York noted that, "At worst, having too many caregivers can cause disruption in a young child's development, such as impaired social relationships, emotional disturbances, or learning difficulties. At least, it frequently causes feelings of anxiety and despondency."[16]

Reliance on Controversial Alternative Methods of Care. The instances of children being supervised by older siblings increased from 3 percent of all arrangements used before the subsidy cut to 8 percent of those used at time of interview. The average age of the sibling babysitters was sixteen

---

16. Community Service Society of New York, *Day Care and the Working Poor: The Struggle for Self-Sufficiency* (New York: Community Service Society of New York, 1982), p. 62.

before the subsidy cut, fifteen at the time of interview. The average age of children being cared for by siblings rose over this period from just over five years to just under eight years. The instances of children left alone part of the day increased from 7 percent of all arrangements used before the subsidy cut to 11 percent of those used at the time of interview. The average age of children twelve or under being left alone part of the day rose from eight years before the subsidy cut to nine years at time of interview. At both points in time, verified cases were found of five- and six-year-olds being left home alone.

Family Attitudes and Children's Adjustment. More than half of survey respondents reported feeling less satisfied with the arrangements they needed to use since their loss of the subsidy. In the opinion of survey respondents, however, almost 70 percent of the children whose adjustment levels were apparent had adjusted over time "very well" or "pretty well" to the new arrangements; 8 percent had adjusted "not very well" or "very badly."

More than 44 percent of the respondents admitted feeling less positive—with respect to their ability to achieve what they wanted for their families—at the time of the survey than when they had been receiving the subsidy. The explanation most frequently cited for this assessment was that the respondent felt "less secure financially" or had had to "downgrade goals for the future."

Work Effort. What effect did loss of day care have on work effort? Approximately 7 percent of survey respondents reported that the loss of the subsidy had caused them to quit work and remain out of the workplace in order to care for their children. Of those who stayed in the work force, 19 percent reduced their work hours as a result of needing to use new arrangements. In addition, 17.5 percent of those who stayed in the work force underwent some other type of job change in order to cope with child-care needs, such as change in place of employment or shift. More than 40 percent of survey respondents reported that they had found it more difficult after losing the subsidy to handle child-care and work responsibilities. More than 80 percent of survey respondents reported using one or more of the listed methods of juggling finances in order to cope with the loss of subsidy. Almost one-third of the respondents reported using all the methods asked about, including not buying adequate food, clothing, or medicines for the family and needing to borrow money from other people, from a bank, or from a lending company in order to handle child care.

Dependency. To what extent did the families losing day-care subsidies become more or less dependent on various forms of assistance? At some time during the twenty-month period covered by the survey, 51 percent of these families were dependent on AFDC, Medicaid, or food stamps. Their dependency can be summarized as follows: not dependent during the survey period, 49 percent; temporarily dependent during the period, 27 percent; dependent at time of survey, 24 percent.

Thus, about a quarter of the families remained dependent at the time of the survey—half of whom had not been dependent at the time of the day-care cut. Although at the time of the cut none of these families was receiving AFDC, approximately 12 percent were on AFDC at the time of the survey twenty months later.

Not surprisingly, the survey showed that this type of family is routinely off and on various forms of welfare. Indeed, this is part of the same population of working poor described earlier—and overlaps the population losing AFDC benefits described later. The families losing day-care subsidies were shown to have only marginally higher incomes (10 percent) than those losing AFDC.

Unfortunately, the survey of those losing day-care was not structured to address the issue of whether the loss increased dependency. However, it is reasonable to conclude, given the very low income of these families, that additional financial burdens—whether day-care, medical, or some other—frequently result in welfare dependency, at least during crisis periods, and in further deterioration in standard of living.

Miscellaneous Problems. Respondents reported that 34 percent of all children had exhibited negative behavioral effects at home or in day-care (attributable to changes in arrangements necessitated by the subsidy loss). Examples of such behaviors mentioned most often were the following: child is more withdrawn, exhibits more aggression or hostility, gets along less well with other children. Four percent of all children were affected positively in their behavior. Respondents reported that 33 percent of all children were currently in at least one child-care arrangement that caused them to worry. The worrisome arrangements most often cited were the following: child is left alone for at least part of day; child is left with a too-young or inexperienced caregiver; the new arrangement involves less supervision. All other children were reported to have no safety problems.

Fourteen percent of children who were in school at the time of subsidy cut exhibited negative changes in school performance (such as receiving poorer grades, losing interest in doing well, or doing homework less consistently)—changes that parents attributed to new care arrangements. Two percent of children were reported to have experienced positive school performance. Of all respondents, 51 percent needed to rely on last-minute emergency backup methods of care more frequently now than before the subsidy cut.

More than half of the respondents reported that their employment status had been affected negatively by the need to make new day-care arrangements. Examples of such negative effects cited were the following: have less regular at work now, am less punctual at work now, cannot work overtime anymore, cannot accept additional responsibility at work. Six percent of respondents reported positive work-related effects.

Of all respondents, 78 percent identified personal problems that they attributed directly to loss of the income-eligible subsidy and the subsequent need to make alternative arrangements. The effects cited most frequently were increased personal stress, common signs of illness such as headaches, and strained personal relationships.

Some of the single mothers losing day-care subsidies made these observations.[17]

"I am taking the risk of leaving them [the children] alone at home after school because I cannot afford a sitter."

"Yes, their [the children's] attitudes have worsened."

"As a grandmother with a very bad heart condition, I needed day-care and it helped eliminate some of the pressure of having two children [mother is deceased]."

"These changes have me on a slow but sure course to heavy indebtedness."

"For the first month I was unable to pay and [I] am now paying additionally each week to catch up arrears. Needless to say, it is most difficult. But I *have* to work."

"I had to accept food stamps and Medicaid. It's almost not worth working, and I have my children split up in different places because I could not afford $120 weekly [for day-care]."

"This cut created an added burden [on the budget]. I may have to apply for public assistance in the future, which I'm against."

"I had to apply for food stamps to cover the change in sitting expenses."

"I have to quit working and go on welfare. . . . (Federal government) should have . . . attacked people on welfare able to work, not people working trying to help themselves."

"I cut my hours and had my eleven-year-old watch my five-year-old."

"My child stays in different places everyday because I can't afford a sitter at all. I guess one day I'll have to quit my job."

Aid to Families with Dependent Children

The AFDC program is the major federal income maintenance program for low-income families. Within New York State this program is administered by county social service departments ("districts").

---

17. Monroe County Department of Social Services, *Cutting Day Care: The Impacts of Reducing Day Care for Low Income Clients* (Rochester, New York: February 1982), pp. 17–18.

AFDC provides financial assistance to low-income families with dependent children who do not have adequate means of financial support because of the absence, death, incapacity, or unemployment of a parent. In New York State, the federal financial participation of approximately 50 percent of program costs is matched by the state (25 percent) and counties (25 percent).

The 1981 omnibus budget act placed new restrictions on both AFDC eligibility and "income disregards" (income excluded for the purposes of determining eligibility). These restrictions increased the income deemed available to recipients, thus reducing grant amounts. Recipients were also entirely eliminated from the welfare roles or shifted to the state's Home Relief category (New York's general assistance program, which has no federal financial participation).

The change that had the greatest effect on AFDC eligibility was the limit placed on total income. This limit required that to be eligible (or remain eligible) a household could not have an income exceeding 150 percent (lowered from 180 percent) of a state's "standard of need." Such a standard is a federally required but state-set concept of income used in determining eligibility for AFDC. At the time of this AFDC rule change, New York State's standard was $5,000 for a family of three—42 percent below the poverty level. At that time, 150 percent of standard of need ($7,500) was 8.5 percent below the poverty level.

Institutional Reactions to the Changes in AFDC

New York has earned a reputation for income maintenance programs that are generous in terms of both eligibility and benefits. The state's constitution, as interpreted by the courts, gives state government an affirmative duty to aid the needy,[18] and political leaders have been liberal in meeting this obligation. Until the 1975 fiscal crisis in New York put a brake on the growth in benefit levels, New York's were among the highest in the nation. In an effort to balance the budgets of the state and New York City, the state standard of need and the maximum shelter allowance were frozen, despite the rapid rate of inflation. By 1981, benefits had fallen relative to those of several other states, but remained well above the national average.

AFDC and Home Relief are administered and partially financed by the state's fifty-eight social service districts. However, localities have no role in setting policy concerning eligibility and benefit levels and are permitted very little discretion in applying the rules and regulations set in Albany.

---

18. See *Tucker v. Toia* (1977) (400 N.Y.S. 2d 728) and cases cited therein.

New York's response to the omnibus budget act was consistent with its tradition of liberal support for the poor given the context of recent efforts to restrain the rate of growth of state spending. Despite his public statement that New York would not increase its own spending to compensate for the federal cuts, former Governor Hugh L. Carey proposed extending eligibility for Home Relief benefits to three groups removed from AFDC by the narrowing of categorical eligibility. His actions may well have been encouraged by New York's constitutional imperative to aid the needy, but could have also mandated automatic extensions in Home Relief to compensate for all of the AFDC cutbacks. To prevent the state from absorbing all these cuts, the governor recommended amending Home Relief to conform to the federal law, except for the groups categorically eligible. The legislature subsequently consented to inclusion in Home Relief of students between the ages of eighteen and twenty-one, women three- to six-months pregnant with their first child, and families in need because a parent is on strike. However, no other legislation was enacted to compensate for the omnibus budget act changes, and its many mandatory provisions were implemented with only minor delay.

As expected, these omnibus budget act changes in AFDC eligibility and benefit levels most affected households with a working member. In Rochester, their effects were felt most directly by working poor families in the city, specifically, low-income, unmarried working mothers with young children.

Effects of the Cuts on Families, 1981–83

In addition to the survey of families losing day-care benefits, described earlier, a survey was undertaken of all 292 families with nearly 600 children who were cut from the welfare rolls because of the application of the 150 percent limit on total income. Most of these families had incomes just above the official poverty level.

As may be seen from the following summary, the findings from this survey indicate that the federal cutback increased the need for local emergency services and demands on local agencies.[19] Lack of flexibility in the income-eligibility regulations decreased the ability of the community to help working mothers when they actually needed help; the apparent result was increased, longer-term dependency on a variety of public programs. The survey also shows, however, that welfare recipients have been conditioned to believe that they should be less dependent on government assistance. More than one-third

19. Center for Governmental Research, "Cutting Welfare Benefits to Working Mothers," working paper (Rochester, New York, Monroe County Human Services Data Sharing Project, December 1983).

of the respondents reported feeling that they were better off, even though their participation in AFDC had been terminated. By an almost three-to-one margin, terminated AFDC respondents felt that life would be better for them in the future rather than worse. In part, this attitude reflects the economic adjustments the families had made and were making, as well as an improving economy. In part, it reflects an apparent relief at being off the welfare rolls.

Characteristics of Families Losing AFDC Eligibility. The 292 low-income families terminated from AFDC included 889 persons—597 of whom were children and 292 were unmarried working mothers. Nearly 21 percent of these families had three children, 32 percent had two children, and 39 percent had one child present. On average, the children losing benefits were just under nine years of age. Nearly 12 percent were under three years old, 18 percent were between three and five years, and 19 percent were between six and eight. Only 6.2 percent were seventeen and older. The average age of the mothers was thirty-two years—nearly 29 percent were between twenty-five and twenty-nine years old, another 29 percent were between thirty and thirty-four years old, and 30 percent were age thirty-five or older. Fifty percent of these families were black, 41 percent white, and 6.5 percent Hispanic.

Income Characteristics and Size of Loss. Families losing benefits averaged gross annual incomes of $8,400 at termination in December 1981. This income level was 8 percent above the poverty level at that time and contrasts with the estimated 1982 median family income in Monroe County of $30,320. On average, the families involved had been receiving $128 monthly in supplementary income from AFDC, or $1,536 annually.

In almost two-thirds of the cases, losses to terminated families went beyond the AFDC check and included food stamps, Medicaid, or both. The average total loss of supplementary income and food stamps was nearly $156 per month. (No value was calculated for Medicaid loss.) In addition, 38 families lost day-care subsidies. By March 1983, the average gross income of the families had remained essentially stable with respect to the poverty line. Income was $9,073, or 110 percent of poverty.

Redependency Issue. Fourteen months after termination, 82 percent of the respondents said they were employed. Contrary to some predictions, large numbers of terminated recipients did not quit their jobs or lose them for the purpose of returning to welfare. Employment in this group remained strong despite the fact that the Monroe County unemployment rate was 6.2 percent at the time of termination in January 1982, and 8.0 percent at the beginning of the survey process in March 1983. Nearly all the employed respondents were working full time, thirty-five or more hours per week. Nine percent had taken on a second job. An additional 22 percent were working more hours.

On average, respondents had spent a little more than three years on the job (with a range of one week to thirteen years).

Of the 292 families that were terminated, approximately 130 (45 percent) had contact with the welfare system over the fourteen months following termination. Of these, seventy-three families had returned to the welfare rolls and forty-five—15.4 percent of the families—were still on AFDC or Home Relief on March 15, 1983. Another 24 families were receiving only Medicaid and food stamps. Sixty-four families had received emergency assistance; twenty-six families had applied for welfare but their applications had been denied. On average, families that had returned to welfare were receiving $384 monthly (AFDC plus food stamps) in 1983 as opposed to $156 in 1981, thus indicating an apparent increase in welfare dependency for the people returning to welfare.

Household heads younger than age twenty-five were more than twice as likely to have cases reopened as older household heads. The younger household head is obviously coping with additional stresses—the demands of young children as well as weak attachment to the work force. Other factors significantly associated with return to welfare were the presence of a child under age three, presence of two children under age six, unemployment of household head, and employment of less than one year on current or last job. Survey respondents usually reapplied for welfare because they had lost their job, suffered reduced wages, or lost some other income source. Other reasons for reapplying related to pregnancy or health. A number of families reapplied because they wanted help with obtaining child support, day care, or medical care.

The attitude of one Rochester mother, reported when results of the survey were released, is typical of many comments made by survey respondents:

Rosemary Jensen, a divorced mother of three, says that only pride, "something inside," has kept her from returning to welfare. If it were just a question of money, Jensen, age thirty-one, said she would have quit her secretarial job long ago and reapplied for welfare. "It's been tough," she said, since she lost her cash benefits and Medicaid two years ago.

Jensen counts herself lucky. She earns about $5 an hour, still receives food stamps, and lives in subsidized housing. But she said she could more easily feed and clothe her children, ages ten, twelve, and thirteen if she were not working at all and received full welfare payments.

If she were eligible for Medicaid again, she says, she could pay for much-needed orthodontic work for her ten-year-old son.

"There are times when you look around and say, 'What am I doing working?' I must be crazy," she said. "I could be home with my kids when they were sick. I could be home when they got home from school."

"My utility bills could be taken care of. I would have a Medicaid card to pay for my son's dental work. . . . It's only pride, something inside that keeps you going."[20]

Hunger and Medical Problems. More than half the respondents indicated that since they had lost their welfare assistance, there had been times when their families had not had enough to eat. For nearly two-thirds of these families, the problem of hunger had increased since they had lost welfare assistance. Fifty-four percent of all surveyed families reported having had to resort to additional methods for obtaining food beyond purchasing it with their own money. Alternative methods for obtaining food included gardening, going to local agencies, and relying on friends or family to supplement available food.

Nearly 40 percent indicated that their children had lacked appropriate clothes for school or for winter weather—with most reporting more of a problem after losing welfare assistance. Even though most of the families had some type of medical insurance, 42 percent said they had had family medical problems for which care was not received. Dental problems were the most common.

Most respondents said they did not seek treatment because they could not afford it. More than half of the respondents said they had been late in making rent or mortgage payments since losing welfare; most said they had been late more often than when receiving assistance. Seventy-two percent of the respondents said they had been late in paying utility bills since losing welfare; at least 15 percent had had their utilities cut off.

Loss of Other Benefits. Sixty-four percent said that they had been significantly affected by the loss of other benefits since the loss of AFDC; food stamps and Medicaid losses were most often mentioned. Indeed, some families felt that the loss of these benefits affected them more than losing AFDC. Slightly more than 45 percent of the respondents lost at least two or three benefits, 10 percent lost four benefits, 8 percent lost five or more benefits (including AFDC). Other lost benefits included child-care subsidies, housing, school lunch, job training, and special nutrition programs as well as Medicaid and food stamps.

General Feelings about Life Situation. Of the respondents, 41 percent said they had felt worse off since losing public assistance, whereas 34 percent felt better off and 21 percent saw no difference. When considering the future, 48 percent of the respondents believed that a year from now things would be

---

20. Carol Eisenberg, "Cuts in Welfare a Hardship, but Pride Keeps Many Going," *Rochester Times-Union*, December 15, 1983.

better for them. However, 17 percent said they thought that life next year would worsen and 18 percent saw no change likely.

Employment Problems. Of the 18 percent of the respondents who lost their jobs after termination, approximately 58 percent had been laid off, and 21 percent had experienced changes in life situations (pregnancy, child-care needs, moving, and so on). Health problems were cited by 12.5 percent of the respondents, and 8.3 percent had been fired. Nearly two-thirds of those out of work were actively looking for employment—using a variety of job search methods. Not surprisingly, unemployed respondents found the lack of available jobs to be the major problem. Lack of specific skills, experience, and transportation also were identified as obstacles to employment in a number of cases.

Day-Care Arrangements. Approximately one-half of the respondent families paid for child-care services. Of these, one-third were receiving a United Way subsidy and had their children in a day-care center. Of the nearly 68 percent of the families not receiving a United Way subsidy, only about 6 percent had applied. This apparent lack of interest in a United Way subsidy may be explained by the type of child-care arrangements chosen by these needy families. Nearly 84 percent had used relatives or private sitters—while the remainder used day-care centers or other arrangements for which a United Way subsidy was not currently available.

Seeking Help. Since losing welfare, only 25 percent of the respondents said that they had gone to agencies other than the Department of Social Services for help. Although the survey structure may have caused an underestimate of those seeking help, this rather low proportion, given the stress on the families in question, suggests that more effort may be required to publicize the availability of certain basic services. This may be particularly true in the case of nutrition services and day care. The findings are consistent with a picture in which poor households do as much as they can to solve their problems on their own, through informal arrangements, rather than going to public agencies for formal dependence.

In general, respondents reported that they had received the help that they had requested. However, more respondents sought help than actually received it from a given service agency. (This finding did not apply to churches.)

Summary and Policy Implications

In Rochester, as in cities across the nation, the effects of the federal budget retrenchment were most directly and deeply felt by the working poor. Cuts in funding for social services, coupled with changes in eligibility for AFDC, were translated into losses of supplements to earned income and of subsidies for day care. Local interviews with affected families—headed by single mothers and concentrated in city neighborhoods—indicate that life has become more difficult. Less satisfactory day-care arrangements, greater difficulty in meeting necessary housing expenses, and more medical, nutritional, and behavioral problems are common among the former beneficiaries of AFDC and Title XX day-care subsidies.

For such families, actions taken by Monroe County (and state government) were central, because the city government has no direct responsibility for administering federally assisted human services. In the case of social services, Monroe County exercised the discretion allowed it by the state, first to eliminate and later to restore nonmandated day-care subsidies. The former action represented a failure of advocacy by day-care proponents, the latter, a success. In contrast, changes in Monroe County services as a result of AFDC cutbacks mandated by the state were regarded as the county's only recourse, particularly in the absence of local advocacy to the contrary.

What are the local policy implications of actions taken in Washington to reduce domestic spending? As we have noted throughout, the locus of action is in those local institutions that have functional responsibilities—not necessarily city hall. Day-care advocates who effectively directed their lobbying at the county legislature were successful in mitigating the local effects of cuts in federal aid for social services. Their success, however, has generated broader issues.

One issue involves the need to determine more comprehensively the importance of day-care relative to other publicly funded services for children, including foster care and protective services. Another issue involves the role of nonprofit agencies in meeting not only day-care needs but also nutrition, housing, and medical needs. The United Way of Rochester, which was helping Monroe County subsidize day care long before the advent of the Reagan administration, has made more than $500,000 in emergency assistance funds available to families through its constituent agencies since 1982. Continuing demand for such aid has generated a joint examination by United Way and county officials of the proper role of governmental and nonprofit agencies in meeting emergency needs.

A final issue involves welfare and work policies. The Rochester surveys found that most of the families dropped from AFDC assistance remained independent of the welfare system—thus vindicating the president's view that Americans prefer work to welfare. A surprisingly high percentage of households terminated from AFDC thought that their life situation had improved; a large number said they expected life to be better a year in the future. These feelings, too, are consistent with the president's view that poor households prefer not to be dependent on government. The decreased availability of ancillary job training, food, and medical services, however, is believed to jeopardize the ability of families headed by women to maintain long-term welfare independence.

In sum, the assumption that cities can manage themselves "more wisely than the federal government can" has been tested in Rochester with results that suggest that the local community dialogue is far from over.

THE PUBLIC SECTOR IN STAMFORD, CONNECTICUT: RESPONSES TO A CHANGING FEDERAL ROLE

W. Wayne Shannon, C. Donald Feree, Jr.,
Everett Carll Ladd, and Carol W. Lewis

For the past five years, the Reagan administration has advanced policies intended to reverse the trend toward an ever larger federal role in domestic affairs. During this time, American politics has been dominated both by a sharp sense of change and by debate over the wisdom of such radical change. The president's "big picture" has been exceptionally coherent. Major cutbacks in the federal domestic budget were to be accompanied by restoration of power and responsibility to state and local governments. Beyond that, many public sector functions were to be "degovernmentalized" altogether, and returned to the disappearing realm of voluntary group activity so strikingly described by Alexis de Tocqueville and others in nineteenth-century America.[1]

Quickly, and somewhat surprisingly, major portions of the president's program were adopted by Congress or otherwise set in motion. Yet, beneath the surface, much remained unclear. How big were the changes? How durable would they prove to be? How would the state and local governments, nonprofit organizations and various sectors of the American public adjust to them? To help answer these and a dozen other questions, we began an inquiry into the impact of changing federal policies on one city—Stamford, Connecticut—in the spring of 1982.[2]

---

1. The president specifically cited de Tocqueville's commentary on Americans' penchant for nongovernment solutions to public problems in his televised address of September 24, 1981. He spoke of the need to recapture the "spirit of volunteerism" and announced his administration's national program toward that end. For an analysis of the president's world view, see W. Wayne Shannon, "Mr. Reagan Goes to Washington: Teaching Exceptional America," *Public Opinion* (December-January 1982), p. 13.

2. The Stamford Community Project was conducted by the Institute for Social Inquiry of the University of Connecticut. Funding for the study was provided by the Stamford Foundation.

Concepts, Study Design, and Methodology

Conceptualizing the Problem: Defining the Public Sector

As we began to tackle our task, we saw that although the Reagan administration's policy initiatives were central to our concern, we were really interested in something more fundamental: the national reexamination of government's role in the provision of public services that predates the present Reagan administration, actively involves partisan groups and interests outside it, and will continue long after President Reagan has left office. The proper question for our study was not how the city of Stamford was responding to the Reagan administration's budget cuts and program shifts, but how Stamford was grappling with a vast, long-term national reexamination of government and the shape of the public sector.

Polities, like social scientists, often pay a considerable price for conceptual confusions. One such confusion that has bedeviled American political discourse stems from a failure to distinguish between *government* and the *public sector*. In the United States, these terms are often used interchangeably. Thus, we talk about the public sector versus the private sector, intending to differentiate between what government does in meeting common purposes and what various private groups and interests do. There is a critical distinction to be made between public and private, but it is not the one just cited. Americans do have private activities and interests that are seen to be separate from those of their fellow citizens. At the same time, they also have public interests—needs and objectives that involve them with their fellow citizens in common or collective ways. This public sector, properly understood, has never been the exclusive province of government. From the beginning of American history, private groups have had a large role in American public life. The churches clearly serve public interests, as do charities, philanthropies, and nonprofit organizations outside government. So, too, do labor unions and business corporations, ethnic associations, fraternal organizations, and a vast array of other groups and institutions that are "private" only in the sense that they are not governmental.

Liberals and conservatives in the contemporary United States are not divided over whether the country should have a large and vigorous public sector. Rather, their disagreements involve how public ends are to be achieved—and specifically, what roles government at its various levels should play, in relation to groups and impulses outside government. The debate now under way in the United States is not really about how the responsibilities of public and private organizations differ, but rather about how the public sector is to be constituted and public values best achieved.

By the 1980 elections, the American public strongly supported government services and favored an extensive, even expanding, role by government in broad sectors of national life. At the same time, this public voiced sweeping criticisms of the federal government—it was too big, too powerful, too intrusive, and too wasteful. In a national survey that the Roper Center designed and directed for the American Enterprise Institute in late 1981, this pattern of public responses was dramatically documented.[3] When asked whether the country is now spending too much in the pursuit of national attainments like more education, better health, and a cleaner environment, Americans said no. If there is a problem, it is that not enough is being spent. At the same time, though, respondents criticized the government's record in promoting the various public objectives and endorsed the idea that institutions other than the central government should play prominent roles in advancing national objectives. They supported a strengthening of the states' role in the federal system, experienced the view that corporations and voluntary organizations should do more in meeting national problems, supported private philanthropy, and reported an inclination to turn to private organizations for help in meeting public problems.

For all this, Americans still saw no substitute for a major role for government in advancing the various public objectives to which government was committed. Most people doubted that other sources could make up for significant reductions in government spending. And although they wanted more private initiative, they recognized that their own recent record through voluntary associations was not impressive. The Roper survey showed that the public recognized the extent to which it had fallen away from the Tocquevillian ideal of an active citizenry vigorously pursuing public sector ends outside government.

This, then, is the larger context in which the Stamford study needed to be set. As our study began, it did not seem at all clear where the larger national debate would eventually lead. But it did seem evident that there was a new willingness to give serious consideration to different approaches. Americans in 1982 were at once committed to a major role for government in meeting public ends, and critical of the enterprise of government. This mix of attitudes was fueling a clear readiness to listen to new ideas. But what promising new answers and directions would be offered? We hoped to monitor closely what was occurring in the public sector of one American city and

---

3. The Institute for Social Inquiry/Roper Survey for American Enterprise Institute, "Private Initiatives and Public Values," which is available through the Roper Center, University of Connecticut, Storrs, Connecticut.

how various actors—from community leaders to the public at large—were assessing these responses.

Stamford as Setting and Case

At the outset, we settled on a community study approach. Other investigators had already begun nationwide studies of the effects of current federal policies on state and local governments and nonprofit organizations.[4] However superior those studies might be in breadth and representativeness, they probably would not permit long hours of interviews with elected officials, administrators, directors of nonprofit organizations, and civic activists. Nor would they provide an opportunity to gauge public opinion. Perhaps most important, they would not provide the "anthropological feel" that can be acquired only by deep immersion in one community.

Of course, Stamford is not a prototypical northeastern central city. That category suggests, with some accuracy, a community of declining population as more and more of its former residents and their children locate in the suburbs; a place with a dramatically expanding black and Hispanic population; a community of relative economic privation compared, for example, with the entire state of which it is a part; and a place of older declining industries. Stamford is none of these. On the contrary, in many ways, Stamford resembles a "Sun Belt city." Its modern population experience has been one of growth rather than decline. In 1940, when Hartford had 166,000 people and New Haven 160,000, Stamford was a small city with 48,000 residents. After 1940 the population of Connecticut's larger cities declined, whereas Stamford's grew steadily until the 1970s, when a modest decline occurred. Stamford's population today exceeds 100,000.

In recent years, the minority population of Stamford has grown significantly. For example, the city was just 5 percent black in 1950, but by 1980 the proportion had tripled, to 15 percent. The Hispanic population also substantially increased, reaching nearly 6 percent of the total in 1980. Still, with nearly four-fifths of its residents from non-Hispanic European origins, Stamford has a far smaller minority population than most northeastern central cities.

---

4. See, for example, the other chapters in this volume. Linked case studies of state and city adjustments have been conducted by Richard P. Nathan and his associates at Princeton University: Richard P. Nathan and Fred C. Doolittle, eds., *The Consequences of the Cuts* (Princeton: Princeton Urban Regional Research Center, 1983). Linked case studies of adjustments by local nonprofit institutions, have been conducted by Lester P. Salamon and his associates at The Urban Institute.

Stamford residents continue to be better off than the Connecticut populace as a whole. In 1980, when the state's median family income was $23,151, Stamford's was $26,692. Similarly, Stamford is an anomaly among northeastern cities in its educational base: its population contains a higher proportion of college graduates than does the state as a whole—even though Connecticut itself ranks high in educational attainment. Property values are far higher in Stamford than in any other Connecticut city and they far surpass the state averages. Unemployment is lower than in other central cities.

The extraordinary development of Stamford as a "home office" city for large American corporations is well known. Whereas most northeastern cities have had to struggle to maintain their job and industrial base, Stamford has had to struggle to manage exceptionally rapid growth. The city's position on the New York border, at a time when many corporations were looking for new corporate homes outside New York, has obviously produced an atypical economic environment.

None of this is to suggest, however, that Stamford is cut off from the American urban experience. The pseudo Sun Belt City does not lack urban problems; it simply has a mix of problems different from older cities. In some important ways, the problems are not different at all. The influx of minority residents characterized overall by lower incomes and greater service needs, for example, presents Stamford with the same public sector demands that central cities across America face. In other ways, too, Stamford has much in common with her sister cities around the country. Public services are delivered in the context of the distinctive American federal system, with its complex mix of federal, state, and municipal funding and direction of government programs. Stamford operates in the American system of fragmented and dispersed government authority—with a multiplicity of participants and jurisdictions: private, nonprofit agencies with and without government monies; local government agencies with local tax funds; local government with direct federal support; and local government with federal funds "passed through" the state.

Methodology

Early on, we proposed a four-phase approach to the study: (1) an investigation of city agencies by mailed questionnaire followed up by personal interviews, (2) the same approach to a broad group of the community's nonprofit organizations providing services of various sorts (in both cases budget data as well as perspectives and attitudes would be sought), (3) a large random sample survey of Stamford residents, and (4) personal interviews with a wide range of community activists.

Detailed budget information for city agencies for four fiscal years (1980 through 1983) was gathered through a mailed questionnaire and long interviews with agency personnel. Both the questionnaire and the personal interviews were used to gather information on perceived impacts of changing federal policies and the agencies' responses, if any, to federal program and funding changes. In addition, interviews were conducted with the mayor and several members of the Board of Representatives (the elected city council) and the Board of Finance.

Stamford, like other American communities, has a large and complex nonprofit sector. In deciding which organizations to study, we relied heavily on informed opinion in the Stamford community. We compiled an initial list of some 230 nonprofit institutions, but, it quickly became apparent that we could not study all these agencies to the extent that we deemed necessary. We therefore divided agencies into categories of apparent importance to the Stamford community, and, on the basis of advice from our local advisory committee, chose approximately one hundred agencies for inclusion in our study. Fifty-five agencies returned mailed questionnaires and consented to follow-up interviews. The nonprofit institutions, like the city agencies, were asked to provide four years of budget data, their perceptions of the impacts of federal policy and funding changes, and information on whatever strategies the agencies were developing, if any, to cope with these changes. Because inflation was so often identified in our interviews in the nonprofit sector, we chose to present constant-dollar budget figures along with current-dollar figures in our analysis.[5] We took every step to verify the budget data of the nonprofit institutions—reading annual reports and other documents when they were available, probing for missing information and seeming inconsistencies or mistakenly classified revenue sources in our personal interviews.

The questionnaire used in the mass population survey was of our own design. The field work was carried out in Stamford by Yankelovich, Skelly, and White. All told, 1,007 telephone interviews were conducted, using random digit dialing. Theoretically, results from the mass population survey have about a 3 percent margin of error.

Our community leadership respondents are not a sample of some known universe of "community decision makers" or "power wielders." We made no attempt to define such a group. Rather, we made a concerted effort to compile lists of persons who could speak for several elements of the Stamford community—blacks, Hispanics, the religious congregations, small business,

---

5. Constant dollars were computed by deflating current dollars by the implicit price deflator for household and nonprofit institutions, as calculated by the Bureau of Economic Analysis, U.S. Department of Commerce.

large business, the government and political sector, human service advocates, labor unions, and people in communications. In all, we conducted interviews with 119 persons representing these sectors from June through late August 1982, and followed up with a small subsample in spring 1984.

Most interviews were based on a slightly modified version of our public survey, which included more opportunity for open-ended discussion of the questions and an opportunity to discuss perceptions on the major elements of the Reagan administration's programs.

The Effects of Federal Policy Changes on Stamford's City Government

Financing City Services

Stamford, as we have already pointed out, is a relatively wealthy central city with greater-than-average resources to meet public service demands. Nevertheless, it is not immune to the revenue-expenditure squeeze now troubling so many American cities. Local taxes have had to support a larger share of city expenditures—rising from 73 percent to 80 percent of the total between fiscal 1980 and fiscal 1983. This trend clearly predated the impact of the Reagan administration's cutbacks. Although nonresidential uses contribute a large share of the city's real property taxes—some 39 percent in 1981— vigorous protests had developed by the summer of 1982 and were being articulated by owners of residential property, who felt a "double whammy" of recent state-mandated reassessments and real-dollar tax hikes.[6]

Stamford does not rely heavily on federal funding to support delivery of city services, and this customary low reliance is further declining. Nonlocal revenues from all sources declined from 18 percent to 12 percent of the total budget between fiscal 1980 and fiscal 1983. The absolute dollar amount dropped by $3.8 million in this period, a decline of roughly 19 percent. Federal funding constituted a significant part of this decline. There was a significant decrease in community development block grant funds and a sharp loss of Comprehensive Employment and Training Act (CETA) revenues. Yet, even at the height of federal aid reductions, virtually all of our respondents saw federal policy changes as less important in Stamford's budget crunch than local problems. They clearly perceived the recent state-mandated reassessment and local tax protests as more problematic than changes in inter-

---

6. The estimate of nonresidential tax contribution is from "The Impact of Residential and Non-Residential Land Uses on Taxes and Municipal Services in Stamford, Connecticut" (Stamford: Stamford Economic Assistance Corporation, 1981).

governmental policies and finance. The mayor, the budget director, the controller, the city grants officer, and other officials echoed one another in asserting that "grants here have always been seen as a supplement." Given the relatively small contribution of intergovernmental funds to the city's budget, even a relatively sharp decline would have a limited budgetary impact in Stamford.

The Impact of Federal Funding Changes

Still, when asked whether "there is any particular area where you think there has been or will be a real loss of services here in Stamford," the twenty-seven city officials and administrators we interviewed responded with a long and varied list. Their statement of expected losses covered virtually every area of service delivery. Specific queries on the actual impact of federal funding changes, however, yielded only marginal evidence of real effects. Throughout our Stamford city data, we found a general climate of anxiety that could not be accounted for by actual agency experience.

Answers to our questions on specific federal funding impacts are summarized in table 27. When we asked the municipal departments and agencies whether their client services had been reduced in response to federal funding changes, only three departments—health, welfare, and CETA—reported substantial service and staff reductions. The Community Development Office indicated that such reductions were of "minor" importance, while the Environmental Protection Commission reported this component as yet "unresolved." For all the other agencies, staff reductions related to federal funding were simply not a factor. Interviews with several administrators in the school system indicated that there had been no loss of educational staff directly attributable to federal funding reductions; rather, layoffs were traced to local budget decisions and were, at most, only indirectly linked to the decline in nonlocal revenues received by the city.

A recent study of Stamford's personnel structure goes far to explain why the impact of federal budget and policy changes on personnel has been so limited.[7] The researchers found not one position among the 1,848 jobs in education that was directly grant-funded. In the city's administration, only thirty-three positions were directly grant-funded through community development block grants. Fire and police departments reported that their staff reductions were wholly city-funded. Major staff reductions in CETA and loss of city employees provided through the CETA program (for example, in the parks department and the Commission on Aging) came as a result of earlier

7. "Report to the Law Department of the City of Stamford: Civil Service and Personnel Structure" (New Haven: Gallant, Mednick, and Gallant, August 1982).

changes in the public employee component. Staff reductions in the housing authority were reported as related only to internal management improvements. According to Stamford's director of personnel, no city employee had been laid off as a direct result of loss of federal funds.

But the impending reductions in federal funding did have some effect on personnel. Of twelve reporting departments, five found "some" deterioration of staff morale attributable to federal budget and policy changes. Still,

TABLE 27

STAMFORD CITY AGENCIES' ASSESSMENT OF THE EFFECTS OF
FEDERAL FUNDING CHANGES

*What, if any, strategies has your agency already undertaken to deal
with federal funding changes? (summer 1982)*[a]

	Importance Attributed			
	Major	*Minor*	*None*	*Not Applicable*[b]
Develop contingency plans	3	2	2	6
Reduce staff	3	1	2	7
Reduce services	3	2	2	7
Restrict number of persons served	2	2	3	7
Increase user fees and charges	1	1	4	7
Increase use of third-party payments	1	1	4	7
Increase number of volunteers	1	2	3	7
Increase private contracting	0	1	5	7
Increase fund-raising efforts directed toward:				
State government sources	3	2	2	6
City government sources	3	4	1	5
Corporate sources	1	1	5	6
Charities, donations by federations and foundations	1	1	6	5
Special events or activities	0	0	7	6
Individual donations	0	0	7	6
Change service priorities	3	0	4	6

Have federal revenue changes already *affected any of the following?*

	Yes	*No*	*Not Applicable*
Number of recipients served	2	6	5
Service levels	3	5	5
Agency staffing	3	5	5
Capital maintenance	1	6	6

TABLE 27 (*Continued*)

*For each of the following areas, please indicate
the effect of federal budget and policy changes.*

	None	Little	Some	Substantial	Not Applicable[b]
Deterioration of agency staff morale	6	1	5	0	0
Deterioration of staff or client relationships	6	1	4	0	1
Decrease in those seeking services	9	2	1	0	0
Deterioration in staff productivity	8	2	1	1	0
Fear of job loss among agency personnel	3	1	4	4	0
Increase in interagency rivalry	8	1	2	1	0
Increase in staff productivity	6	1	2	3	0
Increase in resource planning and utilization	3	1	5	3	0
Agency innovations in services and administration	3	1	4	4	0

SOURCE: Mailed questionnaire and interviews with agency staff, December 1982.

a.   Federal funding refers to grants directly received, funds passed through the state, value of CETA (Comprehensive Employment and Training Act) workers, and so on.

b.   Many departments answered "not applicable" because they do not receive any federal funds that they know of, are wholly city funded, and perceive the department as largely insulated from federal budget and policy changes. "Not applicable" is, therefore, a substantive response.

perceived pressure can contribute to greater productivity, and six departments reported at least some gains in this area.

The city is making efforts to improve revenue collections and to broaden its revenue structure, but the impetus seems to come more from the local taxpayer protests than from a decline in intergovernmental revenues. Among these efforts is the appointment of the Mayor's Alternative Revenue Task Force. The interest rate on delinquent taxes has been increased. And the city is working to collect fees that have gone uncollected for years, such as those for street openings and the police department's burglar alarm system. User fees appear to many administrators to be an attractive option. However, the Board of Representatives has encountered strong resistance to fee increases, and getting them through the board is a major problem. At present, user charges are generally low, even nominal, and they rarely reflect the actual cost of service.

Because budgeting means making choices among departments and programs, the process always involves competition and conflict. The fragmented governmental structure in Stamford underscores this aspect of budgeting; and the retrenchment atmosphere, mill rate increases and reassessment, and perceived budget cuts (some of them absolute reductions, others expressed as smaller-than-usual requested increases) heightened tensions in the fiscal 1983 budget process. Nonetheless, eight of the twelve department heads who responded to our agency survey did not believe that federal budget and policy changes had had any effect on interagency rivalry.

Stamford's corps of professional administrators attests to the problems of governmental performance. Asked if they considered the phrase "efficient and well-run" an apt description of local government in Stamford, twenty-one of the twenty-seven administrators whom we surveyed responded no. This same assessment is suggested by responses to two additional questions. More than half (fourteen) indicated a preference for the delivery of human services through private, nonprofit agencies, whereas only six opted for delivery by government. More than half (sixteen) thought tax money devoted to human services was not well used.

City efforts at securing grants are now more centralized and the Grants Office offers more assistance to city departments. The Grants Office reported more coordination and extensive federal and state contacts. Most department heads concurred, but some reported that they were still reluctant to make a big push for outside grants because of the time and paperwork burden associated with such grants.

From the perspective of the Grants Office, the new federal block grant provisions offer a welcome promise: "Cities would rather have a rational policy at the top than a lot of little grants. It is easier to run a few chosen and fully funded grants." But it is by no means clear the promise will be realized. The Grants Office reported that the state requires more paperwork on the social services block grant than was formerly required by the federal government—and for less money.

Only five of fourteen departments in Stamford reported that contingency plans were being developed to respond to federal funding shifts, and of these five only three assigned this effort "major" importance. Several persons interviewed asserted that no city office or department was actually preparing for impending cuts; this view was corroborated by the director of personnel and several elected officials. This lack of planning seemed to result from the fact that most administrators had not yet felt direct effects. Stamford administrators had a general sense that something important was occurring, but they had not yet been confronted with the practical need to adapt.

In the summer of 1982, there was no city policy on substituting local revenues for losses in intergovernmental funding. Fifteen private, nonprofit organizations and agencies approached the city officials for financial assistance; most of the requests were for small amounts. According to the budget director, his office passed most of these requests along to the Board of Representatives. Directors of nonprofit agencies in the "poverty sector" had thus far made few requests for city support and appeared to be looking more to private sector funding. Both the budget director and the chairman of the board of finance suggested that there was a need for clear guidelines determining the degree and duration of support for claimants outside the ranks of the established city agencies. Overall, a striking lack of strategic thinking and planning in Stamford government was evident, despite the general sense that important funding and policy change was occurring.

The Effects of Federal Policy Changes on Stamford's Nonprofit Sector

The Budget Picture

If Stamford's governmental budgetary structure is characterized by fragmented authority, its counterpart in the nonprofit service sector is even more decentralized. The city, at least, has a central budget document that is more or less understood by civic and political activists in the community. No such central source of information exists for the nonprofit agencies. When we began our research, even the most seasoned local observers could offer little information on the amazing variety of nonprofits pursuing public purposes in the Stamford area. Aside from what the local United Way knew about the agencies it supported, there was no reliable information about the revenue sources of the nonprofits, their current budgetary condition, or the impact on them, if any, of changing federal policies. Clearly, a similar situation exists in cities all over the country, however centralized or decentralized their governments. As Lester Salamon of The Urban Institute recently put it, "The nonprofit sector is the invisible part of the nation's (social services) delivery system. Consequently, it becomes desperately important we know more about the number of organizations and where they get their revenues."[8]

Our careful analysis of the individual budgets of fifty-five of Stamford's nonprofit organizations makes a serious contribution to the task that Salamon

---

8. Quoted in *New York Times*, March 14, 1983.

describes—a detailed case study of one community's nonprofit agencies.[9] Contrary to general expectations and somewhat to our own surprise, we found a very complex pattern of budgetary changes over the period of our analysis. Some agencies experienced substantial increases in funding, while others faced reductions. Our data do not support the conclusion that Stamford's nonprofit agencies as a whole have entered an era of severe revenue decline. In fact, in simple budgetary terms, the financial condition of most agencies improved from fiscal years 1980 to 1982—1982 being the last year for which reliable budget data were available.

Data on Stamford's nonprofit agencies are summarized in table 28. The table shows that only six agencies had fewer current dollars in fiscal 1982 than in fiscal 1980. Of forty-three agencies that had at least some increase in their budgets, thirty had budgetary gains greater than the rate of inflation. Thirteen saw their budgets grow in current dollars—but not enough to offset inflation.

Twenty-eight agencies received no federal aid in any of the years under review. Of the twenty-seven that had federal support, twelve had more in fiscal 1982 than in fiscal 1980; three, exactly the same; and twelve, less support from Washington. In all, these nonprofit institutions received $4,774,286 in federal funds in fiscal 1980; in fiscal 1982 this support had dropped by $307,000 to $4,468,150—a decline of 6.5 percent. This overall decline of federal funding did *not* produce uniform reductions in the agencies' operating budgets. A clear majority of agencies were better off overall in constant dollars in fiscal 1982 than in fiscal 1980. The majority were better off in current dollars.

Less than a third of the agencies in our study (seventeen) reported reliance on federal funds for more than 10 percent of their operating revenue. Only nine of the agencies received more than half of their operating funds from federal sources.

The following shows the constant-dollar classifications (operating funds only) of better-off and worse-off agencies based on a comparison of fiscal years 1980 and 1982 by their degree of reliance on federal funding.

	No federal funds (n = 28)			Reliance of 1–10 percent (n = 10)		More than 10 percent (n = 17)	
	Worse	Better	No Budget	Worse	Better	Worse	Better
Financial position in constant dollars, 1982 versus 1980	7	16	5	4	6	8	9

---

9. Five agencies reported that they had no budget, maintaining that they relied entirely on volunteer activity.

TABLE 28

OPERATING REVENUES OF STAMFORD'S NONPROFIT INSTITUTIONS, 1980–82

Nonprofit Institution	1980	1981	1982	Percent Change in Current Income	Percent Change in Deflated Income
1. Southfield Community Organization	123,854	243,832	330,474	166.8	130.9
2. Person-to-Person	30,000	50,000	70,000	133.3	101.9
3. Center of the Jewish Community	557,605	713,583	1,237,532	121.9	92.0
4. Hartman Theatre	893,077	913,996	1,802,866	101.9	74.7
5. Meridian House	173,000	266,000	320,000	85.0	60.1
6. New Neighborhoods	71,300	109,475	130,200	82.6	58.0
7. Alcoholism Council	132,084	184,084	230,374	74.0	51.0
8. Hospice	0	47,700	82,600	73.2[a]	64.4[a]
9. Literacy Volunteers	0	8,324	12,652	52.0[a]	44.3[a]
10. Rape Crisis Center	20,060	19,715	28,892	44.0	24.6
11. Gateway Communities	106,800	116,900	153,600	43.8	24.4
12. Head Start	238,290	259,845	338,185	41.9	22.8
13. Girl Scouts	475,000	712,000	643,000	35.4	17.1
14. Voluntary Action Center	51,326	54,623	68,679	33.8	15.8
15. Boys' Club	113,127	133,054	150,000	32.6	14.7
16. Visiting Nurse Association	934,000	1,175,000	1,235,000	32.2	14.4
17. Council of Churches & Synagogues	476,000	588,000	622,000	30.7	13.1
18. Easter Seal Rehabilitation	1,285,754	1,462,098	1,646,151	28.0	10.8
19. Jewish Family Service	0	55,000	69,000	25.5[a]	19.1[a]
20. Yerwood Center	269,000	314,000	329,000	22.3	5.8
21. Young Men's Christian Association (YMCA)	1,066,000	1,188,648	1,300,980	22.0	5.6

22.	Aid for the Retarded	759,061	845,333	925,048	21.9	5.5
23.	Rogers School Community Center Organization (ROSCCO)	0	45,670	55,510	21.5[a]	15.4[a]
24.	Family & Children's Service	577,000	622,000	700,000	21.3	5.0
25.	Stamford Museum & Nature Center	506,800	585,000	611,000	20.6	4.3
26.	Child Guidance Clinic	366,377	421,354	440,666	20.3	4.1
27.	Meals on Wheels	102,066	112,254	122,808	20.3	4.1
28.	Southeastern Conn. Commerce and Industry Assoc. (SACIA)	460,000	475,000	543,000	18.0	2.1
29.	Info-line	158,000	165,000	185,000	17.1	1.3
30.	Stamford Girl's Club	78,000	84,000	91,000	16.7	1.0
31.	Young Women's Christian Association (YWCA)	345,430	484,880	396,460	14.8	−0.7
32.	Catholic Families	203,531	220,048	231,661	13.8	−1.5
33.	Red Cross	200,401	219,001	227,617	13.6	−1.7
34.	Elderly Nutrition Program	359,928	396,324	404,858	12.5	−2.7
35.	Boy Scouts	626,000	653,000	702,000	12.1	−3.0
36.	Hot Line	40,434	62,869	45,000	11.3	−3.0
37.	Liberation Program, Inc.	1,156,256	1,142,581	1,270,781	9.9	−4.9
38.	Urban League	318,019	282,205	346,544	9.0	−5.7
39.	United Way	2,209,385	2,233,681	2,341,959	6.0	−8.3
40.	Child Care Center of Stamford	835,642	891,959	880,604	5.4	−8.8
41.	Salvation Army	0	92,000	94,000	2.2[a]	−3.0[a]
42.	Stamford State Opera	83,500	84,400	84,500	1.2	−12.4
43.	Horizons Summer Program	82,206	103,274	83,500	1.5	−12.1
44.	Senior Employment Service	10,000	10,000	10,000	0.0	−13.5
45.	Stamford Economic Assistance Corporation (SEAC)	276,000	191,000	268,000	−2.9	−16.0

TABLE 28 (Continued)

Nonprofit Institution	1980	1981	1982	Percent Change in Current Income	Percent Change in Deflated Income
46. Committee on Training and Employment, antipoverty program (CT&E)	2,279,926	2,150,839	1,958,606	−14.1	−25.7
47. Let's Play House	0	139,000	116,000	−16.5[a]	−20.8[a]
48. Legal Services	180,000	202,478	148,848	−17.3	−28.4
49. Family-Life Workshops	850	700	600	−29.0	−40.0
50. Counseling Center	147,681	156,340	90,000	−39.0	−47.0

SOURCE: Mailed questionnaire and interviews with agency staff, December 1982.

a. Percentage change calculated for 1981–82 only.

Effects on Activities of Nonprofit Institutions

Our inquiry into the effects of federal funding changes on the activities and behavior of Stamford's nonprofits yields few simple generalizations. An overall picture can be gleaned from the data in table 29, which shows the strategies, if any, agencies reported they were using to cope with federal funding reductions. Most agencies, whatever their degree of federal dependency or financial condition, were not cutting staff, reducing services, or restricting the number of clients they served. Increased fundraising effort was by far the strategy cited most often, but even that is being pursued by fewer than half of the agencies with reported budgets. Our interviews confirmed this picture. For most agencies, business was being conducted "as usual." Only the few hardest-hit cases were making substantial changes. They had

TABLE 29

STRATEGIES CITED BY STAMFORD'S NONPROFIT INSTITUTIONS TO COPE WITH
FEDERAL FUNDING REDUCTIONS, BY PERCENTAGE RELIANCE ON FEDERAL FUNDS
AND FINANCIAL POSITION, 1982[a]

Strategy (Number of Institutions Citing Response)	No Federal Funds (n = 28)		1–10 Percent Reliance (n = 10)		More Than 10 Percent Reliance (n = 17)	
	Worse (n = 7)	Better (n = 16)	Worse (n = 4)	Better (n = 6)	Worse (n = 8)	Better (n = 9)
Reduce staff	1	1	...	1	2	...
Reduce services	1	1	...	1	1	1
Restrict number of persons served	...	1	...	1	1	1
Increase user fees and charges	...	2	...	2	2	2
Increase third-party payments	1	...	...	2	1	...
Increase number of volunteers	1	4	...	1	1	1
Increase private contracting	...	...	...	1	1	...
Increase fund-raising efforts	6	3	1	4	5	4
Increase board membership	1	...	...	2	1	1
Change service priorities	1	...	...	1	1	2

SOURCE: Interviews with staff, December 1982.

a. Financial position in fiscal 1982 is compared in constant dollars with the financial position in fiscal 1980 for the operating budget only.

clearly seen their vulnerability in a changing federal policy climate and were seeking ways to cope with it.

Nonprofit Institutions of Stamford: Concluding Observations

Our findings on Stamford's nonprofit sector should be interpreted cautiously in terms of their implications for the future and their applications beyond the boundaries of Stamford. Investigators have only begun to analyze the effects of federal policy and program changes on the nonprofit institutions, and the national picture is not clear. Still, our findings in Stamford raise questions about the accuracy of some preliminary observations that have been made around the country, such as this summary by Richard Nathan and his associates in *The New York Times*: "Nonprofit organizations (particularly community-based organizations) appear to have been among the major victims of the 1981 cuts. They lost CETA workers, and experienced funding cuts under the new block-grant programs; some of them have gone out of business."[10] Another national study, released by The Urban Institute, also reported a dramatic impact by the Reagan administration's programs on the nonprofit sector. One author of this study concluded at a news conference that "the federal government seems to be withdrawing from, curtailing, or dismantling its partnership arrangements with the nonprofit sector."[11] The adjustments we have charted in Stamford point to a more modest and complex set of likely outcomes.

No nonprofit agency in Stamford has died thus far as a result of federal changes. The one agency that did cease operations in 1982 did so as a result of its loss of a contract with a state department—a loss wholly unrelated to federal policies. Several other nonprofit agencies were widely believed to be "unhealthy" by local informants, but their travails had little or nothing to do with current federal policies.

The entire nonprofit sector of Stamford has been living since 1982 in a funding environment that lacks the buoyancy of the 1960s and early 1970s, but some organizations have continued to do quite well. Whether or not they have been living in what one of our respondents called a "fool's paradise," most of Stamford's nonprofit agencies have not experienced fiscal disorders. If federal funds were declining for many, agency heads apparently remained optimistic that they could make up the difference elsewhere, if we are to judge by their fiscal 1983 budget figures. Only three of the Stamford nonprofit institutions submitting 1983 budget figures expected their overall revenue to

---

10. *New York Times*, August 13, 1982.
11. *New York Times*, September 2, 1982.

be lower in 1983 than in 1982.[12] Two of these are Stamford Legal Services and the Committee on Training and Employment, which are clearly in a class by themselves—suffering severe losses in federal funding as a result of federal policy changes and unable so far to find other sources of funding.

The Stamford community will have to assess the effect of the current financial condition of Legal Services Agency and the Committee on Training and Employment on the clients of these programs. There is no escaping the conclusion that the recipients of these agencies' services are the least fortunate citizens of the community—disproportionately black, Hispanic, and poor. It is also apparent that many of these programs have provided advocacy—of a kind unpopular with many people—for the poor and minorities. Administrators at Legal Services Agency and the Committee on Training and Employment believe they have "done their job too well," thus antagonizing people in government at all levels as well as many people in the private sector. If this is the case, these agencies may have a serious problem now and in the future.

Public Opinion

Part of the story of current experience in the delivery of public services in Stamford is told by the budgets of the city and nonprofit agencies. But another part can be told only by the citizens who are directly or indirectly affected by service-delivery programs. To find out what Stamford residents have to say on these matters, a telephone survey was conducted during June and July 1982 with 1,007 randomly chosen Stamford residents.

Services Losses: Expectations and Experiences

Our survey shows that Stamford residents, like Americans nationally, support an expansive public sector. They believe that all manner of services should be provided. Whatever area we asked about, more than two-thirds of the sample said in effect, "Yes, such a service should be provided." When we asked if federal cutbacks would lead to service losses, a substantial majority of the sample answered that they would. When asked to identify a specific area in which they thought there had been or would be a "real loss of services," six in ten mentioned at least one area. One in five named two and almost one in ten suggested three or more. The most commonly named areas were Social Security, college loans, education, and social services for the

---

12. Forty of the agencies in the study provided fiscal 1983 budget data.

poor. There was remarkable agreement across the various demographic groups about expected service losses. A summary of responses for the entire sample is presented in table 30.

However, when respondents were asked about their experience to date—
"Have you or anyone in your family lost or been denied any service because of federal cutbacks?"—and were encouraged to mention as many as three specific service losses, only one in eight respondents (13 percent) reported that someone in the family had lost a benefit. Nonwhite respondents claimed losses at a slightly higher rate (17 percent). The losses cited most frequently—by 5 percent and 3 percent of our sample, respectively—were in student loans and Social Security. Reported losses in these areas were distributed quite evenly across income groups in the sample. Roughly 2 percent mentioned job losses. Somewhat to our surprise, programs targeted specifically to the poor, such as welfare, food stamps, CETA, and legal aid, were cited as areas of loss by very small portions of our sample. Table 31 shows the number and percentage of the sample reporting actual service losses. Here again, as with our city and nonprofit data, we were struck by an apparent gap between expectation and reality. The Stamford public's expectation of the effects of

TABLE 30

SURVEY RESPONSE TO PERCEIVED LOSS OF SERVICES

Is there any particular area where you think there has been or will be a real loss of services? . . . (if so) Where?

Services Reported to Have Suffered a Loss (in Descending Order)	Number of Responses[a]	Percentage of Total
Social Security and the elderly	236	23.4
Education	197	19.6
Welfare	149	14.8
Jobs	59	5.9
Health	40	4.0
Housing	27	2.7
Mass transit	27	2.7
Student loans	25	2.5
Food stamps	18	1.8
Aid for the handicapped	15	1.5
Day care	24	2.4
Youth programs	31	3.1
All others	104	10.3
No loss mentioned	401	39.8

SOURCE: Survey by the Institute for Social Inquiry, University of Connecticut, with fieldwork done by Yankelovich, Skelly, and White, June–July 1982.

a. A total of 606 respondents cited at least one area; the numbers add to more than 606 because of multiple responses. The sample was 1,007 respondents.

TABLE 31

SURVEY RESPONSE TO ACTUAL LOSS OF SERVICES

Have you or anyone in your family lost or been denied any service because of federal cutbacks? . . . (if so) And what was that?		
Services Reported to Have Suffered a Loss (in Descending Order)	*Number of Responses*	*Percentage of Total*
Student loans	49	4.9
Social Security and programs for the elderly	30	3.0
Jobs	20	2.0
Education	8	0.8
Welfare	4	0.4
Health	3	0.3
Housing	3	0.3
Food stamps	3	0.3
Youth programs	3	0.3
Veterans programs	2	0.2
Day care	1	0.1
Aid for the handicapped	1	0.1
Legal aid	1	0.1
All others	13	1.3
No loss mentioned	880	87.4

SOURCE: Same as table 28. At least one area was given by 127 respondents; the numbers do not add because of multiple responses. The sample was 1,007 respondents.

changing federal policies seems to have run far ahead of the actual experience of such effects. To be sure, real losses were being reported, but they seemed much more marginal than expected. So struck were we by this "gap" in our Stamford survey that we repeated the exact questions—on expected and actual service losses—in December 1982 in a Connecticut Poll survey of 500 adults statewide. The results were almost identical.[13]

In another part of the survey we asked only respondents who had said their families currently used such specific services as child care, job training, clinics and health care, housing, and aid for the handicapped and elderly whether they had noticed any change in the service over the past year. Table 32 shows the percentage reporting a decrease in service in each of these areas. Because these percentages are constrained by the number of persons actually using each service, the percentage of users in each case is reported in parentheses. Blacks and other nonwhites in Stamford showed a greater tendency to report recent decreases in service levels. In the areas of housing (for blacks)

---

13. The results of this statewide *Connecticut Poll* survey are reported in G. Donald Ferree, Jr.; W. Wayne Shannon; and Everett Carll Ladd, "Stamford, Connecticut Weathers Reaganomics," *Public Opinion* (February-March 1983), p. 19.

TABLE 32

SURVEY RESPONSE TO PERCEIVED DECREASE IN SERVICES, BY RACE AND INCOME[a]
(Percentage)

Have you noticed any actual change in the level of the service over the past year or so?

Has the level of service provided increased, decreased, or what? Type of service—Child care? Job training? Clinics and other Health Services? Housing? Handicapped? Elderly?

Service Reported to Have Suffered a Decrease	Whites	Blacks	Others (Mainly Hispanic)
Child care	0 (1)	2 (11)	7 (13)
Job training	0 (1)	1 (4)	0 (7)
Health	1 (4)	3 (8)	0 (13)
Housing	1 (2)	7 (10)	4 (9)
Handicapped	0 (1)	1 (15)	2 (7)
Elderly	1 (3)	4 (9)	0 (4)
	Whites, Income Less Than $20,000	Whites, Income $20,000– $50,000	Whites, Income $50,000 and Over
Child Care	0 (1)	0 (2)	1 (1)
Job training	0 (1)	0 (1)	1 (1)
Health	1 (6)	1 (3)	1 (4)
Housing	1 (3)	1 (3)	0 (1)
Handicapped	0 (2)	0 (1)	1 (2)
Elderly	0 (4)	1 (3)	2 (4)

SOURCE: Same as table 28.

a. The percentage of the sample using services is shown in parentheses.

and child care (for other nonwhites) more than half of the minority users of services reported a decline in the level of services. Among whites, although service use in Stamford was generally quite low, those above $50,000 in family income were somewhat more likely to cite decreasing service levels than were those with family incomes below $20,000.

Attitudes toward the Public Sector

The Stamford public manifested the same disquiet about the performance of the government sector and the same willingness to entrust more of the "public agenda" to nongovernment agencies that has been evident elsewhere around the country. By a two-to-one margin, respondents favored provision of human services by private, nonprofit institutions as opposed to government agencies. By a four-to-one margin, they thought that tax money committed to human services was not used well at present. (In this latter perception, they were a bit more skeptical than Americans generally, who reported this view by a seven-to-two margin.)[14] Conversely, a five-to-three plurality maintained that if tax money is given "in large amounts" to nonprofits, it would be well used. (On a similar question, Americans nationally split evenly.) Findings such as these reflect both distrust of the performance of government and an often overlooked willingness to entrust important work to nongovernment agencies.

Only 21 percent of Stamford residents endorsed the statement that the phrase "efficient and well run" accurately describes the federal government. Local government did not fare especially well either: somewhat more than one in four labeled it as efficient and well run. State government came out the best: overall, four in ten found *it* "efficient and well run," almost exactly the proportion saying it was not. The private, for-profit sector was seen as more efficient than government at every level. Respondents were three times as likely to label "big business" efficient and well run as to say that it was not. Attitudes toward small business were similar. Finally, those who had an opinion about "local nonprofit" agencies in Stamford were more than four times as likely to describe them as efficient as to say they were not.

The general perception on efficiency was echoed in dollar-and-cent terms. When asked how much of each dollar spent by the government to help the poor actually goes to people needing assistance, the median amount cited was only 25 percent (as it was on the national survey), and fewer than one in ten thought more money got through than was consumed in overhead. By comparison, when respondents were asked what percentage of the monies contributed to the United Way goes directly to the people who are supposed to be helped, the median was 50 percent (again virtually the same as the national figure), and some 30 percent thought that more than half of the money contributed actually goes to the intended recipients. Overall, the typical Stamford resident (as the typical American) set much higher store in the efficiency of the private, nonprofit sector than in that of the government.

If the perceived choice were simply between government programs and strictly voluntary individual action, this would present a most unpleasant dilemma. Three out of four Stamford residents said they thought people are *less* willing to help their neighbors now than they were twenty-five years ago.

---

14. The references to national data in this section are to the Institute for Social Inquiry/Roper survey cited in note 3 to this chapter.

Half said people today are less willing than they once were to assist in youth activities such as coaching. Fewer than one in six viewed people today as *more* willing. Similarly, they expressed the belief that people are now less prepared to help their elderly parents. In all such views, Stamford residents seemed much like Americans generally. The identical questions about voluntary action were asked of a national sample in the fall of 1981 and Stamford was, at best, only marginally more optimistic about individual readiness to help than was the country as a whole.

Thus, there was widespread skepticism about the capacity for effective voluntarism. Moreover, although three in ten Stamford residents claimed to do volunteer work regularly (roughly comparable to the one in four in the national survey), the amount of time contributed was not large. The median number of hours spent by those who *had* worked during the previous week was only three; taking the amount reported for the "typical week" only raised the median to five hours. Nor was the level of cash contributions impressive. Among those who reported any specific amount, the median total annual contribution was $200. Thus, although Stamford residents seemed to be comparatively more active in volunteer service than their fellow citizens around the country, their level of voluntarism remained quite low.

In sum, Stamford residents reported that they want a vital public sector; they remain attentive to their common needs. A bigger role by nongovernment organizations and voluntary action would be welcome in meeting public needs. But they showed great skepticism about the practical capacity of these "typically American" approaches. In particular, the populace doubted its own readiness to play a larger role through voluntary associations and activity. This is the predicament Americans find themselves in throughout the country. As yet, they do not see a way out.

The Perceptions of Community Leaders

Our interviews with a wide range of community leaders found a climate of opinion much like that of the local public at large. They greatly favored the general idea of a larger role for state and local governments. Dissatisfaction with federal government performance cut across all sections of leadership. Disturbingly, though, for those who would seek a solution by giving more responsibility to the state and Stamford city governments, large majorities also viewed *them* as poorly run and inefficient. The perspectives we found at the leadership level reflected a lack of confidence in the capacity of government at all levels. Thus, the Stamford leadership group opted for private service delivery, wherever possible, by a hefty margin. At the same time, with the exception of corporate spokesmen, the Stamford leaders we interviewed manifested very little support for the Reagan administration's policy initiatives. Only in the case of "New Federalism" was there anything like an even split between those generally for and those against the president's program. In every other area, those outside the big business community expressed much more disapproval than approval. When asked about the Reagan administration's policies, many respondents asserted that the domestic program cuts lacked equity.

With respect to "New Federalism," private initiatives, and voluntarism, the typical response was, "Well, this may be good in theory or in some abstract sense, *but.* . . ." Serious doubts were expressed about the capacity of state and local officials, about the likelihood of significantly greater corporate involvement, and about the prospects for heavier use of volunteers in the delivery of social services. Stamford's leaders were overwhelmingly negative in their assessment of each of these key elements of the Reagan program. So the Stamford community leaders seemed to share the predicament of Americans generally: despite their overwhelming criticism of government performance, they voiced grave doubts that practical alternatives would be found through shifting responsibilities from one level of government to another, or through private sector initiatives and voluntarism.

Despite the general approval that business gives to the policy directions of the Reagan administration, the spokesman for only one of the dozen corporations interviewed said that the president's call for private sector initiatives was a major factor in his firm's response to community involvement and giving. Although most said they were willing to try to accept some responsibility for meeting needs attendant to federal budget cuts, most also expressed skepticism that their efforts would have little effect; none thought it realistic to suppose that a "gap" posed by federal funding reductions could be filled through corporate philanthropy. Several corporate officers raised doubts about corporations making community decisions, on grounds either of propriety— "That's not our business"—or strategic advisability—fear of an eventual backlash. The Stamford corporate community will continue to respond to reasonable requests for community involvement and philanthropy. That involvement, however, will not be much different from present practice.

If the course of domestic public policy development that America has followed for the past half-century has produced serious problems of cooperation, efficiency, and accountability among levels of government, it is nevertheless apparent that many federal policies have achieved goals that both the public and leadership support. This theme was raised again and again in our Stamford leadership interviews. Black leaders, especially, emphasized the view that federal policies show greater sensitivity to the needs of minorities and the poor than do those of state and local government. They argued that these policies contain equity safeguards that are relatively lacking in many state and local programs. Many community leaders agreed that state and local policies are more likely to be subject to personal influences. And for all the criticism of waste in welfare programs, many expressed the belief that the needs of the poor have been much more efficiently addressed by federal than by state and local government.

Conclusions

Stamford, as we completed our initial study in October 1982, was experiencing only minor effects from the federal policy and budget changes under way. Although there had been a visible decline of federal support to the city government, reductions in service were modest and no regular employees had been laid off. Only a small minority of the nonprofit service-delivery agencies had been much affected by federal funding reductions, and local citizens reported relatively small losses of public sector services.

Despite the general feeling that funding cutbacks would ultimately cause substantial disruption in the delivery of human services, neither the city government nor the nonprofit sector was doing much to plan for such a contingency. Aside from a diffuse effort on the part of city and nonprofit agencies to seek additional revenues, the atmosphere was very much "business as usual." Only the most directly affected nonprofits seemed seriously concerned with locating new sources of funding.

In Stamford, as in the nation, criticism of government performance was everywhere. In abstract terms, there was considerable receptivity to a downward shift of functions among levels of government and a larger role for the nongovernment public sector. Nonetheless, doubts about these alternatives were pronounced. There was no certainty that any provider other than the federal government could supply the desired programs and needed resources. The public and community leaders in Stamford expressed only shaky support for the Reagan administration's domestic policy initiatives. People in Stamford, like their counterparts elsewhere in the nation, were left to struggle with this predicament.

What sense is to be made of this general picture? Stamford, we think, is among a class of cities—more affluent than the norm, blessed with a growing economy, relatively low unemployment, and a more than usually capable and enlightened corporate sector—that will be identified as more studies of the effects of federal policy changes are carried out. Stamford and other similar cities may be much more able, despite resistance to local tax hikes, to solve problems locally than less fortunate urban areas. When communities like Stamford do feel the effects of marginal losses of federal support, they probably will not feel enough of a "jolt" to engage much strategic thinking about the future. Studies of the federal cutbacks have found a good deal of denial and efforts to continue business as usual even in places where conditions of austerity have been relatively more pronounced.[15] Experience, too, points to the fact that the future impact of external funding changes typically is exaggerated by people who are apprehensive about the impacts of such changes. Thus it is not surprising that government and nonprofit organizations should persist in established routines as long as no great pinch has been felt. Our reading of the situation in Stamford in 1982 is that, lacking much "jolt," a generalized expectation of future funding and service losses was insufficient to spur contingency planning.

If, as the literature suggests, institutional centralization is an important variable in the capability of systems to adapt to change, Stamford is not well positioned to respond to concerns with the efficient use of resources under conditions of relative austerity.[16] The municipal government is exceptionally fragmented. Although central administrative staff see clearly the problems that declining intergovernmental funds would pose for delivery of city services, there is no effective way to bring this perspective to bear on policy-making. Were the city to face greater problems, its extremely fractured policymaking machinery would surely impede a search for options and solutions. Thirteen commissions over the years have failed to alter the city's thirty-seven-year-old charter to strengthen the city's central government. The last attempt was rejected by voters in a special election on April 10, 1984.

Stamford's nongovernmental public sector is even more fragmented. Aside from the efforts of the United Way of Stamford, there is virtually no forum in which to address concerns with the performance of the sector as a whole. Each agency is on its own. There is no reason to suppose that Stamford is different in this respect from any other urban area. Here, the prospects for "degovernmentalizing" public sector functions run head on into sizable unsolved problems that deserve much more thought and analysis than they have received. Stamford residents, like the American public generally, are favorably disposed toward nonprofit agencies. It remains to be seen, however, how well they would perform the more difficult tasks required by extensive "degovernmentalization." Who would ensure *their* accountability? If profit-mak-

---

15. See, for example, Harold Wolman, "Local Government Strategies to Cope with Fiscal Pressure," in Charles H. Levine and Irene S. Rubin, eds., *Fiscal Stress and Public Policy*, in vol. 9, *Sage Yearbook in Politics and Public Policy*, (Beverly Hills, California: Sage Publications, 1980), pp. 231–48.

16. See, for example, Charles H. Levine; Irene S. Rubin; and George Wolohojian, "Resource Scarcity and the Reform Model: The Management of Scarcity in Cincinnati and Oakland," *Public Administration Review* (November-December 1981), pp. 619–28.

ing corporations are to play a larger role in funding them and in deciding which agencies and programs receive scarce support, do they possess the legitimacy and wisdom to play such a role?

If Americans are to get what they seemingly want—a large and vigorous public sector *and* less powerful and intrusive government—such questions will have to be answered. When we took leave of Stamford, we were struck by how little we really knew about the nonprofits' performance after spending months in the community. Were there too many? Too few? What real difference did the existence of this or that program make? What would be the real impacts, in human terms, of the changes that we had observed in the antipoverty and legal services programs?

Postscript

As Stamford moved into fiscal 1985, the political atmosphere was marked by an apathy apparent in quiet public hearings and low voter turnout for the referendum on charter revision. Observers noted that there simply were no major divisive issues on the agenda. One city official lamented that "it's as if the citizens forgot general government was there at all."

As we renewed contact with selected city administrators and community leaders, we found that public issues had become subordinated to economic growth.

The economy and physical development of Stamford continues to "rage ahead," according to the view of a professional city planner long involved in economic development in the community. A glance from any downtown office window supports that view and attests to both the political fragmentation and booming economy. Since the early 1980s a consensus has emerged that physical development needs to be more carefully pursued and more integrative in design. Much of this "maturation" and planning orientation is attributed to developing concern and initiative, on the part of Stamford's corporations, not to city hall.

City hall has yet to notice any real federal cuts; the federal contribution to the city budget is said to remain fairly constant. Overall, the "New Federalism" is not seen to have had major impact on city services, the city budget, or city government, which is described as "still doing and not doing the kinds of things it always did." As of fiscal 1985, no general government layoffs had been traced directly to federal policy or funding changes.

Several administrators both in city offices and in nonprofit agencies identified the most substantial specific change as the creation of the private industry council (PIC) now responsible for federally funded job-training efforts. The provision of these services is under a new regional consortium, with the result that Stamford has less money and is subject to out-of-town administration. Furthermore, the PIC system is said to be providing inadequate job training for the young, unskilled population.

As for social services within city government, an administrator summed up the general view this way: "One simply can't notice any great difference." That may very well be because the city had insulated itself by not receiving much support in this area. With respect to the change to block grants, the authority that was to have shifted to the state is not quite so threatening to this community as was anticipated two years ago. The state is relying upon a "negotiated investment strategy" to allocate social services block grant monies. This requires that recipient agencies—state, local, and private, non-profit providers—sit down together and work out the distribution of funds and take responsibility for the accommodations and outcomes. A Stamford administrator noted that intergovernment grants now offer less money, have a narrower program focus than the concept of block grants originally promised, and entail substantially more paperwork.

Among the nonprofit agencies, the general outline of our earlier findings continues to hold. No agency has closed and most are seen to be in much the same condition. Those especially hard hit (CT&E and Legal Services) are still financially troubled. The picture today falls far short of the disaster among the nonprofit agencies that some expected in the early years of the Reagan administration.

RETRENCHMENT IN PHOENIX, ARIZONA

John Stuart Hall

Recent changes in the American political and economic condition have enlivened the discussion of Federalism and intergovernmental affairs. Until fairly recently, the topic seemed to generate largely truisms about the diversity of American governments, the range of services provided by similar jurisdictions, and the general complexity and diversity of funding public goods and services. Essays about modern American federalism tended to be descriptive and to reach bland conclusions such as "policy is no longer made mostly in a single governmental unit but is hammered out through a negotiating, bargaining relationship among multiple governmental units."[1]

Between 1978 and 1983, however, several major developments took place, including

- California's Proposition 13, which sharply curtailed use of the property tax and was endorsed by the voters;

I am extremely grateful to the following persons who have helped with this research and written other publications in which together we have attempted to sort out the implications of our findings: David Altheide, Joe Cayer, Paul Dommel, Pamela Eck, Richard Eribes, Nicholas Henry, Alvin Mushkatel, and Jim Musselwhite. I am particularly indebted to national research projects of The Brookings Institution, Princeton University, and The Urban Institute for continued support of my studies in Phoenix. My work could not have been completed without the financial and intellectual support provided by the directors of the following national studies: Richard P. Nathan of the Princeton University Study of Effects of the Reagan Domestic Program Changes on State and Local Government; Lester Salamon of the Urban Institute, Study of Impacts of Retrenchment on the Nonprofit Sector; Robert Cook of the Westat Study of Employment and Training under the Jobs Training Partnership Act; Paul Dommel of The Brookings Institution and Cleveland State Longitudinal Studies of Community Development Block Grant; and Herbert Jacob, Robert Lineberry, and Anne Heinz of the Northwestern University, Government Responses to Crime Project.

1. Catherine Lovell, "Where Are We in Intergovernmental Relations and Some of the Implications?" *Southern Review of Public Administration*, vol. 3 (June 1979), p. 14.

- Limitations on state and local spending or revenue collections were adopted in several other states;

- Ronald Reagan was elected to the presidency;

- Major domestic budget cuts were enacted by Congress in the 1981 Omnibus Budget Reconciliation Act; and

- The national recession of 1980–83 took place.

These events have been hailed as indicators of major change in American politics. Some people have said that a revolution in American federalism was taking place. At a minimum the trend toward growth in government budgets and scope at all levels was said to be reversed:

> The long period of growth in the scope and cost of the domestic programs of the federal government that began with the New Deal came to an end in Reagan's first year in office. Instead of growth and innovation the focus of federal grant programs is now on retrenchment. Now spending initiatives are out of fashion.[2]

Retrenchment, in turn, promised to raise questions about the functioning federalism that had been avoided during the era of rising resources. Now that federal assistance appeared to be shrinking, the question over who would deliver the services and raise revenues in "an overlapping authority" model became far more important both to theorists and to policymakers.

Policy researchers began to turn their attention to two fundamental sets of questions: first, how important were these events? Was retrenchment real? Was a "counterrevolution" in progress, or was the importance of these events being exaggerated? Second, once the magnitude of retrenchment was clarified, what were its effects? What would be the combined and separate effects of national, political, and economic retrenchment on local governments, on human service programs, on recipients of those services, on public officials, on national, state, and local politics, and on the intergovernmental system?

This chapter is a case study of these changes and their effects in the metropolitan area of Phoenix, Arizona. The story is about the way Phoenix area governments, public officials, the public, and program constituents dealt with these events. In telling that story, I show how some of the forces of political and economic expansion and contraction affected local politics and need. In sum, one can see how changes in programs, funds, and economic forces were perceived and responded to in Phoenix. In so doing, I hope to show how federalism really worked in response to the threat of retrenchment.

---

2. Richard P. Nathan, Fred C. Doolittle, and Associates, *The Consequences of Cuts: The Effects of the Reagan Domestic Program on State and Local Governments* (Princeton, New Jersey: Princeton University Press, 1983), p. 2.

The Setting

The Symbolic Importance of Fiscal Constraint

The national move toward fiscal constraint was applauded in Phoenix; the idea fit the prevailing conservative political and fiscal norms. Phoenix city government, Maricopa County government, and the more than twenty independent public school districts in the metropolitan area had operated under a formal limitation on expenditures since 1921—more than a half-century before enactment of Proposition 13. Phoenix voters elected Barry Goldwater to the city council in 1948 and since 1952 have, generally by large margins, favored Republican candidates for president, including Gerald Ford in 1976 and Ronald Reagan in 1980.

Thus political conservatism and the corollary themes of fiscal constraint and limited government have been popular in Phoenix for some time. These values often transcend partisanship; state and local politicians, including Democrats like the state's governor, Bruce Babbitt, have consistently supported the philosophy of fiscal restraint and the tools responsive to that philosophy, including new tax and expenditure limitations on state and local jurisdictions. For example, in November 1974 voters defeated an attempt to enact a more stringent spending limitation in Arizona, yet only one of the nine candidates for governor in the primary election that September had opposed the spending limitation proposal.[3] It was, then, both in keeping with long-standing prevailing state politics and the national spirit of the times that the state legislature proposed, and Arizona and Phoenix voters enthusiastically approved, even tougher expenditure limitations in a special election of June 3, 1980. The politics of retrenchment may have been new and somewhat debatable nationally, but in Phoenix, fiscal restraint was old and popular.

The Reality of Public Sector Growth

Murray Edelman pointed out long ago that political rhetoric need not be connected with policy reality to remain popular.[4] For the past thirty years the reality in Phoenix has been mostly one of public sector growth rather than

---

3. Brent W. Brown, John S. Hall, Sandra Day O'Connor, and Thomas Goodwin, *Arizona's Expenditure and Tax Limitation Proposal: An Analysis of Proposition 106* (Tempe, Arizona: Center for Public Affairs, Arizona State University, 1974). It is interesting to note that one of the primary backers of the spending limitation was Sandra Day O'Connor, then Arizona Senate majority leader; her position was supported by then Governor Reagan, who had proposed a similar limitation for California.

4. Murray Edelman, *The Symbolic Uses of Politics* (Urbana: University of Illinois Press, 1964).

FIGURE 1

ARIZONA EXPENDITURES, FISCAL YEARS 1975–83

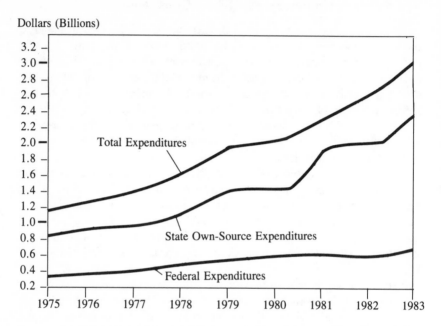

Dollars (Billions)

SOURCE: John Stuart Hall, Richard A. Eribes, and Pamela P. Eck, "The Reagan Domestic
Program from the Arizona Perspective," paper presented at the Research Conference
on the Reagan Domestic Program, Princeton University, June 7–8, 1984.

constraint. Figure 1 charts the steady increases in own-source, federal, and
total expenditures for Arizona and figure 2, federal expenditures for Phoenix,
for the 1975–83 period. Although these figures are based on data from that
period, the growth trends could be traced to the early 1950s. Similar steady
growth trends could also be plotted for Arizona state government and other
jurisdictions in the Phoenix metropolitan area. Yet, fiscal 1982 obviously was
an exception to the steady growth trend. The meaning of that exception is
examined later in this chapter. For now the question of interest is, how did
this general expansion of the public sector occur, given the seemingly par-
amount political importance of the philosophy of fiscal restraint? Why is it
that political rhetoric seems so detached from policy reality? The answer to
this question has at least two parts.

FIGURE 2

FEDERAL EXPENDITURES IN PHOENIX, FISCAL YEARS 1975–83

Dollars (Millions)

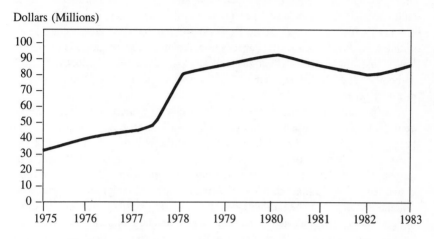

SOURCE: Same as figure 1.

As the Economy Boomed, the Tax System Responded

The principal reason for the steady growth of the city of Phoenix budget is that its revenue structure has promoted automatic and painless response to the area's robust economic growth. Compared with the situations in other municipalities, the revenue structure in Phoenix is diverse, elastic, balanced, and sound. For general fund revenues, the city relies mainly on a combination of sales taxes, state income taxes returned on a population-based formula, and user fees. These three sources, which respond quickly to economic change, have accounted for approximately three-quarters of the city's general fund income over the past two decades.

Conversely, the city's property tax revenue, which has been directly limited by the politics of fiscal restraint, has been a mere sliver of the city's revenue pie. In recent decades it has never exceeded 15 percent of general fund revenues or 10 percent of total expenditures. In the year following the taxpayers' revolt and Proposition 13 (1979–80), Phoenix property tax revenues accounted for 11 percent of the city's general fund budget. By 1983–84 that percentage had declined to 8.4 percent of the general fund budget. In 1979–80 the primary property tax rate was $1.81 per $100 assessed valuation; by 1984–85 that tax rate had fallen to $1.65 per $100 assessed valuation. These decreases were important political responses to perceived public demand for tax limitations, but they have had only minor effects on the overall revenue structure, which relies much more heavily on sales and income taxes and, increasingly, user fees. In response to the electorate's demand for property tax limitation in 1980, city officials supported the idea but simultaneously initiated gradual increases in user fees to make up for any property tax revenue losses that might occur. This strategy worked. User fees increased from 6 percent in 1980 to 18 percent in 1984, more than offsetting the decline in property taxes.

Thus the modern fiscal history of the city of Phoenix has been one of quick revenue response to inflation and economic growth. The growth has been phenomenal. From 1950 through 1980 the population of Phoenix expanded from a little more than 100,000 to almost 800,000 making it the ninth-largest city in the United States. During the same three decades, the city expanded from 17 square miles to 329 square miles. Unemployment generally remained well below the national average, hovering around 5 percent for most of the 1970s. The national recession finally reached Phoenix in 1982; unemployment claimed to 9 percent for the last quarter of 1982 and the first two months of 1983. That average declined rapidly with the national recovery, resulting in a 1984 unemployment rate slightly below 5 percent. Thus three decades of population increase, jobs, and general economic growth have made Phoenix one of the most prosperous cities of the developing Sun Belt. The local tax system allows for a portion of the economic boom to be rolled over automatically into the public sector. This arrangement is convenient for conservative politicians who face reelection from a conservative electorate. In Phoenix, service expansion has not been inhibited by messy debates about significant local tax rate increases or new taxes.

Limitations and Loopholes

The prevailing pattern of economic growth and the responsive tax system have led to continued public sector growth that could not be curtailed by property tax limitations. But what of an overall cap on local government spending? There have been formal limits on municipal government expenditures in Arizona since 1921. They have not significantly limited local government spending, however, because they were not designed to do so. The 1921 statute that remained in effect until 1978 limited municipalities and counties to a 10 percent increase over the budget of the previous year, but local governments did not really have to live with these limits. Important categories such as intergovernmental revenues were exempted from budget limitations. Clever accounting and knowledge of loopholes meant that "half or more of typical local budgets may be free of the

10 percent limitation.''[5] A new expenditure limitation now in effect—approved by voters in a special election June 3, 1980—plugged some of the loopholes of the old 10 percent limitation. Under this cap, the budget increases of Arizona cities and towns are limited to a ratio based on annual population and inflation adjustments to their fiscal 1980 budget base. However, the new limitation exempts thirteen types of revenues, including federal grants-in-aid of any type. Furthermore, these legal constraints provide four options by which voters can override expenditure limitations in their own jurisdictions. On November 30, 1981, Phoenix voters did just that by voting to allow the city to exceed state expenditure limits through fiscal years 1985 and 1986 for spending in connection with large capital budget programs of aviation, water, wastewater, and the Civic Plaza.

Similarly, there is no limit on the city's ability to pass special bond issues to finance important capital and public works projects. In 1979 Phoenix voters approved a $253 million bond issue for a variety of public works improvements. In June 1984, they sanctioned $525.7 million more in bond revenues for various capital projects.

According to one study, the behavior of local officials in Arizona may provide a preview of strategies and responses likely to follow newly enacted fiscal controls in other states.

> As the Arizona experience indicates, fiscal limitation also produces incentives for budget obfuscation. Local governments can also be expected to devise stratagems for loosening or circumventing fiscal controls, especially when demographic or economic change cause pressures far exceeding the legal limits. Such unanticipated reactions may serve to exacerbate the increasingly Byzantine process of budgetmaking.[6]

Who Provides Public Services in the "Private City"?

The scope and strength of public sector growth in Phoenix seem to run counter to the political speeches, but the cynic's response might be, "What's new?" Moreover, it can be argued that conservative pro-growth political culture promotes not only the "invisible hand" approach to revenue generation but a similar system for public spending. Indeed, as we have argued elsewhere, the growth of Phoenix has been managed more by the marketplace than by local government.[7]

---

5. Anthony H. Pascal et al., *Fiscal Containment of Local and State Government* R-2494-FF/RC (Santa Monica, California: Rand Corporation, 1979), p. 71.

6. Pascal et al., *Fiscal Containment of Local and State Government*, p. 78.

7. David Altheide and John Stuart Hall, "Phoenix: Crime and Politics in a New Federal City," in Ann Heinz, Herbert Jacob, and Robert L. Lineberry, eds., *Crime in City Politics* (New York, Longman Incorporated, 1983), pp. 193–238.

The perceived place of city government in Phoenix's development has colored the city's agenda, priorities, operations, and patterns of decision making. Basic city services such as police, firefighting, sanitation, and streets have benefited most from increased revenues. At the same time the city's elected officials and administrators have shied away from social services, comprehensive planning and regulation, and other areas of greater concern in other municipalities. At least until recently, Phoenix local government has grown but its functional service agenda has remained limited. The city conforms closely to Salamon's model of the "private city" which he portrays as having

> a tradition of 'privatism' that confines city government to a largely passive role as the facilitator of private economic activity. What distinguishes the private city is the ad hoc character of government actions and the extent to which governmental power is put at the disposal of business elements in their private pursuit of wealth.[8]

The "private city" model is just that, a model. Thus neither Phoenix nor any other real city fits the model perfectly. Nevertheless, the recent history of the politics of Phoenix is a history of public assistance to growth and development. This means that supporters of a conservative private sector philosophy indirectly benefit from the growth of the public sector. These people may prove less resistant, therefore, to overall growth than to the distribution of public benefits of that growth. In Phoenix and in any other "private city" some questions of interest are: Who benefits from public activity? Who receives what proportions of public sector growth? Who provides public services in a private city? If these questions are interesting during periods of growth, they are even more so in times of retrenchment.

The Context: Federal Programs and the Political Agenda of Phoenix

Municipal government reform hit Phoenix late—1984—and hard. The nonpartisan council-manager form of municipal government that emerged from the 1948 reform movement was a reaction to the corruption and ineffectiveness of the rather strange hybrid commissioner-manager form of city government that preceded it.[9] The group of reformers called the Charter Government Committee dominated the electoral process in Phoenix for almost

---

8. Lester M. Salamon, "Urban Politics, Urban Policy Case Studies and Political Theory," *Public Administration Review*, vol. 37 (1977), pp. 422–24.

9. For more details on the history of Phoenix city government, see Leonard E. Goodall, ed., *Urban Politics in the Southwest* (Tempe, Arizona: Institute of Public Administration, 1967), pp. 110–26.

three decades through a steering committee of local bankers, developers, and large-business owners. The group perpetuated itself through recruitment of people who shared the group's perception of the city's business and problems. Until 1975, only two candidates for city council were elected without the endorsement of the charter committee. In that year, four independent candidates broke the committee's exclusive dominance; by 1981, the group's endorsement had lost much of its importance.

In 1983, Phoenix voters amended the charter to create a larger council, the members of which were to be elected by district rather than citywide, as had been the practice for the previous thirty years. The new district system, which has been in operation since January 1984, remains officially "nonpartisan." The strong city manager and his staff, which has grown to approximately 9,000, continue to play a key role in implementing and developing city policy. It is far too early to speculate on the precise impact of the new system.

The important point here is that for much of the development of the modern city of Phoenix, a small group of advocates of a "business approach" to government served as the principal architects of the Phoenix model, which includes the following elements.

- A city council that is composed of amateur politicians who believe in limited city government, act as a "board of directors" for the government, and have exclusive policymaking control over all functions carried out by the city government;

- A city government that is obligated to provide traditional services such as police and fire protection, street, sewer, and sanitation services and to expand those services to new residents and newly annexed portions of the city;

- Avoidance of special-purpose boards, commissions, and districts and consequent incorporation of recent programs such as antipoverty, public housing, and neighborhood development into regular city departments; and,

- Avoidance of municipal responsibilities for some of the costly activities provided by municipal governments elsewhere such as welfare, corrections, public health, and public education. These functions are handled by the Maricopa County government, by independent school boards, by state government agencies, or by nonprofit organizations.

Thus the notion of "limited government" has been important in Phoenix politics in ways other than providing support for the concept of fiscal constraint and tools of tax and expenditure limitations. The limited government concept has undergirded the development of local and political institutions and organizations.

Expanding Local Government with National Resources

The view of Washington, D.C., from Phoenix is summed up in this serious comment of one local official in 1977: "The federal government is evil."

But many local leaders who may have shared this view were also pragmatists. They began to consider federal aid as useful. The first pragmatist was Milton Graham, the mayor elected in 1963. Graham, a member of the community elite, had been nominated by the Charter Committee and shared the conservative views of his colleagues on many issues. But he saw federal revenue available for urban problem solving and began making trips to Washington to learn how some of that money could be channeled to Phoenix. Succeeding mayors and council members have followed Graham's lead,[10] without abandoning the philosophy and rhetoric of local control.

Throughout the 1960s, federal aid to Phoenix represented a minute fraction of the city's total revenues, but in the early 1970s the city entered the federal grants game in a big way. In fiscal 1972 federal aid accounted for only 3.2 percent of total city expenditures; by 1975, that proportion had increased to 14 percent. Table 33 depicts the subsequent expansion of federal grants-in-aid to Phoenix. The amount of federal aid rose from a little over $30 million in fiscal 1975 to a peak of $93 million in 1980. Federal aid represented an increasingly large proportion of the city's total budget through fiscal 1979, then declined but remained well over 10 percent of the total through fiscal 1983.

Participation in federal programs, of course, meant that local officials had to conform to federal civil rights, minimum wage, and environmental quality requirements. They also had to accept federal targeting of benefits on particular geographic areas and constituencies and had to use the funds for specific "eligible" activities.

The growth in federal aid and programs seems inconsistent with the predominant local political philosophy to many people, including the state's most prominent conservative, Senator Barry Goldwater, who has commented, "the most vociferous citizens of the cities of my state against high taxes and

---

10. For more of this history, see John Stuart Hall, "Phoenix, Arizona," chapter 3 in Paul R. Dommel and Associates, eds., *Decentralizing Urban Policy*, (Washington, D.C.: The Brookings Institution, 1982), pp. 47–83.

federal control are also the most vociferous citizens calling for federal aid to the cities."[11] But local politicians tended to accept large shares of federal aid and the accompanying involvement of the federal government in local politics and policy for two rather easily understood reasons: (1) the automatic nature of formula block-grant distribution, and (2) the high priority local people place on maintenance or reduction of local taxes combined with the need to expand municipal services.

Although city reports on federal aid in the 1970s listed more than 100 federal grants, a large proportion of these funds were derived from a few block-grant entitlements. The community development block grant program, the Comprehensive Employment and Training Act program, Title XX of the Social Security Act, urban mass transit assistance, and general revenue sharing accounted for more than 70 percent of the city's federal grant activity for most of the years reported in table 33. These programs were entitlements requiring applications and plans but no competition of the sort required for categorical grants. In addition, funds for these programs had few strings; they were flexible programs. Hence city officials could use the revenues to meet pressing infrastructure problems without resort to local taxes.

TABLE 33

TOTAL EXPENDITURES FOR THE CITY OF PHOENIX, FISCAL YEARS 1975–83[a]

Fiscal Year	Total Operating and Capital Expenditures ($ Thousands)	Federal Grants and Revenue-Sharing Expenditures ($ Thousands)	Federal Aid as a Percentage of Expenditures
1975	236,793	33,509	14
1976	250,067	40,048	16
1977	296,469	44,840	15
1978	355,306	80,405	22
1979	389,349	85,964	22
1980	469,448	93,058	20
1981	537,590	83,247	15
1982	488,391	79,573	16
1983	621,958	83,145	13

SOURCE: City of Phoenix Annual Financial Reports: "Financial Highlights, Total Expenditures Summary" page for each year and tables of operating and capital grant encumbrances and expenditures. Figures are rounded.

a. Includes operating and capital project funds.

11. As stated in a television interview, on the program "The High Cost of Everything," *CBS Report*, June 26, 1979.

Finally, these federal programs represented political decentralization from the national to the local government. As a result they were easier to rationalize. This rationalization rested on the importance placed on limited functions of local government. Many local officials and constituents accepted the reasoning of a former mayor, Margaret Hance, that federal programs and functions can be separated from traditional local government services. Said the mayor in a 1979 interview with *Fortune* magazine, "The poor are a federal not a local responsibility. If Washington cannot afford these programs, we certainly can't. Local people do not feel the welfare programs should be financed by local taxes."[12]

Thus, according to this *Fortune* author, the growth of federal aid in Phoenix in the late 1970s seems to have stemmed from a "take what you can get" perspective. Local officials seemed to believe that Phoenix could either take federal money or leave it. The retrenchment of the early 1980s, however, provided some direct tests for the take-it-or-leave-it philosophy.

Trouble in Paradise, or the Effects of Retrenchment in Phoenix

Enactment of the 1981 Omnibus Budget Reconciliation Act and media reports speculating on further cuts in domestic programs created major uncertainties for officials in Phoenix. Even more worrisome was the recession, which resulted in sales and income tax revenues well below the amounts forecast for fiscal years 1981 and 1982. Other events combined with recessionary forces to promote a climate of gloom not evident in Phoenix for the previous thirty years. In addition to new tax and expenditure limits placed in effect in 1980, the legislature responded to perceived taxpayer demands by eliminating the state sales tax on food and indexing the state's income tax. These and other retrenchment decisions reduced the state's capacity to transfer funds from state to local governments.

Thus, in 1981 questions were being raised about the fiscal future in Phoenix: what would retrenchment mean for local governments in general and the city of Phoenix in particular? What would happen to the people and organizations that had become used to receiving federal funding? How would the changes affect local politics and programs? Could Phoenix actually take federal aid or leave it in an era of economic recession and state local gov-

---

12. Quoted by Julie Vitullo-Martin, "A City that Can Take Federal Money or Leave It," *Fortune*, July 28, 1980, p. 75.

ernment retrenchment? To answer questions like these, I examined the effects of federal aid cutbacks on budgets and programs of the city of Phoenix and on nonprofit service providers in the Phoenix metropolitan area.[13]

The first task was to determine the impact of federal budget cuts in the Phoenix area. Figures 1 and 2, presented earlier, show the overall pattern of funding before and after the changes of 1981–82. City revenues declined between these two years to break a growth pattern that spanned the eight years represented by the figures (1975–83) and most of the thirty-year period from 1950 to 1980. Figure 2 displays a modest decrease in federal funds beginning in late 1980 and continuing until 1982. The figure suggests that 1982 was an anomaly, at least when considered in relation to total city expenditures over this eight-year period; in 1983, spending was virtually back to the place on the trend line that had been developing since 1975, and 1984 and 1985 (not shown in the figure) saw a resumption of historical growth.

Table 34 shows federal aid to Phoenix in the program areas that experienced the largest cuts of the omnibus budget act of 1981.[14] The largest dollar reductions and percentage decreases were in employment and training, community development, and the Maricopa County maternal and child health program. The city's community service program suffered large percentage decreases, but the total dollar decreases were relatively modest. Most program areas experienced stabilization increases in funding after fiscal 1982, rather than further reduction.

Restoration came from two principal sources: Congress and the Arizona legislature. Congress restored the funds for several of the programs that the Reagan administration's domestic budget architects had attempted to cut; the restoration came through such legislation as the Emergency Jobs Appropriations bill and the Jobs Training Partnership Act. One national study showed that federal funding for the fifty states, on the average, increased 4 percent between 1982 and 1983 and 8 percent between fiscal 1982 and fiscal 1984.

---

13. For a full report of the effects of federal aid shifts in Arizona and the Phoenix governments, see John Stuart Hall and Richard A. Eribes, "The Reagan Domestic Program from the Arizona Perspective," in Richard P. Nathan and Fred C. Doolittle, eds., *Reagan and the States* (Princeton, New Jersey: Princeton University Press, forthcoming in 1986). For an assessment of effects of retrenchment on nonprofit organizations in the Phoenix metropolitan area, see John Stuart Hall et al., *Government Spending in the Nonprofit Sector in Two Arizona Communities: Phoenix/Maricopa County and Pinal County*, (Washington, D.C.: The Urban Institute, 1985).

14. For a detailed examination of those cuts and the rationale for looking at these particular program areas most closely, see John William Ellwood ed., *Reductions in Domestic Spending* (New Brunswick, N.J.: Transaction Books, 1982).

TABLE 34

SUMMARY OF CHANGES IN FEDERAL AID TO PHOENIX, FISCAL YEARS 1981–84

Type of Federal Aid and Location	Amount ($ Millions)				Percentage Change	
	1981	1982	1983	1984	1981–82	1982–84
Community Development, city of Phoenix	13.0	12.8	11.4	11.2	−1.5	−12.5
Community Services, city of Phoenix	1.0	0.8	0.7	0.7	−20.0	−12.5
Social Services, city of Phoenix	1.2	1.1	1.4	1.1	−8.3	0.0
Education, Phoenix Union	0.1	0.1	0.2	0.3	0.0	200.0
Highway aid, city of Phoenix	3.0	3.1	4.5	4.2	3.3	35.5
Mass transit, city of Phoenix	6.6	5.8	7.4	8.9	−12.1	53.5
Housing, city of Phoenix	6.1	5.4	5.8	6.0	−11.5	11.1
Health care Maternal and child Maricopa County	0.9	0.7	0.6	0.7	−22.2	0.0
Alcohol and drug abuse Maricopa County	2.3	1.7	1.8	n.a.	−26.1	21.8[a]
Employment and training (CETA and JPTA)[b] City of Phoenix	13.7	8.7	7.8	5.5	−36.5	−36.8
Maricopa County	9.4	5.7	5.0	6.1	−39.4	7.0

SOURCE: John Stuart Hall, Richard A. Eribes, Pamelia P. Eck, "The Reagan Domestic Program From the Arizona Perspective," paper prepared for presentation at a research conference on the Reagan domestic program, Princeton University June 7–8, 1984.

n.a.   Not available.

a.   Data for 1981–83.

b.   Comprehensive Employment and Training and the Jobs Training Partnership Act.

Federal aid to Arizona increased 26.5 percent between 1982 and 1984, the largest increase among all fifty states.[15]

Just as restoration proceeded somewhat unevenly among the states, a somewhat uneven pattern of restoration and increases could be seen among most major domestic programs affecting Phoenix. But the overall message is

15. Rochelle L. Stanfield, "Federal Aid to States Resumes Its Upward Course, But Not for All," *National Journal*, December 17, 1983, p. 264.

clear. Phoenix did well for different reasons, including population-based formulas that made the area's population increase particularly valuable. In addition, because of the structure of the state's Aid to Families with Dependent Children (AFDC) program and the impact of the recession, entitlement areas boomed.

The state legislature and the city council also helped account for the return to normal levels of spending in Phoenix. State legislative decisions, not directly linked to federal programs, began to pay off in fiscal 1983. The state lottery, which had been implemented to increase revenues and to improve highways throughout the state and mass transit in Phoenix and Tucson, yielded nearly $4 million for the city of Phoenix alone. The state's temporary sales tax and other responses to the 1981–82 recession responded predictably well to improved economic conditions; a share of that sales tax went to the Phoenix city treasury. The city council's decision to gradually increase user fees produced more revenue to operate the city of Phoenix. Shifts in state and local revenue sources and improved state and local economic conditions coincided with federal program restoration.

All this means that the overall fiscal effects of retrenchment on Phoenix city government and other local jurisdictions in the Phoenix metropolitan area where minimal compared with initial expectations. But in a few important program areas such as employment and training and community services, retrenchment was relatively severe. How did Phoenix cope with the instances of retrenchment that did surface?

Local governments cope with uncertainty all the time. In Phoenix the threat of retrenchment elicited responses consistent with the city's traditional methods of dealing with uncertainty. The city's productivity program has been described as "one of the best governmental productivity programs in the country."[16] As a part of that program, city officials increased their reliance on private contractors for services ranging from landscaping to water bill processing on the assumption that contractors would do a better job for less money. We have already mentioned the increases in user fees, and in 1981-82 there were some modest service cuts and a hiring freeze. For the first time in twenty-five years, a small number of civil servants (fifty-two) were laid off and others were demoted or transferred.

How did Phoenix absorb relatively important cuts in some service areas without widespread layoffs or major reorganization of government? The two major ways were anticipatory behavior and carryover of unused funds.

---

16. Jeremy Maine, "Why Government Work's Done," *Fortune*, August 10, 1981, p. 156.

Officials in Phoenix had for some time forecast the demise of the Public Service Employment program created by the Comprehensive Employment and Training Act (CETA). Accordingly, throughout the late 1970s, several million dollars of local revenues were budgeted in steps to reduce reliance on CETA employees and to increase new slots in areas important to the operation of the city, such as police, fire, street maintenance, and parks.

The effects of reductions in various social services and community service programs and in the Phoenix community development program were minimized by carryover of unused 1981 funds. If the cuts had been ratified at the national level during fiscal 1983, much of the carryover would probably have been depleted and the fiscal effects would have been more severe. But because 1983 was a year of restoration, the carryover procedure proved wise.

Thus the three-year field examination revealed few important fiscal, organizational, or programmatic effects from retrenchment in Phoenix government. But what of the effects on people in this politically conservative environment? To some degree I have not collected the appropriate information to respond to that question. I did, however, look closely at the Phoenix metropolitan area nonprofit sector to assess the effects of retrenchment on this important segment of the social, health, and human service delivery system.[17]

Some might assert that the findings of minimal effects on local government jurisdictions are in keeping with bureaucratic survival strategies, which also include coping by passing funding reductions on to other groups, especially the nonprofit organizations that help provide public services. Because retrenchment involved public sector cutbacks at a time of economic recession, it was hypothesized that the nonprofit institutions would face an "unavoidable squeeze" as they attempted to respond to rising expectations with ebbing resources. Much of this speculation was based on the assumption that many nonprofit associations depended heavily for their existence on a variety of public funds including federal funds passed through governments in different ways. In addition, the demand for nonprofit voluntary activities was thought to be increased by the economic recession. Because little was known about these matters in Phoenix, it was ideal as one of the sixteen sites for a comparative assessment of the nonprofit sector organized by The Urban Institute. Two forms of data from that study are available and useful for understanding initial impacts of retrenchment on nonprofit organizations.

---

17. For a full report of the initial phase of this study, see Hall and Altheide, "Government Spending in the Nonprofit Sector in Two Arizona Communities."

The first such set of useful information comes from a basic community information system that was created largely from scratch. One objective behind the creation of this information system was to determine the full range of public resources—federal, state, and local—falling into program areas of concern to nonprofit organizations in Phoenix. This system controlled for double accounting among levels of government and was comprehensive, that is, it examined public revenues from all sources relevant to the Phoenix metropolitan area. The second principal objective of this budget information system was to identify the extent to which this total public resource was channeled to private, nonprofit organizations to carry out public purposes. A third objective was to examine the changes that occurred in both total resources and resources to nonprofit institutions during fiscal years 1982 and 1983. Research in Phoenix focused on six major program areas considered to be most relevant to private nonprofit organizations: health services, social services, housing and community development, subsidized employment and training, culture and arts, and income assistance.

In a sense, this analysis represents a different way to cut the same pie, and thus it serves as a check on the large amount of research on the effects of federal budget cuts in Phoenix. The findings of this study almost exactly parallel those of the study of effects on state and local governments. Total public support for the six areas under review *expanded* for Maricopa County—the Phoenix Metropolitan area—between fiscal years 1982 and 1983. The dimensions of fiscal change in these program areas are laid out in table 35, which shows that total public spending in areas of concern to nonprofit institutions declined modestly in social services and more significantly in employment and training and housing and community development. The table also displays percentage increases in the program areas of health care, arts and culture, and income assistance. These totals areawide conform with earlier assessment of changes in federal spending for the same period.

Five of these six program areas represent potential spending in direct support of nonprofit organizations. Income assistance is an exception as a program that can affect the demand for nonprofit services but not provide direct support to nonprofit organizations. Table 36 summarizes evidence on the direct impact of public budget changes between 1982 and 1983 on nonprofit organizations. An overall modest decrease in public spending was accompanied by an overall modest decrease in spending for these programs through nonprofit organizations. From this table and other evidence gathered on the project, it appears that nonprofit organizations were disproportionately cut back between 1982 and 1983, particularly in the program areas that attracted the lion's share of public support.

TABLE 35

PUBLIC SPENDING CHANGES IN MARICOPA COUNTY PROGRAMS OF CONCERN TO
NONPROFIT INSTITUTIONS, FISCAL YEARS 1982–83

Type of Institution Offering Program	Extent of Public Spending		Percentage Change, 1982–83
	1982	1983	
Social services	80,190	76,103	−5.1
Employment and training	22,746	18,535	−18.5
Housing and community development	31,132	26,433	−15.1
Health care	555,851	576,719	3.8
Arts and culture	7,276	7,710	6.0
Subtotal	697,195	705,500	1.2
Income assistance	166,760	178,028	6.8
Total	863,955	883,528	2.3

SOURCE: John Stuart Hall and David L. Atheide, "Government Spending in the Nonprofit
Sector in Two Arizona Communities: Phoenix/Maricopa County and Pinal County,"
working paper (Washington, D.C: The Urban Institute, June 1984).

TABLE 36

CHANGES IN PUBLIC SUPPORT FOR MARICOPA COUNTY PROGRAMS OF CONCERN TO
NONPROFIT INSTITUTIONS, FISCAL YEARS 1982–83

Type of Institution Offering Program	Percentage Change in Public Spending	Public Support of Nonprofit Institutions		Percentage Change, 1982–83
		1982	1983	
Social services	−5.1	38,834	38,933	0.3
Employment and training	−18.5	9,271	6,033	−34.9
Housing and community development	−15.1	3,117	1,507	−51.7
Health care	3.8	211,132	215,129	1.9
Arts and culture	6.0	843	709	−15.8
Total	1.2	263,199	262,312	−0.3

SOURCE: Same as table 35.

But this finding needs to be understood in the context of data from other
sources in the larger study of the nonprofit sector. Tables 37 and 38 report
information gleaned from a survey of Phoenix area nonprofit agencies engaged
in the delivery of social and human services. Table 37 shows that total
government funding of these organizations represented slightly more than 40
percent of their total funding. Like the other eleven metropolitan areas and
four nonmetropolitan counties in The Urban Institute study, Phoenix nonprofit

TABLE 37

REVENUE SOURCES OF SELECTED NONPROFIT INSTITUTIONS IN THE PHOENIX AREA,
FISCAL YEARS 1982–83[a]

Revenue Source	Percentage of Total Revenue (n = 128)
Government (combined federal, state, and local)	40.5
United Way	5.3
Other federated funders	1.2
Religious organizations	1.2
Other individual donations	11.6
Corporate grants	2.4
Foundation grants	1.5
Dues, fees, charges	26.8
Endowment, investment income	2.2
Other[b]	7.1
Unspecified	0.2
Total	100.0

SOURCE: "The Phoenix Nonprofit Sector in a Time of Government Retrenchment," Lester Salamon, series editor, report (Washington, D.C.: Urban Institute, forthcoming), p. 3-3.

a. Based on institutions that responded to the 1983 Urban Institute survey.

b. Includes such items as product sales, special fund-raising events, and rental of facilities to others.

institutions received over two-thirds of their income from government and user fees and charges. More than three-quarters (77 percent) of Phoenix nonprofit institutions surveyed reported some reliance on service charges, making this the most common source of nonprofit revenue in Phoenix. Thus, Phoenix nonprofit institutions in 1982, like the Phoenix city government, were already relying heavily on fees.

The study of the nonprofit sector also indicates that there are widely different types of nonprofit organizations and different effects of budget changes on those organizations. Table 38 shows that 61 percent of the organizations surveyed expected a decrease in government funding for fiscal 1983. Whether that decrease actually occurred is one subject of a follow-up survey, the results of which are not yet available. (Preliminary results indicate that nonprofit agencies' projection of government revenue loss proved to be exaggerated.) That table also indicates that cutbacks in federal spending would be particularly strong in the areas of health and mental health care, culture and arts, and institutional and residential care organizations.

Table 39 shows the demand side of the retrenchment equation and illustrates the diversity of nonprofit organizations. From that table one can see

TABLE 38

CHANGES IN PROJECTED GOVERNMENT FUNDING, SELECTED NONPROFIT
INSTITUTIONS IN THE PHOENIX AREA, FISCAL YEARS 1982–83[a]

Type of Institution	Number of Institutions	Percentage with Change in Government Funding		
		Increase	No Change	Decrease
Social services	24	13	33	54
Institutional and residential care	16	6	50	64
Health and mental health care	18	0	17	83
Employment and training	8	25	38	38
Legal and advocacy/housing and commu- nity development	5	20	20	60
Culture and arts	10	10	10	80
All organizations[b]	97	8	31	61

SOURCE: Same as table 37.

    a.   Based on institutions that responded to the 1983 Urban Institute survey.

    b.   Institutions that have at least 50 percent of expenditures in the specified category and receive government funding. "All Organizations" includes additional agencies that report multiple service categories.

that demand has increased for employment and training services and health and mental health services. Because these types of organizations have experienced disproportionate cuts in the Phoenix area, we find some evidence in support of the "squeeze" hypothesis.

In general, the nonprofit sector study suggests that although there is some evidence to support stories about the tragic effects on some people as a result of the service cutbacks, Phoenix's nonprofit organizations continued to be sustained by looking to different sources of revenues. Table 40 shows that almost half of the responding organizations reported increases in user fees in 1982 and exactly one-half expected similar increases in 1983.

In interviews, personal tragedies were occasionally uncovered that were parallel to those described in the media reporting the effects of cutbacks on individuals. In general, however, much more evidence was found of organizational survival, and in many cases expansion was noted.

Conclusions

From studies of federalism in Phoenix, by separate analysis of different measures of both cause and effect, it became clear that retrenchment in Phoenix was less than expected. Substantial evidence of adjustment, anticipation, and compensation was found at all levels of government. Public

TABLE 39

CHANGES IN DEMAND FOR SERVICES, NONPROFIT INSTITUTIONS IN THE PHOENIX
AREA, FISCAL YEARS 1982–83[a]

Type of Institution	Number of Institutions	Percentage with Change in Demand for Services		
		Increase	No Change	Decrease
Social services	53	36	60	4
Institutional and residential care	17	53	29	18
Health and mental health care	24	58	29	13
Employment and training	10	80	20	0
Education and research	11	18	82	0
Legal and advocacy/housing and community development	7	57	43	0
Culture and arts	15	20	80	0
All organizations[b]	158	44	48	8

SOURCE: Same as table 37.

a. Based on institutions that responded to the 1983 Urban Institute survey.

b. Institutions that have at least 50 percent of expenditures in the specified category and receive government funding. "All Organizations" includes additional agencies that report multiple service categories.

TABLE 40

INCREASES IN FUNDING FOR SELECTED NONPROFIT INSTITUTIONS IN THE PHOENIX
AREA, BY SOURCE, FISCAL YEARS 1982–83[a]

Revenue Source[b]	Percentage with Increase, 1980–82	Percentage with Increase, 1982–83
Government	18	13
Foundations and corporations	27	41
Private donations, United Way	43	52
Earned income (dues, fees, and investment income)	47	50

SOURCE: Same as table 37.

a. Based on institutions that responded to the 1983 Urban Institute survey.

b. The number of institutions in each category are as follows: government, 123; foundations and corporations, 113; private donations, 136; earned income, 144.

managers were using various combinations of carryover funds and productivity innovations in combination with minor and not-so-minor revenue adjustments. Many of these measures were a part of long-term local public finance strategies.

In fact, retrenchment as it was originally defined simply did not take place in Phoenix. Restoration occurred quickly and on many fronts. The scope and swiftness of restoration are not really surprising because, although the domestic budget cut aspect of retrenchment fit well with a local political rhetoric, economic recession did not. The Phoenix public finance system is geared to economic growth. Economic growth is perceived as desirable; it automatically fuels the local finance system. Moreover, political rhetoric does not stand in the way of astute use of federal and other external funds when they are available.

Clearly, nothing like a revolution in American domestic relations occurred in Phoenix during the early 1980s. But state and local governments in Arizona made changes because of the threat of, and to some degree the manifestation of, retrenchment. In keeping with local priorities, local public officials reexamined their revenue structure and renewed their commitments to avoid reliance on federal funds and other external revenue sources. In his statement to the Advisory Commission on Intergovernmental Relations on March 1, 1984, Phoenix Mayor Terry Goddard endorsed the general position of several of his predecessors concerning the need to avoid reliance on federal funds, but he also made the following suggestions to improve the relationships with the federal government: (1) any reduction in federal funds should allow for a gradual transition period; (2) any federal mandates for new state and local government programs should incorporate federal funding; (3) the federal government should transfer funds when it transfers program responsibility; (4) the federal government should not preempt state and local tax structures without arranging for compensation; (5) the federal government, in allocating resources, should consider the problems of both distressed and growth cities; and (6) federal support for infrastructure maintenance is essential.

Few people are arguing the need of a "New Federalism" these days. At least in Phoenix, the old federalism appears to be alive and well because, political rhetoric aside, it works. In another paper, written when the rhetoric of the "New Federalism" was at its high point, I argued that anything as neat and decisive as the Reagan administration's proposed separation of national, state, and local functions was unlikely to be accepted, given the original reasons for establishment of the federal system: "What seems enduring in the history of American government is the federal-state-local assistance relationship. The understanding, tolerance, and anticipatory behavior required to make this unique arrangement work does not seem in danger of drastic change in Arizona."[18]

In Phoenix, federalism has played an important part in expanding the public agenda and the distribution of public benefits. It has resulted in short-term successes like the community development block grant. That program alone has enlarged the public agenda directly through targeting and indirectly by providing an intellectual resource for local officials to treat urban problems.

Most important, American federalism survived, indeed mediated, the political and economic event we called retrenchment. Therein lies an important lesson: American federalism is unique and multifaceted. At its best it can be a catastrophic insurance plan. When depression, recession, budget cuts, political error, and pure human stupidity seem about to unravel the American political fabric, federalism compensates. When the dam breaks, federalism fixes it. Under stress, American federalism forces American governments to cooperate.

But because public problems like crime, poverty, inequality of educational benefits, and ill health remain, and because most public officials claim that the solution is not their responsibility alone, the American system of federalism raises a tough question for conservatives, liberals, and patriots: does this uniquely successful approach to insuring against public catastrophe cost too much?

---

18. John Stuart Hall, "Reagan Domestic Program in the Arizona Context," paper delivered at the 1982 meeting of the American Political Science Association, Denver, Colorado, September 1982.

ENTREPRENEURIAL CITIES AND THE NEW POLITICS OF ECONOMIC DEVELOPMENT

Dennis R. Judd and Randy L. Ready

American cities are "unwalled," vulnerable to buffeting by social and economic forces beyond their control. For the past half-century, a whole class of cities—not exclusively the old industrial cities of the North—have been unwilling participants in a reshuffling of economic resources and populations. The postwar urban crisis literature chronicled white flight and business relocation to the suburbs, as well as rising levels of racial segregation, poverty, crime, and disorder in the central cities. Recent urban scholarship has changed focus, but once again cities, especially the old industrial cities, are characterized as victims of social and economic transformations that take place beyond their borders. The new research documents economic growth in the Sun Belt, decline in the Frost Belt—and it is instructive that both terms entered the popular lexicon only in the past decade. The spirit of recent analysis is succinctly captured in the 1980 report of the *President's Commission for a National Agenda for the Eighties*:

> As industrial activity becomes increasingly freed from specific locations in post-industrial America, economic gains of productivity and efficiency are secured by capital shifts and are registered in new locations. Such disinvestment patterns are accompanied by a residue of social costs that are anchored to the places, and experienced by the people, left behind.[1]

The leaders of declining cities have never been willing to accept their "fate" as losers in the postindustrial economy. When faced with the deterioration of housing and downtown business districts, they pursued redevelopment strategies that were remarkably similar from city to city. Through

---

1. President's Commission for a National Agenda for the Eighties, *A National Agenda for the Eighties* (Washington, D.C.: U.S. Government Printing Office, 1980), p. 42.

federally sponsored urban renewal programs, executive-centered downtown coalitions sought to reclaim valuable urban land for "higher and better" use rather than for housing poor people.[2] An inward-looking redevelopment machine dominated the politics of many cities during this phase.[3]

Over time, the municipal development agenda has been transformed. Economic development strategies have become much more elaborate and complex. Growth cities as well as cities in decline have turned to the national market and scrambled to make themselves attractive to footloose private firms. All cities are engaged in aggressive campaigns to secure their share of national economic growth.

Well before the 1980 election, cities were actively trying to gain more control over their own economic destinies. They have been pushed further in this direction by the policies of the Reagan administration. Cities have been instructed to wean themselves from dependence on federal aid and to prepare themselves for free-market competition. According to the Reagan administration, cities must compete with one another for market shares, just as firms do: "State and local governments have primary responsibility for making their urban areas attractive to private investors."[4] Cities gain control over their own destinies, in this interpretation, not by insulating themselves from national market forces but by accepting the responsibility for achieving success in national market competition.

Entrepreneurial strategies make up the heart of the municipal policy agenda and municipal politics in the mid-1980s. Most cities have accepted the Reagan administration's mandate that city governments cooperate with the private sector and compete with one another to provide a favorable climate for business. In some cities, however, the political constituency has challenged conventional thinking about which groups should control local economic development and how the benefits of local economic growth should be allocated.

2. Robert H. Salisbury, "The New Convergence of Power in Urban Politics," *Journal of Politics* (November 1964), pp. 775–97.

3. Harvey Molotch, and John Logan, "Tensions in the Growth Machine: Overcoming Resistance to Value-Free Development," *Social Problems*, vol. 31, no. 5 (June 1984), pp. 483–99; Susan S. Fainstein, Norman I. Fainstein, Richard Child Hill, Dennis Judd, and Michael Peter Smith, eds., *Restructuring the City: The Political Economy of Urban Redevelopment* (New York: Longman, 1983); John H. Mollenkopf, *The Contested City* (New Jersey: Princeton University Press, 1983); Roger Friedland, *Power and Crisis in the City: Corporations, Unions and Urban Policy* (New York: Schocken Books, 1983); and Alan Wolfe, *America's Impasse: The Rise and Fall of the Politics of Growth* (Boston: South End Press, 1981).

4. U.S. Department of Housing and Urban Development, *The President's National Urban Policy Report: 1982* (Washington, D.C.: U.S. Government Printing Office July 1982), p. 23.

The election of minority mayors is a political development that potentially challenges conventional growth politics. As of May 1985, only about 1 percent of all the mayors in the United States were black, but there are now seventeen black mayors of cities with populations of 100,000 or more. Baltimore is the only city in this category with a majority black population that has not elected a black mayor. Black mayors preside in four of the ten largest cities: Chicago, Detroit, Los Angeles, and Philadelphia. Two major cities, Denver and San Antonio, have elected Hispanic mayors.

Of course, the presence of a minority mayor does not automatically translate into a new municipal agenda. Coleman Young and Andrew Young, for example, preside over conventional, old-style, "downtown growth" politics in Detroit and Atlanta.[5] Lionel Wilson, the mayor of Oakland, California, has led a fight to cut municipal expenditures and to bring more business investment to that city. Wilson Goode campaigned for the mayoralty of Philadelphia in 1983 on a classic reform platform, promising to streamline city bureaucracies, build a convention center, improve the port, and promote economic development.[6]

But it is likely that new political pressures will be brought to bear on black mayors. For more than twenty years public opinion polls have consistently shown that blacks favor a much higher level of social welfare spending and government services than do whites.[7] The differences in black and white attitudes toward government programs have remained remarkably stable over time.[8] There is a higher degree of congruence between the policy orientations of black representatives and their constituencies, regardless of social class, than between white government representatives and the white electorate.[9]

Black municipal leaders tend to focus on issues of inequality in housing, health care, employment and income, and education.[10] But when they hold municipal office, do they try to implement policies different from those implemented by white mayors? The most comprehensive study to date found that in cities with black mayors and council members, the proportion of the municipal budget spent for health, education, and housing was higher than

5. Coleman A. Young, "Detroit: Moving Forward in the Frost Belt," *USA Today* (November 20–22, 1981); and Thulani Davis, "Black Mayors: Can They Make The Cities Work?" *Mother Jones*, vol. 9, no. 6 (July 1984).

6. Davis, "Black Mayors," p. 36.

7. Karnig and Welch, *Black Representatives and Urban Policy*; and Terry Nichols Clark and Lorna Crowley Ferguson, *City Money* (New York: Columbia University Press, 1983).

8. Susan Welch and Michael W. Combs, "Interracial Differences in Opinion on Public Issues in the 1970s, "*Western Journal of Black Studies*, vol. 7, no. 3 (Fall 1983), pp. 136–41.

9. Karnig and Welch, *Black Representatives and Urban Policy*.

10. Ibid., p. 11.

in white-governed cities.[11] These findings confirm what might be expected from observing the first black mayors of major American cities, Richard Hatcher of Gary, Indiana, and Carl Stokes of Cleveland.[12, 13] And in their study of ten California cities, Browning, Marshall, and Tabb reported that when minorities gained representation on city councils, as well as in mayors' offices, they achieved far-reaching changes in city policies.[14]

On balance, we would expect many minority mayors to seek policy changes, or at least to put a new face on old policies. Nearly all black mayors win office by gaining an overwhelming proportion of black votes, usually more than 95 percent, and much smaller percentage of white votes, typically 10 to 20 percent. The key to victory is a combination of large black majorities and heavier-than-usual voter turnout. For example, Wilson Goode received 97 percent of the black vote in the Philadelphia primary election in May 1983, while attracting 23 percent of the vote in white areas. In Chicago's general election of April 1983, Harold Washington received 98 percent of the black vote, 58 percent of the Hispanic vote, and 18 percent of the white vote. When black candidates run for office, voting usually divides along racial lines.[15]

When Hispanic populations help to elect Hispanic mayors, pressures for policy changes also will be exerted. Hispanics have high rates of unemployment and poverty, and they often live in substandard housing in segregated neighborhoods. They fall far below the general population on all indicators of economic well-being. In Denver, which elected a Hispanic mayor in June 1983, racial tensions between the Hispanic and white communities have existed for a long time.[16]

Several relatively small cities are currently pursuing well-publicized alternatives to the usual economic growth strategies. These municipal policies are remarkably similar across the country because they are informed by several movements of the 1970s—the environmental crusade, the search for "appropriate" technologies and alternative energy systems, and a political struggle for grassroots democracy and local self-reliance. Santa Monica, California, for example, whose city council is dominated by representatives of the Cam-

---

11. Ibid.

12. Levine, *Racial Conflict and the American Mayor*.

13. William E. Nelson, Jr., and Philip J. Meranto, *Electing Mayors: Political Action in the Black Community* (Columbus: Ohio State University Press, 1977).

14. Rufus P. Browning, Dale Rogers Marshall, and David H. Tabb, *Protest Is Not Enough: The Struggle of Blacks and Hispanics for Equality in Urban Politics* (Berkeley: University of California at Berkeley, 1984).

15. Karnig and Welch, *Black Representatives and Urban Policy*.

16. Dennis R. Judd *The Politics of American Cities*, 2d ed. (Boston: Little, Brown, 1984) pp. 248–52.

paign for Economic Democracy, imposes on developers requirements for construction of low-income housing, day care centers, and provision of special services. Davis, California, has targeted much of its public money to solar energy, energy conservation, and neighborhood-run services. Burlington, Vermont, has elected and reelected a socialist mayor. Saint Paul, Minnesota, has embarked on an unusually well-defined program to become an energy-efficient city with a "self-reliant" local economy.

Economic Development Policy in Three Cities

We have conducted field studies in three cities in an effort to discover the ways in which the economic development agenda is changing. Denver, Chicago, and Saint Paul were selected because they are each well-publicized examples of cities where politics-as-usual is being challenged. Our research in these cities has revealed the degree to which economic growth programs reflect local political conditions. Denver is a city in the process of repackaging the old downtown-growth, executive-centered coalition into a bright new wrapper more attractive to minorities and neighborhoods. Chicago has elected a mayor, Harold Washington, who redefines the city's growth priorities to create local jobs and rejuvenate neighborhoods: all in the context of the tremendous restraints imposed by continued opposition from entrenched city bureaucracies and the remnants of an old party machine. Among American cities, Saint Paul is frequently held out as the premier example of a city that is attempting to implement alternative energy systems and conservation, neighborhood power, and control over its local economy.

Is a transformation in city politics taking place that may produce new municipal policies? Three case studies cannot definitively answer this question, but they can describe the mobilization of new political constituencies and the rise of a new breed of political leaders. They also can reveal what new municipal growth agendas may look like in the future.

The case studies are presented against a background composed of two principal elements: the mandates contained in federal urban policy, and the municipal growth agenda pursued by most cities. We now turn to these topics.

These new municipal growth agendas (since World War II) compare to conventional growth policies, and to one another, in a manner described in the following display:

1940s	*1950–1970s*	*1980s*
Local business organizations: First example—Allegheny Conference, Pittsburgh	Executive-centered growth coalitions. Vehicle: urban renewal. Goal: reclaim downtown	Redevelopment Coalition: Recent example—Baltimore's Harbor Place

These coalitions are increasingly being replaced by four types of growth strategies:

1.	2.	3.	4.
Create "good business climate"; pursue private investment (for example: Houston and many cities)	Repackage downtown-growth coalition: first comes business investment; neighborhoods, minorities next in line (example: Denver)	Redefine growth objectives: job creation and neighborhood revitalization given priority. Constraints: politically divided city (examples: Chicago and many cities)	Attempt to create "appropriate" technologies; alternative energy use; grassroots democracy; local self-reliance (Saint Paul and Davis, California)

The Federal Policy Mandate

Throughout his political career, Ronald Reagan has evinced a preoccupation with the ideal of self-reliance. He returns to the themes of self-reliance, autonomy, and individual responsibility over and over again in his speeches. This perspective has informed his view that welfare programs undermine individual self-respect, moral character, creativity, and the motivation to work. In applying the themes of individual responsibility and self-reliance, however, the president makes few distinctions between individuals, institutions, political systems, and cultures.[17] It is as much a desideratum for cities to become self-reliant as for people.

Perhaps reasoning that the president's well-known views on welfare were being directed at them, the cities' mayors reacted angrily to the draft of an urban policy report by the Department of Housing and Urban Development (HUD) that was circulated at the U.S. Conference of Mayors meeting in early July 1982. The document, drawn up as a preliminary version of the official

---

17. Robert K. Dallek, *Ronald Reagan: The Politics of Symbolism* (Cambridge: Harvard University Press, 1984).

national urban policy report required every two years by Congress, asserted that the swelling volume of federal urban aid had transformed mayors "from bold leaders of self-reliant cities to wily stalkers of federal funds."[18]

Although the controversial language was meticulously removed from the final version, when *The President's National Urban Policy Report* was issued on July 8, it hardly reassured the mayors. Rhetoric to the contrary, urban policy was being virtually abandoned in favor of a national Economic Recovery Program, principally embodied in federal tax reductions. According to the Reagan philosophy, the fortunes of individual cities, like the fortunes of other parts of the country, would be determined by their success at adapting to national economic transformations such as the growing service and high-technology sectors. Urban leaders were instructed to become entrepreneurs, to take responsibility for their own destinies, and to compete for economic growth: "State and local governments will find it is in their interests to concentrate on increasing their attractiveness to potential investors, residents, and visitors."[19]

Long before hearing such advice, local public officials had put in place strategies designed to reverse the decline in local economies and to accelerate growth. Aggressive mayors had become wily stalkers of both federal funds and private investment.

The Municipal Growth Agenda

The federal mandate is clear: cities must make themselves more attractive to private firms and must provide fertile ground for local entrepreneurship. To accomplish these objectives, HUD suggests that localities form public-private partnerships. The Committee for Economic Development has elaborated on the advantages it sees in these arrangements:

> The evidence clearly indicates that many of the goals of American society can best be realized by developing a system of incentives for private firms to do those social jobs which business can perform better and more economically than other institutions. Indeed, the entrepreneurial thrust of business . . . may well be indispensable in achieving a permanent solution to urban and other socio-economic problems that have badly overtaxed the capacity of public agencies.[20]

Nearly all cities have created public-private partnerships to promote economic growth. Some 15,000 local nonprofit and quasi-public organizations

18. John Herbers, "Administration Seeks to Cut Aid to Cities, Charging It Is Harmful," *New York Times*, June 20, 1982.

19. U.S. Department of Housing and Urban Development, *The President's National Urban Policy report: 1982*, p. 14.

20. Committee for Economic development, *Public Private Partnership: An Opportunity for Urban Communities* (New York: Committee for Economic Development, 1982).

currently administer much of the economic development activity that is occurring.[21] Although economic development organizations designed as public
agencies under the auspices of city government (as in Saint Paul and in
Portland, Oregon), or as private corporations accountable to the chamber of
commerce or other private sector representatives (as in Philadelphia and in
Milwaukee) continue to exist, joint public-private representation on a quasi-
public corporation is the most typical structure.[22] The Committee on National
Urban Policy believes that "there is some possibility that public-private partnership will become the nostrum for the 1980s that community participation
was for the 1960s."[23]

Development campaigns have become "internecine and aggressive,"
with each state and municipality trying to outbid its neighbors for new investment.[24] The race for high-technology industries has been particularly keen.
For example, when the Microelectronics and Computer Technology Corporation—a research and development consortium formed by industry—announced that it would entertain competitive bids for its location, cities formally
proposed no fewer than fifty-seven sites, each with state and local tax subsidies, higher education connections, infrastructure support, land assembly
and financing assistance, and other special concessions. The array of in-
ducement techniques now available to local governments and economic development organizations is awesome and rapidly growing in cost.[25]

Despite the popularity of the incentives, there is evidence that most of
them have had little influence on investment patterns. The most damning
evidence comes from the vast number of industrial location studies that have
been conducted over many years and in all parts of the country. Michael

21. Vernon Levy, *Economic Development Programs for Cities, Counties and Towns* (New York: Praeger Special Studies, 1981).

22. R. Scott Fosler, and Renee A. Berger, *Public Private Partnerships in American Cities* (Lexington, Massachusetts: Lexington Books, 1982); and Ruth Knack, "Setting Up Shop for Economic Development" *Planning*, vol. 49 (October 9, 1983), pp. 14–15.

23. Royce Henson, ed., *Rethinking Urban Policy: Urban Development in an Advanced Economy* (Washington, D.C.: National Academy Press, 1983), p. 150.

24. Roger J. Vaughan, *State Taxation and Economic Development* (Washington, D.C.: Council of State Planning Agencies, 1979), p. 98.

25. L. L. Ecker-Racz, *The Politics and Economics of State-Local Finance* (Englewood Cliffs, New Jersey: Prentice-Hall, 1970); Lawrence Litvak and Beldon Daniels, *Innovations in Development Finance* (Washington, D.C.: Council of State Planning Agencies, 1979); Neal R. Peirce, Jerry Hagstrom, and Carol Steinback, *Economic Development: The Challenges of the 1980s* (Washington, D.C.: Council of State Planning Agencies, 1979); Vaughan, *State Taxation and Economic Development*; Barry M. Moriarty, et al., *Industrial Location and Community Development* (Chapel Hill, North Carolina: University of North Carolina, 1980); and Terrence E. Cook, "The Courtship of Capital: Political Implications of Increasingly Portable Capital and Fixed Territorial Jurisdictions of Government," paper presented at the 1982 annual meeting of the American Political Science Association, Denver, September 2–5, 1982.

Wasylenko, in his study of geographical location studies conducted since the 1920s, concluded:

> Taxes and fiscal inducements have very little, if any, effect on industrial location decisions. Thus, state and local policies designed to attract business are generally wasted government resources, since businesses that ultimately locate in a jurisdiction would have made the same decision with or without the fiscal incentive.[26]

There are many reasons why most financial incentives are ineffective. For one thing, the actual "differences" between localities and thus the true "incentives" are usually small. In the case of tax differences, there is a tendency toward convergence of the actual tax payments that similar firms make, regardless of region. As for financial incentives, they are becoming more and more universally available. If all jurisdictions offer them, they benefit no one but the business firms, which receive a subsidy regardless of where they locate.[27]

But economic development incentives need not be effective to be popular, partly because they fit so comfortably with prevailing political ideologies. As pointed out by Henry Aaron, their popularity among local politicians "derives from a peculiar alliance among conservatives, who find attractive the alleged reduction in the role of government that would follow from extensive use of tax credits, and liberals anxious to solve social and economic problems—by whatever means—before it is too late."[28]

Consider the dilemma facing cities. On the one hand, city officials are told that they must find solutions to their own problems, and they are instructed to be entrepreneurial. On the other hand, they are faced with diminishing resources with which to implement effective policy responses. So public officials have turned to financial incentives and tax concessions as "costless" programs; these at least have the appearance of positive action. As Theodore Lowi has pointed out, "Most cities find themselves literally too small to handle their policy problems but politically too weak to resist trying."[29]

A final reason why most city officials cannot resist offering investment incentives is related to the overwhelmingly important symbolic value of incentives as indicators of the "business climate" in a particular city:

---

26. Michael Wasylenko, "The Location of Firms: The Role of Taxes and Fiscal Incentives," in Roy Bahl, ed., *Urban Government Finance: Emerging Trends* (Beverly Hills, California: Sage Publications, 1981).

27. Barry M. Moriarty, *Industrial Location*; and Wasylenko, "The Location of Firms."

28. Stanley S. Surrey, *Pathways to Tax Reform: The Concept of Tax Expenditures* (Cambridge, Massachusetts: Harvard University Press, 1973).

29. Theodore J. Lowi, "The State of Cities in the Second Republic," in John P. Blair and David Nachmias, eds., *Fiscal Retrenchment and Urban Policy* (Beverly Hills, California: Sage Publications, 1979), p. 47.

A company may find clues about a community's willingness to host industry by its willingness to grant tax and financial incentives. Industry may find these programs to be mere tokens, insignificant compared with other influences on locations, but they are tokens, nonetheless. The community that actively disdains such incentives, especially the more mundane programs affecting location, may do so at its peril.[30]

The compelling nature of the economic development agenda has led almost all cities to embrace it in broad outlines. But local political leaders also realize that economic development programs must be sold to their political constituencies. City leaders will tackle the economic development task differently, depending on their own inclinations and on the nature of their constituencies that elected them into office. In the case studies that follow we sketch three different responses.

Denver, Colorado: Repackaging the Growth Agenda

Defining the Problem: Growth or Decline?

An outside observer might not expect Denver to get caught up in the competition for economic growth. Historically, Colorado's problems have been associated with too much development rather than with insufficient growth. Air pollution, urban sprawl, water shortages, traffic snarls, the despoliation of mountain environments: these are the issues that capture public attention. According to Governor Richard Lamm, westerners have become wary about growth:

> Slowly at first, then with a rush, "quality of life" issues gained dominance.
> . . . The West had learned that it had sold itself too well. It learned that it could never assimilate the massive immigration that resulted from it. So yesterday's ethic of "growth at any price" changed to a mood of skepticism and caution.[31]

Preoccupation with the side effects of growth was a natural reaction to the runaway pace of development in the 1970s. Following the 1973 oil embargo, a surge of interest in oil shale development led the way to massive speculation in Western Colorado. By 1980, ten megaprojects were being planned and the state was bracing itself for an influx of thousands of workers and billions of dollars. Between 1972 and 1982, the value of total mineral production increased from $400 million to more than $2.5 billion.[32]

---

30. Roger W. Schmenner, "Industrial Location and Urban Public Management," in Arthur P. Solomon, ed., *The Prospective City* (Boston: The M.I.T. Press, 1980), pp. 446–68.

31. Richard D. Lamm and Michael McCarthy, *The Angry West: A Vulnerable Land and Its Future* (Boston: Houghton Mifflin Company, 1982), p. 122.

32. Peter Warren and Jennifer Sussman, "Natural Resources: Role in the Colorado Economy," vol. 2, no. 1 *Public/Private* (March 1983), p. 19.

Denver became the headquarters for literally thousands of energy companies. Between 1973 and 1982, fifty new buildings shot up; between 1979 and 1982, more than $2 billion was invested in the skyscraper boom.[33] Between 1970 and 1978, office space in the core areas of twenty of the largest American cities expanded by 38 percent, but in Denver during the same period there was a 103 percent increase.[34]

The metropolitan area's 34 percent increase in employment from 1970 to 1978 was second only to Houston's growth rate during the same period.[35] In the 1970s per capita income increased by 27 percent, retail sales grew by 12.6 percent annually, and the unemployment rate increased by only 0.5 percent.[36] Certainly all expectations in 1980 were for "continued economic expansion for the Denver metropolitan area economy for at least the next decade."[37] Coping with growth and protecting the quality of life appeared to be the greatest challenge for the region and for Denver as well.

But the energy boom was short-lived. The national recession of 1981 and falling oil prices substituted disinvestment for the problems associated with development. Optimism about sustained regional growth had fueled downtown office construction that far exceeded demand once the recession hit. By 1984, Denver had the highest downtown office vacancy rate in the nation, 28.1 percent—more than double the national rate.[38] As one policy analyst for the city remarked, "If there was a boomtown that was hurt by the [Exxon pullout] it was Denver, not Battlement Mesa."[39]

A new language of economic decline entered the mayoral race of 1983. In large part, Federico Pena was able to build his campaign on the idea that Denver needed dramatic new leadership; his campaign theme was "Imagine a Great City." By the time he delivered his first State of the City address in July 1984, Pena had thoroughly adopted the view that Denver had to devise strategies to promote investment:

---

33. "Dynamic Downtown Denver," *Empire Magazine* (Denver Post), January 3, 1982.

34. J. Thomas Black, "The Changing Economic Role of Central Cities and Suburbs," in Arthur P. Solomon, ed., *The Prospective City* (Cambridge Massachusetts: The M.I.T. Press, 1980).

35. Gladstone and Associates, *Economic Impact and Implications of the Transitway/Mall* (Denver: Regional Transportation District and Downtown Denver, Inc., 1978), p. 3.

36. Data provided by the Denver Regional Council of Governments. See their *Profiles of 1970–80 Socio-economic Change by County and Census Trace* (Denver, Colorado: DRCOG, 1983).

37. Gladstone and Associates, *Economic Impact and Implications of the Transitway/Mall*, p. 3.

38. E. Wilkinson, "Downtown Vacancy Rate Highest in the U.S.," *Denver Post*, July 24, 1984.

39. Interview with Liz Orr, Denver City Office of Policy Analysis, July 19, 1984.

We are in jeopardy of losing our place as the dominant center of commercial activity in the metro area. If we cannot succeed in expanding the economic base of our city by creating new jobs, increasing retail sales and adding new development, we will be unable to avoid cutbacks in services, meet the needs of our disadvantaged, or reinvest in our neighborhoods at a level sufficient to insure their continued health.[40]

City Leadership during the 1970s

An active interest in promoting investment was hardly new to Denver. In fact, the late 1970s expectation of self-sustaining growth was an anomaly; as in other cities, there had been well-organized efforts to reclaim the downtown from small, marginal businesses and run-down neighborhoods. Growth policies in Denver had always been narrowly targeted toward downtown projects.[41] During the years when Denver's central business district changed from older, redbrick and sandstone commercial buildings to a forest of skyscrapers, William H. McNichols served as mayor.

McNichols, who took office in 1968, had served as manager of public works for years. A progrowth Democrat, McNichols aimed chiefly "to keep the city's services functioning smoothly and the residents' taxes low."[42] He spent much of his time encouraging private sector initiative and development downtown. During the 1970s a new arts center, a sports arena, an expanded sports stadium, and a higher education complex were completed. McNichols was instrumental in getting more than $400 million in bonds approved for public improvements, a feat that earned him the nickname, "Bill the bondsman."[43]

The Denver skyline changed dramatically during McNichols' tenure. The conversion of valuable land was not left to chance. Through the Skyline Project, the Denver Urban Renewal Authority presided over the reconstruction of a twenty-seven-block area in downtown Denver. By the fall of 1984, nearly a billion dollars of public and private funds had been spent on construction in the Skyline Project.[44]

In addition to all this activity, in 1980 corporate and development interests founded the Denver Partnership, a downtown development corporation that took the lead in determining the future of the central business district.

---

40. Federico Pena, State of the City address. July 5, 1984.
41. Dennis R. Judd, "From Cowtown to Sun Belt City: Boosterism and Economic Growth in Denver," in Fainstein et al., eds., *Restructuring the City*, pp. 167–201.
42. Interview with Orr.
43. George V. Kelly, *The Old Gray Mayors of Denver* (Boulder, Colorado: Pruett Publishing Co., 1974), p. 259.
44. Denver Urban Renewal Authority, *Denver Urban Renewal Authority Skyline Project: Summary of Developments* (Denver, Colorado: DURA, 1984).

The partnership planned much of the conversion of a major sector of downtown into the pedestrian 16th Street Mall retail and office area.

Other development activity during the McNichols era centered on the use of federal funds such as community development block grants and urban development action grants. The Urban Renewal Authority focused its attention on the downtown area, so the Community Development Agency devoted most of its efforts to neighborhood revitalization. This latter agency spent $44.6 million that it received for the first three years primarily for housing rehabilitation grants and loans, neighborhood business revitalization programs, and other neighborhood development and upkeep activities.

The Community Development Agency also established a Mayor's Advisory Council in 1974 to serve as the decision-making group concerning community development funds; the mayor appointed ten members of the council and each city council member made one of the other thirteen appointments. The creation of the council was politically significant because, by creating an intermediary council to allocate federal funds going to the neighborhoods, the mayor essentially washed his hands of neighborhood issues and the potential conflicts inherent in allocation decisions.

Thus urban renewal activity downtown constituted the majority of the McNichols administration's economic development initiatives. The city did receive some planning funds from the Economic Development Administration in the mid-1970s that were earmarked for comprehensive economic development planning. Staff from various city agencies along with several community leaders set out to use those funds for data collection and policy development. Two planning documents resulted from those efforts.

The first, published in 1977, outlined the city's economic problems and suggested goals and strategies to make the city more financially secure. The city's main problems included pockets of high unemployment, the outward movement of firms, saturation of prime industrial land, deterioration of industrial and commercial areas, financing problems in older areas and for small business, and restricted city revenue sources.[45]

The committee maintained that the three main goals for the city's economic development ought to be to increase employment opportunities for residents, to create a more attractive investment climate, and to expand the fiscal capacity of the city.[46]

The litany of problems and proposed solutions is familiar to observers of older industrial cities, but the severity of the problems in Denver in the

---

45. City and County of Denver, *Economic Development in Denver; Agenda for Action* (Denver, 1977), p. 3.

46. Ibid., p. 4.

1970s was minimal compared to many other cities across the country. The mayor and city council officially adopted the report, but little action was taken.

An elaboration of the initial work took place in 1979. This document, known as the overall economic development program and comprehensive economic development strategy, placed the city's objectives in priority order and proposed more specific projects to meet those objectives. The report also specified a "special impact area" within the city to receive targeted economic development attention. The area centers on the core of the city and includes the downtown business district as well as the city's oldest industrial sectors and neighborhoods with the highest black and Hispanic concentrations.

The report again gained council approval but little implementation occurred. The city did follow through on one proposal and hired an economic development coordinator. The position was eliminated just two years later during staff cutbacks. One participant in the formation of the policy reports later noted that "visible prosperity was the greatest single factor working against the city's development of an economic development effort."[47]

The end of the energy boom in the summer of 1981 signaled the end of McNichols' career as mayor. The city had been balancing the general fund with transfers from the capital fund for years. The recession aggravated the fiscal situation and Denver residents began to suspect that their boom town had problems.

A series of scandals then rocked the McNichols' administration: millions of dollars were lost through faulty city contracts. The city's chief tax collector was indicted for embezzling city funds. Police moonlighting and social involvement with known drug users attracted widespread press attention. The city government reacted slowly to a Christmas Eve blizzard in 1982 that dumped more than two feet of snow and left many streets impassable for weeks. And three top police officials were suspended for their roles in an alleged bingo scandal.

A New Electoral Coalition

On June 21, 1983, thirty-six-year-old Federico Pena captured the mayor's office after what appeared to be the longest of long shots. As his campaign manager proclaimed, "Taking someone with a 5 percent name recognition who happens to be Hispanic in a city with an 18 percent Hispanic population—that has got to be something of a major political event in the city's history,

---

47. Interview with Orr, 1984.

if not the state and region."[48] In fact, Pena's election marked the first time that a Hispanic mayor had been elected in a major U.S. city that was not itself predominantly Hispanic.

Pena started his campaign by announcing, "I think we're going to put together a coalition in the city in a way that nobody has ever done before."[49] The coalition he put together included blacks, Hispanics, labor, homosexuals, business leaders, women's groups, environmentalists, neighborhood groups, elderly people, handicapped people—even McNichols' own brother, former governor Steve McNichols, and three of the candidates Pena had defeated in the primary.

Pena's campaign strategy was twofold. First, he attempted to build a broadly based coalition that included the thousands of liberal Denverites who had consistently voted for Representative Patricia Schroeder and Senator Gary Hart, but who had never been to the polls during a mayor's race.

Second, Pena ran a campaign based on the issues. He distributed to the public a series of issue papers in which he detailed his position on air pollution, airport expansion, neighborhood planning, Denver's financial future, economic development and job creation, and the physical development of the city. He promised to open city hall to neighborhood groups, minorities, and others who had previously been shut out of the city government, and he also stressed the need for long-term planning. Pena criticized McNichols for trimming the city planning staff and all but eliminating neighborhood planning. He asserted that Denver should grow, but that the growth should be directed so that Denver did not become another Houston or Los Angeles.

Most of the campaign staff had close ties to Lamm and Hart, whose campaigns had been hard-hitting and confrontational. In contrast, Pena's campaign staff decided early on that Pena would not win if he were presented as a confrontational Chicano activist out to take over city hall with a "divide and conquer" approach. Pena therefore portrayed himself as a "young, bright, and articulate activist who did his homework, maintained his principles, and who happens to be Hispanic."[50]

The campaign and election were notable for their lack of overt racism, especially in contrast to the bitterly divisive campaign in Chicago that same year. Pena's Hispanic background was seldom mentioned; he managed to avoid the topic almost entirely. Pena believed that "When I have a chance to meet people and talk to people, the last thing they think of is that I'm

---

48. Gary Delsohn, "Pena's Early Coalition a Winner," *Denver Post*, June 22, 1983.
49. Ibid.
50. Patrick Yack, "Pena Has Overcome One Issue Political Label," *Denver Post*, April 26, 1983.

Hispanic."[51] Pena has persisted in downplaying his minority status while in office. He has repeatedly turned down offers to participate in nationwide Hispanic political forums. He carefully avoided the spotlight during the Hispanic delegates' movement to abstain on the first ballot at the 1984 Democratic National Convention in protest over the Simpson-Mazzoli immigration bill.

When Pena first won a seat in the Colorado legislature in 1978, he was branded a one-issue politician. He had spent the years since his arrival in Denver in 1972 as an activist lawyer with the Mexican-American Legal Defense and Education Fund and later with the Chicano Education Project, fighting for improved education for minorities and for underprivileged people. Once in the legislature, Pena dispelled the one-issue label. After being elected for a second term, Pena's popularity with his Democratic colleagues led to his selection as House minority leader.

When Pena announced his decision to run for mayor, many politicians, including some influential leaders of the Hispanic community, felt uneasy about his candidacy. For example, Ed Romero, director of the Latino Chamber of Commerce, refused to support Pena because he believed that Denver was "not ready for a minority."[52]

But Pena maintained that Denver had "gone beyond questions of ethnic background."[53] Analysis of the primary election results revealed that, indeed, Pena had forged the coalition that he had sought. An extensive voter registration drive fell far short of its goal of registering 16,000 new Hispanic voters before the primary; not even one-fourth of that number had registered. As it turned out, Pena did not have to rely heavily on new Hispanic voters to win in the primary.

Pena finished first in a field of seven candidates in the May 17 primary. His 36.4 percent of the vote easily outdistanced third-time candidate and former district attorney Dale Tooley's 30.8 percent and McNichols' 19.1 percent. Despite a heavy spring snowstorm, more than 63 percent of the city's voters had gone to the polls to send Pena into the runoff against the forty-nine-year-old Tooley.

In the month before the runoff election, Pena attempted to consolidate his coalition, while Tooley attempted to characterize Pena as too liberal and lacking in administrative experience. Pena supported collective bargaining for city workers; Tooley opposed it. Pena criticized police sweeps of Denver neighborhoods to arrest street-gang members; Tooley thought the sweeps were a good idea. Pena continued to charge that the city was in the midst of a

---

51. Ibid.
52. Ibid.
53. Bill Walker, "Old Guard Joins in Praise for Victor," *Denver Post*, June 22, 1983.

fiscal crisis; Tooley believed that the rebounding national economy was improving Denver's fiscal condition.

On June 21, 1983, a record 155,000 voters, 71.5 percent of those registered, went to the polls. Pena received 79,453 votes—51.4 percent of the total—to Tooley's 75,043 votes—48.6 percent of the total.

Pena had sealed the victory by adding more than 5,000 new voters to the rolls in the heavily minority-populated western and northern districts of the city. He won the northeast districts (52 percent black) by almost a two-to-one margin and the north central districts (51 percent black and 21 percent Hispanic) by four to one. In the end, Pena had needed the new voters, blacks and Hispanics, to carry the general election. Tooley captured most of what was once considered to be McNichols' territory in the heavily Republican and conservative Democratic districts of southwest and southeast Denver.

Repackaging the Growth Agenda

Federico Pena captured the mayor's office on the strength of a coalition of diverse groups that had never before had much influence in local politics. The new mayor moved quickly to follow through on many of his campaign promises. He had pledged to open city government leadership positions to women and minorities, and he established a twenty-two-person transition team to select the key members of his administration. After several weeks the cabinet was in place. It included three women and two members of minority groups.

With regard to the neighborhoods, Pena had pledged that they would "have a partner, rather than an adversary" in the mayor's office.[54] To increase input from neighborhood groups he began a series of "town meetings" in each council district. Pena increased the size of the neighborhood planning staff from three to eight people and ordered a traffic study of the one-way streets running through the neighborhoods toward downtown.

It would be misleading, however, to concentrate on Pena's overtures to the neighborhoods, for economic development has become the administration's principal priority. The Pena administration's overall economic development strategy is borrowed directly from the 1979 Economic Development Program and other plans adopted under the McNichols regime. Pena's economic development team advises that "while some refining and elaboration of this work is needed . . . this should not be the main concern of a City economic development program at this point. Instead the City should focus

---

54. Federico Pena, *The Pena Neighborhood Program: Neighborhood Planning, Preservation and Development* (March 19, 1983), p. 3.

on the proposed new initiatives which are directed at implementing or *doing* economic development, not further planning for it.''[55]

The major initiatives all are focused on one objective, enhancement of the city's economic condition:

> unless the City's revenue base substantially is enhanced, further reductions in service delivery and increases in taxes will be required. Such actions could easily make Denver less attractive for both residential and business locations which would further aggravate the City's economic condition. This is the single most compelling reason for the City to undertake a strong economic development program.[56]

The message was unmistakable. Denver had enlisted in the competitive race to attract new investment, sales, and jobs.

As one symbol of this competition, the city has been working fervently to develop a new convention center as "the major economic development project Denver undertakes in this decade."[57] A new convention center and better marketing of the cultural attractions downtown are seen as integral to attracting more visitors.

One other recent initiative of the Pena administration is indicative of the city's priorities for economic development. On July 8, 1984, Pena announced that his administration and the Denver Partnership, the downtown development corporation, would collaborate on a downtown master plan. Expected to take eighteen months to be completed, the plan is to direct and promote development in and around the central business district. A twenty-seven-member panel serves as the steering committee for the project.

Some neighborhood groups were concerned about what they considered to be overrepresentation of downtown interests on the committee. Five representatives of the Denver Partnership were included, but only three seats were offered to neighborhood leaders. Other concerns about the influence of business interests surfaced when it was learned that the partnership would provide three-quarters of the initial funding and two-thirds of the staff for the eventual $3 million planning project. William Fleissig, Denver's newly hired downtown planner, explained that the Denver Partnership would play the lead role in the downtown plan only because "we just didn't have the core staff or the money to do it ourselves."[58]

---

55. City and County of Denver, *Economic Development Action Program* (Denver: CCD, 1984), p. 1.
56. Ibid.
57. Ibid., p. 6.
58. Kevin Flynn, "Firms, City to Plan Core Area," *Rocky Mountain News* July 9, 1984.

One of the highest priorities defined by the planning group was to determine how best to attract a major anchor retail store to the central business district. For a long time Denver has been trying to lure a high-fashion retail store (such as Saks Fifth Avenue or Neiman-Marcus) to its downtown 16th Street Mall. The efforts still were unsuccessful in late 1985, but the team working on the master plan hoped to put together an irresistible package of incentives. Garrick Hill, a former high-fashion store executive, knew that the task would not be easy:

> To get anything major, it's going to take major public involvement. To get an anchor, you're going to have to give him a 40,000–50,000-square-foot pad for $1 a foot or something ridiculous to get him to come in. I don't think it will happen without some subsidizing.[59]

Elsewhere in the country the cost of attracting a national retailer has been high. For example, Saks Fifth Avenue recently opened in downtown Cincinnati at a cost to the city of $16 million for the land and the construction of the basement and first-floor levels.[60]

Big-name retailers are seen as a linchpin in a plan to revive the image of downtown and to increase sales tax revenue. Pena has said, "If in a major city like Denver you have a downtown which is not full of people and where people are literally gone at 5:30 in the afternoon, then you begin to have questions about how exciting that city is."[61]

Leveraging private investment downtown is the first goal of the Pena administration. Other development priorities must follow the revitalization of the central business district. As one administrative assistant put it, "Downtown is going to have to pay the bills. . . . We probably will be criticized by some for focusing too much on downtown. People will ask, 'What does Saks Fifth Avenue have to do with the neighborhoods?' The answer is that downtown retailing has everything to do with the neighborhoods. The city needs the revenue."[62]

Response from the Neighborhoods and Minorities

Soon after his election, Federico Pena attended a symposium for recently elected mayors at Harvard. Pena was surprised at the issue that most of the new mayors consistently raised as the primary obstacle that they faced in

59. Kevin Flynn, "Downtown Retailers Could Be Costly," *Denver Post*, April 1, 1984.
60. Ibid., p. 24.
61. Ibid., p. 25.
62. Interview with Tom Gougeon, administrative assistant to Denver Mayor Federico Pena, July 17, 1984.

governing their cities: animosity between the central business district and the neighborhoods over development priorities. Most of the new mayors (including Pena) had been elected as advocates of the neighborhoods. They now faced the problem of heightened expectations yet inadequate resources. Pena did not sense the same intensity of conflict in Denver and wondered why.[63]

Part of the explanation may be that Pena has successfully invoked the symbols of open and responsive government. Pena was careful not to make specific promises that he could not keep. He promised openness, and he proceeded to hold town meetings. He promised representation, and he began appointing minority and neighborhood representatives to a variety of posts. Perhaps most important, Pena promised to improve the city's economic condition and to ensure the vitality of its neighborhoods. Initially, it appears that he was successful in persuading most groups that his downtown-centered development program was the way to do both.

In Denver in 1984, groups that were previously excluded feel as if they have a voice in city government for the first time. People are involved and informed. Minorities and neighborhood groups have assumed a "wait and see" approach with Pena. As one neighborhood activist said, "You have to give the man some time. He's honestly trying to do what's best for all of us."[64]

Within the administration there is concern that "as the city gets more involved with economic development there will be more conflict, both internally and externally" over such issues as the strategic use of community development block-grant funds. The city council will have to be included in policy decisions, of course, and the effect of its input is far from certain but probably divisive.[65]

An interesting political experiment is being conducted in Denver. Can conflicts be managed by implementing an economic development program that justifies downtown revitalization by its potential spillover effects into neighborhood and minority communities? Is this the repackaging of progrowth politics what may be expected of minority mayors who are elected by broadly-based coalitions? Certainly, the coalitions that elect Pena and other minority mayors to office will begin at some point to expect more than openness and symbolic sharing of power. Until then, Denver's program provides a glimpse into what may become a familiar development strategy in cities all across America: a reworking of familiar progrowth politics by minority and "reform"

---

63. Interview with John Parr, director, Center for Public-Private Cooperation, University of Colorado at Denver, July 19, 1984.
64. Interview with Kay Gingenbock, Brothers Redevelopment, Inc., August 2, 1984.
65. Interview with Orr.

mayors to make downtown development palatable both to dominant business interests and to minority and neighborhood constituencies.

Chicago, Illinois: A Reform Agenda in a Hostile Environment

Immediately to the left of the LaSalle Street entrance inside Chicago's city hall is a door; above it in bold, back-lit letters cut in an aluminum panel one reads: "Neighborhoods" in capital letters. Awkwardly sandwiched between this panel and the door jam is a neatly lettered but much smaller sign that says, "Mayor's Office of Inquiry and Information." A subtle but important lesson can be gleaned from these two messages. Mayor Harold Washington wanted to have an accessible, prominently located office that would coordinate neighborhood information, plans, and programs, but the city council refused to approve the funds.

An important struggle is going on between the remnants of Chicago's machine organization and a broad coalition of blacks, Hispanics, and white reformers who elected Harold Washington mayor on April 12, 1983. But this struggle should be understood as far more than the expected battle between two factions, both of which sought to control the reins of power; and it is not a fledgling political machine replacing a tired old one. Washington ran for office on a reform platform emphasizing more efficient and open government, an end to patronage, a redistribution of power and benefits away from downtown to the neighborhoods, and job-oriented economic development. What is ultimately at stake in Chicago's current political struggle is the definition of the municipal agenda.

Many of the Washington administration's programs fall firmly within the tradition of progressive urban reform. One writer has said that Washington "deeply believes in the possibilities for honest government that can work for all the common people."[66] Thus, he has dedicated himself to "good government" goals of ending the patronage system, streamlining the city's bureaucracies, and giving citizens access to city hall. For example, one of his first acts in office—it is mentioned over and over again in city documents—was to issue a freedom-of-information executive order making government information and documents available to the public. In the past, Chicago's city government was an inaccessible fortress. Now a multitude of documents such as "A Citizen's Guide to City Hall" explain the responsibilities of the

---

66. David Moberg, "The Man Who Wants to Break the Mold," *Chicago* (October 1983), p. 182.

various departments, provide telephone numbers, and encourage citizens to attend hearings or inquire about programs.

This type of reform hardly constitutes a unique urban agenda. Only in Chicago would antimachine reform seem new. Still, a new municipal agenda is being tried. Its three main elements are a redistribution of power and resources to neighborhoods, the enfranchisement of previously politically inactive powerless groups, and "a substantial downward redistribution of benefits toward the many blacks who occupy the lower rungs of the socioeconomic ladder."[67] These three themes were sounded throughout the mayoral campaign and can be summed up in the thesis that "power and resources had too long been concentrated in City Hall and in the Central Business District, which has long been seen by many as either the handmaiden of City Hall or as the key component in city government with City Hall as the handmaiden."[68]

The Chicago Development Plan

In early April 1983, about two weeks before the mayoral election, the Research and Issues Committee of the Washington campaign released a fifty-two-page document called "The Washington Papers." It is doubtful that the detailed outline of his proposed policies had any effect on the election, but it did confirm that Washington was running a reform campaign. A striking feature of the collection of papers was the omission of economic development per se from the list of policy areas. But there was a reason for this ostensibly curious omission. By subsuming economic development under two policy categories, "Jobs for Chicagoans" and "Neighborhoods," economic development was defined as a divisible public good with specific economic and political purposes.

That the city government is being redefined in entrepreneurial terms is obvious in "The Washington Papers," but the principles guiding the entrepreneurial strategies are vastly different from those that would be suggested by the standard municipal development model. "The Washington Papers" became the guiding philosophical and strategy document leading to the weighty, detailed Chicago Development Plan published in May 1984. The five development goals of the new reform agenda are as follows:[69]

---

67. William J. Grimshaw, "Is Chicago Ready for Reform? or, A New Agenda for Harold Washington," in Melvin G. Holli and Paul M. Green, eds., *The Making of the Mayor: Chicago 1983* (Grand Rapids, Michigan: William B. Eerdmans Publishing Co., 1984), p. 8.

68. William A. Sampson "The Politics of Adaption: The First Year of the Washington Administration," in Samuel K. Gove and Louis H. Mascotti, eds., *Chicago Politics in Transition* (Urbana: University of Illinois Press, forthcoming).

69. City of Chicago, "'Chicago Works Together': 1984 Chicago Development Plan," (Chicago, Illinois: May 1984).

Goal I.   Increase Job Opportunities for Chicagoans
            Policies: Targeted Business Investment in Support of
                    Job Development
                    Local Preference in Buying and Hiring
                    Skilled Labor Force Development
                    Infrastructure Investment for Job Development
                    Affirmative Action

Goal II.   Promote Balanced Growth
            Policies: Balanced Growth between Downtown and Neighbor-
                    hoods
                    Public-Private Partnerships Strengthened Tax Base
                    Equitable Distribution of the Tax Burden

Goal III.   Assist Neighborhoods to Develop through Partnerships and Coordi-
            nated Investment
            Policies: Neighborhood Planning
                    Expanded Housing Opportunities
                    Linked Development

Goal IV.   Enhance Public Participation in Decision Making
            Policies: Increased Citizen Access to Information
                    Increased Opportunities for Citizen Involvement

Goal V.   Pursue a Regional, State, and National Legislative Agenda

The appointment of Robert Mier as acting commissioner of the Department of Economic Development confirmed the new policy directions. Formerly the director of the Center for Urban Economic Development at the University of Illinois, Chicago campus, Mier had been recruited to serve on one of the policy task forces during the Washington campaign. He is a rare breed: a specialist on neighborhood economic redevelopment in a profession where most people are oriented to downtown development.

The idea of "balanced growth" represented a radical departure from previous development policies. According to Mier, under previous administrations his department had been addicted to "blockbuster" downtown projects involving large amounts of money and real estate. Only one deal involving small business had ever been processed through the department in its history.[70]

More was involved in the Washington program than the redistribution of development money to the neighborhoods. Under the machine virtually all the development money that had not gone downtown had been distributed to neighborhood chambers of commerce, on the basis of the powers and electoral successes of the ward committeemen.[71] It may have been called development money, but everyone knew it was patronage. Now the plan was to target

---

70. Interview with Robert Mier, commissioner, Department of Economic Development, City of Chicago, July 24, 1984.

71. Interview with Kari Moe, assistant commissioner, Policy, Planning and Research, Department of Economic Development, City of Chicago, July 25, 1984.

money to redevelopment objectives openly obtained and distributed to neighborhood redevelopment corporations, cooperatives, and private business. Over the first three years the Economic Development Department staff planned to create ten to twelve neighborhood corporations through which it would funnel grants.

A successful distribution of money in this manner not only constitutes a direct attack on Chicago's patronage system, but lays the groundwork for creating a new political base in the city. The neighborhoods, represented through black ministers and community organizations, were significant components of the Washington campaign. Thus, intense battles between the city council and Mayor Washington are being fought over the new programs. It comes as no surprise that the council has resisted the proposal for an Office of Neighborhoods.

Mier believes that development should be tied to the creation of local jobs and used to nurture small businesses and neighborhood organizations. Most of the loans being negotiated in the Department of Economic Development involve small businesses. Mier also wants to encourage the development of neighborhood cooperatives, like food-buying clubs and minority credit unions.

The Chicago Development Plan for 1984 outlines a formidable number of programs and projects designed to bring recovery to the city's economy and direct benefits to minorities, city residents, and small businesses. For the year beginning with the plan's publication, May 1984, the list of job creation "targets" is impressive indeed:[72] (1) create or retain more than 8,000 jobs, directly and indirectly, through financial assistance for business expansion and start-up; (2) provide technical assistance to more than 4,000 businesses; (3) establish public-private task forces for at least two Chicago industries; (4) increase City of Chicago local purchasing from 40 percent of total purchasing to approximately 60 percent—about $80 million; and increase private sector local purchasing by 5 percent—an estimated $250 million; (5) increase City of Chicago purchasing from minority-owned and women-owned firms to 25 percent of total purchasing—$100 million; and (6) train 12,000 persons in employment skills.

Included in the list of specific programs intended to meet these targets are "micro loans" to small neighborhood businesses; "business incubators" (low-rent space for small businesses in city-owned buildings); "linked development" (agreements on local hiring, affirmative action, and local purchasing in exchange for big-business development approval or assistance);

---

72. Ibid., p. 14.

and enterprise zones. According to the development plan, a newly established Mayor's Office of Employment and Training will target job training to employers' needs, and (among other programs) use "neighborhood-based organizations to screen unemployed and economically disadvantaged residents for placement in jobs with area businessmen."

The development program and its methods of implementation are extraordinarily ambitious. Neighborhood organizations are encouraged to review programs and submit requests. Capital improvement programs are to be reviewed and implemented through the Neighborhood Infrastructure Renewal Task Force. All city contractors and businesses receiving financial assistance from the city are expected to participate in an aggressive affirmative-action program. Twenty-five percent of city purchasing is to be targeted to companies owned by minorities and women; this is overseen by the Purchasing from Minority and Women-Owned Firms program.

A multitude of programs are designed to stimulate citizen participation and neighborhood institution building. The philosophy guiding these programs is described in the development plan as follows:

> Successful neighborhood planning cannot be a "top-down" process. It must be based on an awareness that neighborhood problems and assets are best known to neighborhood residents and the local organizations devoted to the betterment of their neighborhoods.[73]

Thus, according to the development plan, more than 100 community-based organizations already receive development services. To build neighborhood institutions, the Department of Planning, through the Neighborhood Planning Service, is supposed to help neighborhood residents participate in drawing up local development plans. Community development block-grant money in the amount of $200,000 is being set aside for planning grants to low- and moderate-income neighborhoods.

Economic Development and Political Realities

A planning document with such ambitious goals creates high expectations, but failure to implement its programs is likely to create immense cynicism. This is what happened in the federally funded Model Cities program during the 1960s.

Most of the programs just described have been slow to get off the ground. As of August 1984, for example, no cooperatives had actually received loans or technical assistance, unless one counts as a cooperative the one Hispanic

---

73. Ibid., p. 3.

credit union that received a loan. Neighborhood development corporations were being set up, or were they? (The answer varies with the source.) No neighborhood infrastructure task forces were in operation. The capital improvement projects dated from Jane Byrne's administration, having been in the pipeline before the 1983 election. The promised studies of Chicago's sectoral priorities and the appropriate role for public and private cooperation had not even begun.

The plans to transform city political power also have been slow to materialize. Many observers have commented on Harold Washington's deliberate style: "He tends to hold back commitments, listen to all parties, then make a decision."[74] This style may be appropriate for someone who is dedicated to fundamental reform, but his inability to deliver large numbers of jobs and favors quickly almost certainly will create problems with his own constituency.[75]

National news coverage has focused almost exclusively on Washington's clashes with Edward Vrdolyak, the Cook County Democratic chairman and the real leader in the Chicago City Council, and Alderman Edward Burke, who chairs the council's powerful finance committee. Shouting matches make good news coverage. The antagonism is bitter and often racial. Racial fears often are used as a device to organize opposition to the Mayor's policies. Much is at stake. The machine is fighting for its very life against the first reform movement to capture the official reins of power in Chicago.

Probably the most important obstacle to reform are the city bureaucracies. In every agency, a few Washington appointees, often no more than two or three, occupy the top positions. Most employees were there long before the latest mayoral election, and they are securely ensconced in their jobs. It is clear that these employees are in a position to slow policy changes or sabotage them altogether. For example, after Washington's election, restaurant inspectors employed by the Consumer Affairs Department began to issue a large number of citations. For the first time in memory, they were following the letter of the law. When restaurant and shop owners complained, the inspectors claimed they were following orders issued by the new regime.[76]

---

74. Moberg, "The Man Who Wants to Break the Mold," p. 175.

75. Ibid., and Grimshaw, "Is Chicago Ready for Reform?"; William J. Grimshaw, "The Election of Mayor Harold Washington: Reconciling Race and Reform" and "Class, Culture, and Race in Chicago Politics," in Samuel K. Gove and Louis H. Mascotti, eds., *Chicago Politics in Transition* (Urbana: University of Illinois Press, 1982).

76. Interview with William J. Grimshaw, associate professor, Illinois Institute of Technology, July 25, 1984.

Of course, any mayor who launches an assault on the established order will meet resistance. Chicago's bureaucracies, like those in other big cities, have grown up over a long period. But in Chicago's case, normal bureaucratic inertia is compounded by the unique way city agencies are accustomed to delivering services. Under Mayor Richard Daley, the bureaucracies were virtually administrative arms of the machine. Bureaucrats were expected to be loyal to the party; many of them participated actively in precinct-level work before and on election day. The everyday delivery of services, too, was political. The most loyal Democratic wards got first attention in basic services like street sweeping, road repairs, and utility improvements. Chicagoans have always known that their city government was thoroughly political and that the Democratic party controlled politics.

Mayor Washington's reforms were aimed squarely at the traditional ways of doing business. Only a wholesale purge of old employees could prepare the way for rapid acceptance of the new norms: openness in government; coordination with neighborhood groups—including the neighborhoods in black and Hispanic wards.

But Harold Washington was denied even the usual amount of house-cleaning. For fourteen years before the 1983 election, Michael Shakman had led a fight to get the federal courts to declare the patronage system illegal. Despite the persistent legal assault, the Democratic party had been able to preserve 8,000 patronage employees. Then just weeks before the mayoral election, Federal District Judge Nicholas Bua handed down a landmark decision: only 250 appointments, plus department heads, could henceforth be exempted from civil service.

Washington supported the decision, in principle, because it conformed to his reform ideals. But he desperately needed more appointments to carry out his programs. After protracted negotiations with the court, a compromise was reached allowing him to make 792 appointments. No doubt exhibiting an unprecedented burst of civic virtue, the Democratic party now became a powerful foe of patronage politics, arguing that even 250 appointments were too many (for years, Democratic party lawyers had been defending patronage jobs).

The inability of the Washington administration to appoint more people was a devastating blow. As of August 1984 fewer than 600 appointments had been made. Under the judge's supervision, hiring procedures were slow and cumbersome; an open position could take months to fill. For example, in the policy, planning, and research division of the Department of Economic Development, three top staff positions remain unfilled. Of ten top staff people, only three were hired by Washington. It was the same in all the departments and agencies—a thin sprinkling of Washington appointees are to be found: "It is like trying to win a reform war with someone else's army."[77]

There are other constraints as well. Washington came into office facing a gap between resources and expenditures of more than $100 million. Obviously the mayor does not have excess funds to distribute to his constituency, even if he were disposed to do so.

The Chicago View of Urban Policy

In a sense, Chicago is now attempting to implement, at the local level, an urban policy similar to that pursued by the federal government for much of the 1960s and 1970s. One of the five development goals of the Chicago Development Plan calls for the city to influence urban programs in Illinois and to help formulate a national agenda for the cities.

The urban agenda proposed by Mayor Washington, however, is not in harmony with the programs of the Reagan administration or even the national Democratic party. In June 1984, just in time for the U.S. Conference of Mayors meeting and the Democratic national convention, the mayor's office printed 5,000 copies of a booklet entitled, "Mayor Harold Washington: A Federal/Urban Partnership to Renew Our Cities."[78] The document proposed a national full-employment jobs program, a federally assisted effort to build capital infrastructure, and a new federally funded housing program. The key programs proposed included: a national Production and Jobs Board "that develops industrial policies in coordination with similar local economic development bodies"; a Community Renewal Employment Act, a National Capital Investment Bank to "provide a revolving fund at lower than private interest rates for local capital investment," to be matched by locally raised capital; and a National Capital Investment Council to "advise governments on national resource allocation and local investment planning."[79] Democratic candidate Walter Mondale did not endorse any of these themes in his 1984 campaign. Taken together, the Washington proposals implied a faith in the power and desirability of government intervention in the marketplace that seemed outside the national political debate of 1984.

Chicago's program of local economic development depends critically on local government intervention. It presumes that city government can stimulate an alternative model of economic growth, by sowing seed money for economic development projects in the neighborhoods, by involving neighborhoods and

---

77. Interview with Moe.

78. *Mayor Harold Washington, A Federal/Urban Partnership to Renew Our Cities* (Chicago, Illinois: Office of the Mayor, June 1984).

79. Ibid., p. 4.

small businesses in economic planning, and by using the city government's own purchases to generate business for small and minority-owned firms. There is reason to believe that an urban political constituency exists for redefining economic development goals in this way. Whether Chicago's government has the financial, managerial, and policy capacity to transform local economic development, however, remains an open question.

Saint Paul, Minnesota: A Rebirth of Municipal Mercantilism?

Following the example set by English towns and boroughs, early American cities regulated important aspects of local commercial life: they authorized market houses; adopted regulations to prevent fraud, the sale of spoiled goods, inaccurate scales, and hoarding; even controlled the details of local commerce through publicly owned wharves, fairs, and streets.[80] Before the Revolutionary War, municipal corporations held "a unique role as a center of trade and commerce," and thus were important in its regulation.[81]

Adam Smith, in the book that established the fundamental premises of classical economics, attacked such practices. Commenting on the economic regulations imposed by English municipalities, he concluded that "the pretense that 'municipal' corporations are necessary for the better government of . . . trade is without any foundation."[82]

One wonders what Adam Smith might make of Saint Paul's experiment in municipal governance. In attempting to assert control over the city's economic future and to protect its local economy from the vicissitudes of national economic change, its mayor has said he wants to "gradually shift from a reliance upon imports to greater self-reliance. This can be accomplished by redefining the city's role in the development of the economy and the community."[83]

When George Latimer was first elected mayor in 1976—he is now in his fifth term—his platform amounted to classic urban reform. He wanted to bring efficiency to the city government. First, he brought the budgetary power into his office in order to satisfy his standards of "accountability." He also

---

80. Richard C. Wade, *The Urban Frontier: Pioneer Life in Early Pittsburgh, Cincinnati, Lexington, Louisville, and St. Louis* (Chicago: University of Chicago Press, 1959), pp. 79–83.

81. Jon Teaford, *The Municipal Revolution in America: Origins of Modern Urban Government, 1650–1825* (Chicago: University of Chicago Press, 1975), p. 3.

82. Ibid.

83. *Saint Paul's Homegrown Economy Project: A New Economic Policy and Program for the Self-Reliant City* (Saint Paul, Minnesota: Office of Mayor George Latimer, August 1983), p. 10.

brought several city agencies into a newly organized Department of Planning and Economic Development.

The mayor also wanted to explore new ways of delivering municipal services. In his first term, he suggested that neighborhoods ought to be able to "buy" some of their own services, instead of having a uniform mix of city services provided to all neighborhoods. The idea was motivated by his populist orientation toward local democracy and by distrust of "bigness": "What we should avoid is monopolistic practices of public bureaucracies. But monopolistic practices are just as deadening when they're in the private sector."[84]

The most distinctive element in Saint Paul's economic development strategy is its Homegrown Economy Project. In his October 21, 1982 State of the City address, Mayor Latimer announced that the city would embark on the program to "put Saint Paul on the map as the first of the new generation of self-reliant cities," and that its economic development program would make it unnecessary for the city to "recklessly compete with other cities for established businesses."[85]

In August 1983 the mayor's office distributed the first detailed public description of the programs making up the city's new economic development strategy. The booklet, titled "The Saint Paul Homegrown Economy Project: A New Economic Policy and Program for a Self-Reliant City," cited an interesting mix of urban scholarship. The definition of a city was borrowed from Jane Jacobs (*The Economy of Cities*): "a settlement that consistently generates its economic growth from its own local economy."[86] Research by M.I.T. Professor David Birch was cited to argue that small businesses create most new jobs.[87] Robert Reich, the author of a series of articles critical of large industrial corporations, is quoted on the point that "large conglomerate enterprises" are unwieldy and bureaucratic in comparison with the small-scale firms that should make up creative and adaptive economy.[88] And finally, David Morris, president of the Institute for Local Self-Reliance, is quoted on the virtues of the self-reliant city:

> The self-reliant city views itself as a nation. It analyzes the flow of capital within its borders and evaluates its "balance of payments." It recycles money as much as it recycles goods. Every added cycle increased the community's wealth.

---

84. Interview with Mayor George Latimer, July 27, 1984.
85. George Latimer, "Saint Paul at the Crossroads," State of the City Address, Congressional Record—Senate, S16027-S16028, December 21, 1982.
86. Jane Jacobs, *The Economy of Cities* (New York: Vintage Books, 1969), as quoted in Saint Paul Homegrown Economy Project report.
87. David Birch, "Who Creates Jobs?" *Public Interest* (Fall 1981).
88. Robert Reich, "The New American Frontier," *Atlantic Monthly* (March 1983).

Businesses are evaluated not only for the services and products they offer but for the way they affect the local economy.[89]

In its Homegrown Economy Project Saint Paul has set forth eight basic criteria for deciding which businesses contribute to a healthy local economy:

An emphasis on *local ownership* to foster economic spinoff purchasing in the Saint Paul economy and to increase the likelihood that business assets remain in the area. Locally owned firms also tend to demonstrate a greater civic commitment.

An emphasis on creating a *growing job base of quality (skilled) jobs* in relation to the resources consumed (amount of land needed, degree of public subsidy, or amount of public support services required).

An emphasis on *diversifying the local economy* through the proliferation of many smaller businesses rather than a handful of larger ones, enhancing the stability of Saint Paul's business climate and encouraging innovation.

An emphasis on *high inter-industry dependence* in Saint Paul to increase the economic multiplier effects of local purchasing and procurement activities.

An emphasis on products and services which *directly benefit the local population* or add to the wealth of area consumers by reducing or avoiding costs resulting from the diseconomies of the existing economic environment.

An emphasis on the *community or employees having a stake in the enterprise* as a way of building community cohesion and encouraging functional management-labor relationships.

An emphasis on *generating net tax benefits* to the community in relation to resources or public studies used.

An emphasis on *attracting capital and funds from outside of the area* by encouraging export industries that have a higher economic multiplier effect on the local economy while holding promise for future growth in world markets.[90]

The programs being used to implement these objectives are a mixture of the conventional and unusual. Nearly all the programs are motivated by the objectives of efficient energy utilization, neighborhood improvement, small-business assistance, and creation of local jobs. Consider, for example, the following: the city shares a building with a private developer and uses its share of the space to offer below-market rentals to nine small companies. All the businesses in this "incubator" facility receive assistance, using some combination of loan repackaging, technical assistance, and subsidized jobs. There is a local procurement program through which local companies can use the city to negotiate for nondefense contracts. A set-aside program requires that 20 percent of small-business loans and city purchasing be targeted to businesses owned by minorities, women, or handicapped persons.

---

89. David Morris, "The Self-Reliant City," *Western City* (October 1982), as quoted in *Saint Paul Homegrown Economy Project* report.

90. *Saint Paul's Homegrown Economy Project.*

As of August 1984 the Job Creation Incentive Program had made more than 500 job placements. In this program, the city underwrites a wage of up to four dollars per hour per worker for up to six months, provided the employer keeps the worker at least six months. This program, because of its success at placing workers into permanent jobs, has become the model for the state's current jobs program.

The people involved in the Homegrown Economy Project want to encourage the growth of cooperatives. They also want the city to become involved in equity financing of individual businesses. With its share of the profits, the city would create a revolving fund for small-business loans. The city already owns an asphalt-making business. But no equity financing ventures have got off the ground. In April 1983 city voters turned down a proposal that would have made a cable television company a city-owned enterprise. Mayor Latimer believes that this decision was a serious setback to the principle of city-owned businesses and equity financing.

Originally the main focus of Saint Paul's Homegrown Economy Project was energy conservation. Saint Paul helped negotiate a large energy park that includes a mixture of businesses, condominiums, and apartments. The projected energy savings from the pooling of energy demand is 20 to 40 percent. The city was also installing a district heating program using the latest European technology. A Neighborhood Conservation Program was funding four neighborhood conservation companies. In addition, there is an active home energy improvement program for individual home and apartment owners. All these efforts have produced results: according to the mayor, the city's energy needs have declined significantly. But the urgency energy self-sufficiency and the ability of that self-sufficiency to shape local economic development have subsided with the drop in oil prices.

In January 1983, the mayor's office announced a Neighborhood Partnership Program to help neighborhood corporations and groups. Through this program the city made $2.25 million available for distribution to the neighborhoods to fund minor public improvements such as rehabilitation of businesses and residences, economic development (loans, loan packaging, interest subsidies), and assistance to cooperatives. Neighborhoods make formal application for the grants. Matching funds, which can take the form of sweat equity or volunteer activities, are required.

But the scale of the Homegrown Economy Project is tiny compared with the volume of federal and state funds and the amount of large-scale private investment pouring into the city. A total of twenty to thirty jobs that would not otherwise have existed could be directly traced to enterprises of the Homegrown Economy Project in late 1984. A shutdown by one large company would put many times more people out of work than have been employed in the project.

Of course, the project has not had much time to do more than to get off the ground. Even its chief architect, Richard Broeker, acknowledges that the main effect of the project has been to create optimism that Saint Paul can control its own destiny. For example, he says, the Homegrown Economy idea increased the enthusiasm for the small-business loan program. Thus the main effect of the project on Saint Paul has been cultural and political rather than economic. It gives people who work in the city government, and some other people in Saint Paul, the sense of engaging in a community endeavor.

It will never be easy to assess the independent effect of the Homegrown Economy Project. The task is made especially difficult by the fact that Saint Paul has been remarkably successful at generating intergovernmental aid and private investment. The city will prosper with or without the language and logic of the self-reliant city. For example, five major foundations have given significant money for job training, energy assistance, neighborhood programs, and cultural development. Even more important, from 1978 through 1984 sixteen urban development action grants were awarded to the city, bringing in a total of about $57 million. The city has also been successful at obtaining higher-than-usual awards for housing, energy assistance, and small-business development. City officials describe Saint Paul as at or near the top in the amount of federal funding received in several categories. It also should be added that, as the state capital, Saint Paul has a large amount of public sector employment: 14,000 state employees work in the city.

The project that overwhelms almost every other endeavor is the World Trade Center, the thirty-fourth such center officially designated by the World Trade Center Commission and the ninth in the United States. Construction on this $250 million complex began in August 1984.

The center will be a massive structure, forty stories of glass, steel, and aluminum towering over the Saint Paul skyline, "the focal point of the city." When complete, it will be the most expensive project ever built in the downtown area. Construction on the various phases will employ thousands of construction workers for many years. The main tower is to be connected by skyways to other structures in a sixteen-acre area that will eventually include a 300-room hotel, condominiums, a medical and high-technology center, and a museum. Dozens of retail shops, restaurants, and service shops also will be located there. The project is a classic public-private undertaking of the sort praised so highly by the Reagan administration in its *National Urban Policy Report*. The trade center development will directly employ about 2,000 people. In addition, 11,000 to 15,000 export-related jobs will be created, many of them in Saint Paul. The World Trade Center will provide services for companies throughout the state of Minnesota. To increase exports from the state, there will be a library, trade support division, a world trade education division, translation services, a satellite link, and other services.

Saint Paul was awarded the trade center in January 1984 by a nine-member state commission. Five cities had made proposals, including the larger city across the river, Minneapolis. Broeker claims that the self-reliant city idea, the emphasis on the city as an exporter and importer of goods with its own balance of payments, led Latimer and himself to see, early on, the potential for a world trade center.

It is tempting to conclude from the Saint Paul study that the city's success is unrelated to the Homegrown Economy Project, energy initiatives, or other endeavors associated with the "self-reliant" city ideal; that its economic vitality is a consequence of classic, successful competition for government aid and private investment; and that the Homegrown Economy Project language is a mythical reworking of the facts. But such a conclusion could be wrong. The economic goals that motivated the Latimer administration infused the city's diverse programs with an unusual degree of coherence. As local politics, at least, they have a good deal of reality.

The Future of Growth Politics

Downtown redevelopment, slum clearance, and highway construction were the main sources of community turbulence in cities during the 1950s and 1960s.[91] Conflict between neighborhoods and urban renewal, housing, and highway authorities was frequent and intense probably because the benefits and costs of redevelopment were so visible. Housing removal and displacement and destruction of neighborhoods constitute a dramatic statement about political winners and losers. For example, by 1967 urban renewal had destroyed 404,000 housing units, most of them occupied by low-income tenants, but only 41,580 units of replacement housing suitable for low- and moderate-income families had been built.[92] Large clearance projects that

---

91. John H. Mollenkopf, "On the Causes and Consequences of Neighborhood Political Mobilization," paper presented at the annual meeting of the American Political Science Association, New Orleans, September 4–8, 1973; John H. Mollenkopf, *The Contested City* (Princeton, New Jersey: Princeton University Press, 1983); Roger Friedland, *Power and Crisis in the City: Corporations, Unions and Urban Policy* (New York: Schocken Books, 1983); Manual Costells, *The City and the Grassroots: A Cross-Cultural Theory of Urban Social Movements* (Berkeley: University of California Press, 1983); and Clarence N. Stone, *Economic Growth and Neighborhood Discontent: System Bias in the Urban Renewal Program of Atlanta* (Chapel Hill: University of North Carolina Press, 1976).

92. Friedland, *Power and Crisis in the City*, p. 85.

destroyed homes and neighborhoods in such numbers clearly illustrated that an attempt to reclaim the downtown for "desirable" business and residents, far from benefiting all the city's residents, made more business and living space available for some at the expense of others.

The divisiveness of this kind of development politics is well documented in the urban literature. Yet Paul Peterson has written, "When development policies are considered, attempts to ascertain the power of one or another individual or group are probably pointless, if not misleading. In this policy arena the city as a whole has an interest that needs to be protected and enhanced. Politics of benefit to the city contribute to the prosperity of all residents."[93] Peterson identifies the "politics of benefit" as policies that promote local economic growth. Peterson says that economic development policies are so manifestly beneficial to everyone that they are consensual in nature: "The consensual politics of development is illustrated by the frequency with which responsibility for development policy is granted to groups and entities outside the mainstream of local politics."[94]

In other words, businessmen often locate such politics in private or quasi-public development authorities because economic development is "nonpolitical." This is a curious logic, indeed. It is at least as logical to suppose that independent authorities have been established to take development policies out of city politics precisely because of their divisive character. In fact, the literature on economic development strategies documents that this is often the motive for establishing independent authorities.[95]

Nevertheless, is it correct that growth strategies are now removed from urban electoral politics? And are the current economic development strategies less divisive than in the past or, even, consensual?

Current growth strategies are less targeted than those of the 1950s and 1960s. Neighborhood commercial revitalization, tax incentive programs like enterprise zones, and below-market loan programs all seem to be economic and not political. They address the market; discussion of their merits and mechanisms proceed in a market language. Most of the time, voters have no immediate contact with them. It is indeed true that these policies have been located in development agencies that are neither public nor private, and rarely do they fall neatly within the jurisdiction of a single city. Thus, the institutions that promote economic development have changed venue and enlarged their territory. Often this has occurred as a result of conscious decisions: "Cos-

---

93. Paul E. Peterson, *City Limits* (Chicago: University of Chicago Press, 1981), p. 147.
94. Ibid., p. 123.
95. Friedland, *Power and Crisis in the City.*

mopolitan capital tries to ensure that important decisions are made at levels of government at which it has more influence.''[96]

Growth politics has lost some of its divisive quality. Part of the reason is that most urban officials and their electoral coalitions have come to believe that growth is the only lasting solution to local public problems. The federal government's policies also have had an effect: "The Reagan Administration's cuts in urban aid have stimulated localities to intensify their search for . . . investments. . . . Under desperate conditions, the mere possibility that subsidies may work is apparently enough to prompt politicians to offer them.''[97]

Current economic development strategies may also be less divisive because their benefits and costs are more widely distributed than was the case in the past. Cities spend large amounts of money and give up potential tax revenues to promote economic growth. John Friedland has demonstrated that cities that have spent more to promote growth have higher property taxes and higher debts than other cities, although all three of these characteristics may merely reflect the fact that such cities find themselves in difficult straits to start with.[98] But higher taxes, spread among thousands of taxpayers, are less tangible than the immediate threat of displacement by the bulldozer.

Thus, growth politics has been partially depoliticized. Nevertheless, it will continue as the subject of political controversy. Urban political leaders and their constituencies often have been reminded that economic decisions carry important political consequences. Plant closings or the fact or the threat of disinvestment by mobile national and international corporations have become the focus of community protest.[99] The lack of local or even national ties by big corporations has been well documented.

Strong political pressures are encouraging cities to reevaluate their developmental policies. Federal policy initiatives combined with federal aid cutbacks, local fiscal stress, and continuing local economic decline can lead cities to seek conventional growth at any price or search for alternatives.

The mobilization of new urban constituencies may well repoliticize economic development policies. The promises that accompany local versions of supply-side economics may not satisfy coalitions made up of poor people and minorities. Minority electorates are likely to demand that economic devel-

---

96. Molotch and Logan, "Tensions in the Growth Machine," p. 493.
97. Ibid., p. 494.
98. Friedland, *Power and Crisis in the City.*
99. Barry Bluestone, and Bennett Harrison, *The Deindustrialization of America: Plant Closings, Community Abandonment, and the Dismantling of Basic Industry* (New York: Basic Books, Inc., 1982).

opment be directly targeted to providing local jobs and housing and to improving neighborhoods. This was a theme of Jesse Jackson's presidential campaign and of Operation PUSH, the organization he headed in Chicago. In 1982, the editor of *Black Enterprise*, writing about the connection between "economic power and political clout" concluded, "In cities with a strong black political presence, requirements for minority employment, minority participation in business dealings with City Hall, and stiff enforcement of anti-discrimination laws have been instituted. Conversely, cities where blacks have little clout have often done less than they should to ensure economic justice."[100]

Our case studies indicate that growth policies in the 1980s may be subject to political challenge. In Denver, for example, the election of a Hispanic mayor has resulted in a repackaging of economic development policies without any substantive changes in how they operate. The neighborhoods are offered a secondary benefit sometime in the future. Boston is pursuing a similar policy under a newly elected white mayor. The "new politics" in many cities may well consist of an attempt to build consensus support for downtown development policies that, in addition to benefiting landowners and developers in the city center, promise to generate a fiscal surplus that is shared with the rest of the city. Such consensus politics depends both on the economic ability to generate surplus revenues and on the political will to share them.

In contrast, Chicago illustrates a frontal attack on the old downtown-oriented policies, but within the context of powerful political restraints. The policy directions being charted in Chicago may provide a model for other cities seeking control over their development process. For example, in examining New York City's economic development policies, John Mollenkopf has proposed that "city assistance to growing sectors should be limited to those instances where aid induces employment expansion." He has further proposed that the city require firms to hire and train New York City residents in exchange for economic assistance.[101]

One piece of evidence that cities of all sizes are trying to keep their resources within city boundaries is the widespread adoption of residency requirements for public employees. Since 1970, 81 percent of cities surveyed in a major study have adopted residency requirements for public employees.

---

100. Earl G. Graves, "Why Black Mayors Are More Than Symbolic Figures," *Black Enterprise* (January 7, 1982), p. 7.

101. John H. Mollenkopf, "Economic Development," in Charles Brecher and Raymond P. Horton, eds., *Setting Municipal Priorities, 1984* (New York: New York University Press, 1983), p. 154.

A close relationship exists between the degree of fiscal stress and adoption of these requirements.[102] Presumably, cities are eager to find other means as well to stop dollars from flowing out of local economies.

Cities have a political logic that may be driving toward a confrontation with "economic logic." Mayors may find it necessary to promise more immediate and visible benefits to their constituencies than in the past. If that is the case, "trickle down" promises will not work; these may be replaced by a definition of economic growth as a divisible public good, as in Chicago. At that point, with neighborhoods and groups seeking their share of neighborhood grants, loans, and designation as enterprise zones, political consensus will be difficult to maintain. Conflict over the targeting of local economic development efforts is also likely to intensify when national economic growth slows, removing the appearance that virtually all cities and all neighborhoods can simultaneously win from the granting of local development subsidies.

Saint Paul is an example of a third variation of economic self-reliance. Its experiment in building a locally programmed economy may appeal to other cities. The Conference on Alternative State and Local Public Policies, a clearinghouse for reform and progressive politicians, had identified, up to 1983, a number of cities that had "radical" governments or had adopted what the conference labeled "progressive" programs: Anchorage, Spokane, Santa Cruz, Santa Barbara, Santa Monica, Saint Paul, Duluth, Austin (Texas), San Antonio, Harrisburg, Durham (North Carolina), Hartford, and Burlington (Vermont). All these cities had adopted some combination of growth controls; rent controls; special programs for minorities, women, elderly people, and handicapped people; equity financing of business or neighborhood groups; promotion of alternative energy production or consumption; and other programs.[103] Even cities that are not characterized as "progressive" in the sense of adopting new programs like these may support attempts to manage as well as to promote growth.

For all the rhetoric of self-reliance and local entrepreneurship, cities are part of the national economy, and their ability to deliver economic gains to local residents will depend in part on their national competitiveness. Denver's economic strategy expressly acknowledges this fact. Chicago's strategy starts from the assumption that external demand for Loop development will continue

---

102. Peter K. Eisenger, "Municipal Residency Requirements and the Local Economy," vol. 64, no. 1, *Social Science Quarterly* (March 1983), pp. 85–96.

103. Richard J. Margolis, "Reaganomics Redux: A Municipal Report," *Working Papers for a New Society*, vol. 10, no. 3 (May-June 1983), journal published by Cambridge Policy Studies Institute, Cambridge, Massachusetts; see also *America's Cities and Counties: Citizen's Guide 1983-1984* (Washington, D.C.: The Conference on Alternative State and Local Policies, 1985).

and needs no subsidy, so that new development efforts can be concentrated on the neighborhoods. Saint Paul may have given intellectual priority to development of the Homegrown Economy Project, but it has given practical priority to sharpening its ability to compete successfully for external business development and governmental assistance.

Cities are not in a position to define themselves as independent local economies. They remain as unwalled cities. Even so, it is likely that urban leaders in the next decade will be forced to address, much more directly than in the past, questions about the distributional benefits of economic investment and growth. Such questions are inherently contentious but unavoidable.

ABOUT THE AUTHORS

Marc Bendick, Jr., is a co-principal member in the firm of Bendick and Egan Economic Consultants, Inc., in Washington, D.C. An economist, Bendick specializes in issues of employment, economic development, human resources development, and the evaluation of programs serving the poor and disadvantaged.

Judith Feder is co-director of the Center for Health Policy Studies at Georgetown University. She is a political scientist; her published work includes books and papers on Medicare, Medicaid, long-term care, and hospitals' care for the poor.

G. Donald Ferree, Jr., is associate director of the Institute for Social inquiry at the University of Connecticut and director of the Connecticut polls. He is the author of several articles on American political attitudes and behavior.

John M. Greiner is a private consultant based in Alexandria, Virginia, and specializing in measuring and improving the productivity of public services. A former senior research associate at The Urban Institute, Mr. Greiner is the author of numerous books and articles on measuring state and local government productivity, responding to fiscal stress, and the use and impacts of incentives for public employees, including *Productivity and Motivation: A Review of State and Local Government Initiatives,* "The Impacts of Massachusetts' Proposition 2½ on the Delivery and Quality of Municipal Services," and *How Effective Are Your Community Services? Procedures for Measuring the Effectiveness of Municipal Services.*

249

Jack Hadley is co-director of the Center for Health Policy Studies at Georgetown University. He is an economist and has published papers on hospitals' care for the poor, physician payment, and the relation between medical care use and health outcomes.

John Stuart Hall is director of the School of Public Affairs at Arizona State University. He has written widely on American federalism and domestic policy. Recent co-authored books include *Government Spending and the Non-Profit Sector in Two Arizona Communities, 1985; Reconsidering American Politics, 1985; The Politics of Decentralization, 1982;* and *Studying Implementation, 1982.*

Dennis R. Judd is associate professor of political science and fellow at the Center for Metropolitan Studies at the University of Missouri, St. Louis. He has published numerous articles on urban revitalization, nationanl urban policy, and state politics. His books include *The Politics of Urban Planning* (co-authored, 1973), *The Politics of American Cities* (2d ed., 1983), and *Restructuring the City* (co-authored, 1983). He is currently writing books on public policy and American politics. He is co-editor of *Urban Affairs Quarterly.*

Everett Carll Ladd is professor of political science and executive director of the Roper Center for Public Opinion Research at the University of Connecticut. He has written extensively on American political parties, elections, and public opinion. His most recent book is *The American Polity: The People and Their Government* (1985).

Carol W. Lewis is associate professor of political science and associate director of the Institute of Urban Research at the University of Connecticut. She has written extensively on various aspects of urban policy and public budgeting.

Sarah F. Liebschutz is professor of political science and public administration at the State Unviersity of New York, College at Brockport. She is the author of numerous articles and reports to federal agencies on the community development block grant, job training partnership, and other federal intergovernmental aid programs. She was New York State field associate for the national study of the Reagan domestic program, directed by Richard P. Nathan at Princeton University. Her most recent book is *Federal Aid to Rochester* (1984).

George E. Peterson is director of the Public Finance Center of The Urban Institute. He has served as a member of the Committee on National Urban Policy of the National Academy of Sciences. His most recent book is The Urban Institute publication, *The Reagan Block Grants: What Have We Learned?* He has graduate degrees in philosophy from Oxford University and in economics from Harvard University.

David W. Rasmussen is professor of economics at Florida State University. A specialist in urban economic development, Rasmussen has also worked at the U.S. Department of Housing and Urban Development and the U.S. Department of Commerce.

Randy L. Ready holds a master's degree from the Department of Sociology, University of Denver. In 1984–85 he was a fellow in the New York City Fellowship Program.

W. Wayne Shannon is professor of political science and assistant director of the Institute for Social Inquiry at the University of Connecticut. He is the author of *Party, Constituency and Congressional Voting* (1981) and has written on Congress, the presidency, and American public policy.

Alan J. Taddiken is principal research analyst at the Center for Governmental Research, Inc., in Rochester, New York. He directed a project on the impacts of federal budget cuts in the Monroe County area, which received commendation from the Governmental Research Association in 1984. He is currently directing research on performance issues in elementary and secondary education, both public and private.